STUDY GUIDE

WITH PROGRAMMED UNITS AND LEARNING OBJECTIVES

for Hilgard, Atkinson, and Atkinson's

introduction to

PSYCHOLOGY

SIXTH EDITION

RITA L. ATKINSON
Stanford University

RICHARD C. ATKINSON
Stanford University

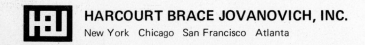

HARCOURT BRACE JOVANOVICH, INC.
New York   Chicago   San Francisco   Atlanta

Cover: detail of Circular Forms—Sun and Moon (1912-13), by Robert Delaunay. Stedelijk Museum, Amsterdam.

ISBN: 0-15-543658-9

Printed in the United States of America

contents

Each chapter in this *Guide* consists of Learning Objectives, a Programmed Unit, Terms and Concepts for Identification, Self-Quiz, and Individual and/or Group Exercises.

To the instructor

To the student

to the instructor

The *Study Guide* is designed to assist students in mastering the content of the introductory course. In preparing the *Guide* consideration was given to four major difficulties students often encounter: First, they may be uncertain about what to learn from each chapter—how to distinguish crucial material from less important details. Second, they may fail to learn the meanings of specific psychological concepts and terms. Third, they may have no satisfactory way of knowing how well they have mastered the material until after an examination (which often is too late). Fourth, they frequently find it difficult to understand or appreciate the role that research plays in psychology.

The five sections of each chapter in this *Guide* have been designed to help students in each of these areas. The first section is a list of *learning objectives* to help students focus on what they should learn from the chapter. Next is a *programmed unit,* which gives students a preliminary acquaintance with some of the terms and ideas covered in the chapter. Students should work on this unit *before* reading the corresponding text chapter. Next is a list of the important *terms and concepts* in the chapter. After reading the programmed unit and the text, students should be able to provide brief identifications for each of these. Items missed then become an object for further study. Next is a multiple-choice *self-quiz,* which provides students with an opportunity to practice exam-taking and, at the same time, points out their areas of weakness. Finally, there are *individual and class exercises,* which give students a closer look at one or more of the concepts discussed in the chapter, a chance to explore some interesting aspects of human behavior, and a feeling for the way information is derived from research. A few of the exercises must be done in class, but most have been planned so that students can carry them out on their own if the instructor does not want to take class time. The usual procedure is for each student to collect data, which he or she can then analyze or bring to class, where it can be combined with those of other students for analysis and discussion.

The authors are grateful to John C. Ruch of Mills College for preparing the self-quizzes and several of the exercises.

to the student: how to use this guide

The *Study Guide* is designed to help you in several ways: It tells you what you should learn from each chapter; it introduces the concepts and terms you will encounter in the text; it provides examination questions that will enable you to determine just how much you have learned; and, finally, it suggests exercises that will give you an understanding of the interests of the psychologist and, in most cases, a look at psychological research methods.

Each chapter in the *Guide* parallels one in the text, and there are five sections for each chapter. The first section of each chapter in the *Guide* lists the *learning objectives*—the ideas and facts you should learn from the chapter. Look them over before you start to read the chapter. You may want to refer back to each objective after you have covered the appropriate section in the text. Or you may prefer to complete the chapter and then see if you have mastered all the objectives. In any event, the learning objectives cover the important ideas in each chapter; they ask about topics you will probably be expected to know on an examination.

The second section of each chapter uses a technique of learning called *programmed instruction,* a method of self-instruction. This technique, based on certain principles of learning explained in Chapter 9 of your text, aids in the understanding and mastery of material.

These programmed units are intended as a *preview* of the corresponding chapter in your textbook. From each programmed unit you will acquire an acquaintance with *some* of the key ideas and concepts presented in the text; as a result, you should be able to read the text chapter with increased understanding. Although the programmed units are intended chiefly as a preview of the text, they also may be profitably used later as a review before examinations.

A word of warning: The programmed units cannot serve as a substitute for the text chapters. They do not treat all the important ideas presented in the text—for the programmed units to do so would require a book many times the size of this one. And even the ideas they do cover are treated in much greater detail in the text. If you work through the programmed units, however, and then go on to study the text, you will master the text treatment more easily than if you had not gone through the programmed material.

The programmed unit consists of a series of short steps called "frames." Each frame requires you to make a *response*—either by filling in a blank or by circling one of two words. To the left of the frame, on the same line as the blank, is the correct response.

Use a paper or cardboard strip to cover the answer column to the left of the program. After you have written your answer in the appropriate blank in the frame, move the strip down only far enough to reveal the correct answer. If you have made a mistake, cross out your answer and write the correct one above it.

Once you have completed the programmed unit, read the corresponding chapter in the text. After you study the text chapter, turn to the *terms and concepts for identification* section of the *Guide* and see how many you can identify correctly. If you have trouble, consult the appropriate section of the chapter or look in the glossary. The list of terms and concepts may seem long for some chapters, but if you learn them all you will have a good grasp of the material that is likely to appear on an examination.

Next, turn to the *self-quiz* section of the *Study Guide* and answer all the questions. Check your answers against the answer key; for questions on which you made an error go back to the text and review the appropriate material.

The final section of each *Study Guide* chapter presents one or more *exercises* designed to illustrate various aspects of psychological research. A few of the demonstrations require special equipment and must be presented by the instructor in class, but most are designed so that you can carry them out on your own. Sometimes you may be asked to do an exercise on your own but to bring the data to class so that the data from all students may be combined for analysis and discussion. The exercises in the *Guide* are designed to give you a better understanding of scientific methodology, some interesting insights into human behavior, and a feeling for how psychologists investigate the types of problem presented in the chapters.

To summarize: There are five sections in each chapter of the *Guide:* learning objectives, programmed unit, terms and concepts for identification, self-quiz, and individual or class exercise(s). First look over the learning objectives and complete the programmed unit for a chapter, then read the chapter, and then proceed to the terms and concepts for identification, the self-quiz, and the exercise(s). These sections are designed to help you understand the concepts in the text, to allow you to evaluate your learning, and, finally, to introduce you to the methods of psychology. It is important to remember, however, that the *Guide* is designed as a supplement, not a substitute, for the text. Used properly, the *Guide* will enhance your comprehension of the text's contents.

1 the nature of psychology

LEARNING OBJECTIVES

Describe five psychological approaches to the study of man.

State the definition of psychology given in the text.

Be familiar with current fields of specialization within psychology.

Describe the various research methods of psychology. Make certain that you can identify the independent and dependent variables in a number of different experiments.

Explain how experiments are designed to study the effect of one or many variables; know the function of a control group.

Distinguish between experimental and correlational methods. Be able to interpret the significance of correlation coefficients.

PROGRAMMED UNIT

psychology
(or people)

1. Psychology studies people from a number of different viewpoints. This book will cover five approaches to the study of _____.

2. The *neurobiological approach* attempts to relate a person's actions to events taking place within the nervous system. If you measure the activity of nerve cells in different parts of the brain when a person is angry, you would be

biological

studying emotion from the <u>neuro</u>_____ approach.

1

3. The neurobiological approach to psychology studies the relation between a person's thoughts or actions and events taking place within the
nervous
_____ system.

4. A study relating changes in nerve-cell structure to the learning of a new task is an
neurobiological
example of the _____ approach to psychology.

nervous

5. Instead of studying events occurring in the _____ system, we can focus on the individual's *behavior*.

6. Behavior refers to those activities of an organism that can be *observed*. When we
behavior
observe a child laughing or talking, we are observing _____.

7. Behavior refers to any action of an organism that can be
observed
_____.

8. If we measure the neural hormones secreted when a person is angry, we are using
neurobiological
the _____ approach to study emotion. If, instead, we count the number of times the person strikes his fist on the table when angry,
behavioral
we are using the _____ approach.

observable
internal
9. The *behavioral approach* focuses on (*observable/internal*) events; the neurobiological approach studies (*observable/internal*) events.

10. Some behaviorists do study events occurring within the body, provided they can be objectively measured. But a strict behavioral approach, called *stimulus-response psychology,* focuses on the *stimuli* that elicit behavioral *responses* and is not concerned with what goes on inside the organism. Stimulus-response
responses
psychologists study stimuli and _____ rather than internal events.

11. An experimenter studying how quickly a person can press a lever in response to
stimulus-response
the onset of a tone would probably be a _____ _____ psychologist.

12. Strict stimulus-response psychologists are not concerned with the mental processes that intervene between hearing a tone (the stimulus) and pressing a lever (the response). They are interested only in the stimulus and the
response
_____. *Cognitive* psychologists, on the other hand, study the way the mind *processes* sensory information.

13. A psychologist who studies how the mind processes incoming information is
cognitive
called a _____ psychologist. Cognition refers to those mental processes by which sensory information is transformed in various ways, coded and stored in memory, and retrieved for later use.

14. As you read this sentence your mind transforms the stimuli of "marks on paper" into visual images and compares those images with others stored in memory to arrive at meaning. The events that intervene between stimulus input and your
cognition
response are what we mean by _____tion. Perceiving, remember-
processes
ing, and thinking are all cognitive _____.

thinking

cognitive process

15. Cognitive processes include perceiving, remembering, and _____.
Perceiving is a _____ _____, and so is remembering.

remembering

conscious

16. Cognitive psychologists are usually interested in *conscious* mental processes, such as perceiving, _____, and thinking, rather than *unconscious* processes. Conscious processes are mental events of which we are *aware*.
Perceptions, memories, emotions, and dreams are all _____ processes of which we are aware.

aware

conscious

17. Conscious processes are those internal psychological events of which we are fully _____. If you are angry and are aware that you are angry, this is a _____ process.

18. Some internal events are unconscious; these are emotions, repressed memories, and desires of which we are not aware. Internal psychological events of which we are not aware are called _____ processes.

unconscious

19. If you are angry at your mother but are not aware of this anger, then it is an _____ process.

unconscious

unaware
(or not aware)

20. The *psychoanalytic approach,* originated by Sigmund Freud, assumes that much of our behavior is influenced by unconscious processes of which we are _____.

unconscious

21. Freud believed that many of the forbidden or punished impulses of childhood are driven out of awareness and become _____. He assumed that such unconscious impulses are expressed indirectly in dreams, slips of speech, and other forms of behavior.

psychoanalytic

22. The assumption that many of an individual's impulses are unconscious is basic to the _____ approach.

aggressive

consciousness
(or awareness)

23. Freud believed that unconscious impulses are usually concerned with *sex* or *aggression.* Sexual and _____ impulses are those most often punished in children, and thus those most apt to be banished from _____.

human

24. A fifth approach to the study of psychology emphasizes those "human" qualities that distinguish people from the animals—primarily their *free will* and their drive toward *self-actualization.* This approach is called *humanistic* because it focuses on the _____ qualities of people.

self-actualization

will

25. The humanistic approach emphasizes the individual's free will and drive toward _____-_____. It rejects the view that we are mechanically controlled either by external stimuli or by unconscious impulses. We are responsible for our own actions and thus are said to have free _____.

26. The psychological approach that focuses on self-actualization and free will is

humanistic   called _____. Self-actualization refers to our need to develop

our potential to the fullest.

self-actualization   **27.** Our natural tendency to actualize our potential to the fullest is called _____

_____.

28. For review, identify each of the following approaches to the psychological study

of man.

neurobiological   **a.** Relates actions to events in the brain and nervous system._____

behavioral or
stimulus-response   **b.** Relates stimuli to observed responses._____

cognitive   **c.** Focuses on the way the mind processes information. _____

psychoanalytic   **d.** Emphasizes unconscious processes. _____

humanistic   **e.** Emphasizes free-will and self-actualization. _____

29. Because there are so many different approaches to the study of psychology, it is

difficult to define the field precisely. For our purposes we will define psychol-

ogy as *the science that studies behavior and mental processes.* Behavior refers to

observed   any action of the organism that can be _____. Mental proc-

are not   esses are internal events that (*are/are not*) directly observable.

behavior   **30.** Psychology is defined as the science that studies _____ and

mental processes. If we are aware of our mental processes, they are

conscious   _____. Unconscious mental processes are not available to one's

awareness   _____.

mental processes   **31.** Psychology is the science that studies behavior and _____

_____, both conscious and unconscious.

32. The aim of a science of psychology is to discover *relationships among variables.*

A *variable* is something that changes, something that can take on different

values. "To vary" means "to change"; therefore a quality that is subject to

variable   change is called a _____.

is   **33.** A person's rate of breathing in different situations (*is/is not*) likely to change.

variable   Breathing rate is thus a _____.

34. Many experiments in psychology study more than one variable. If we wished to

discover the effect of fear upon breathing rate, we would have

two   _____ (*number*) variables in the study. We would be trying to

relationship   discover the <u>rel</u>_____ between the variables of breathing

rate, fear   _____ and _____.

35. *Time* is a variable in many experiments. A psychologist who wants to determine

the effect of the passage of time on forgetting might ask several subjects to

memorize the same set of materials and then have them recall the materials after

varying intervals of time. In this case the variable whose effect the psychologist

time   was trying to discover would be _____.

36. The psychologist studying the rate of forgetting by varying the passage of time is able to manipulate the time variable by deciding when he will test the memory of his subjects. A variable that is directly controlled or *manipulated* by the experimenter is called an *independent variable.* Time, in the experiment we have

independent   been describing, is a(n) _____ variable.

37. We call such a variable independent because its value does not depend upon the

manipulated   values of any other variable. Instead, it is controlled or _____
by the experimenter.

38. The experimenter can control or manipulate time in an experiment, but he cannot directly control or manipulate forgetting. If he finds, however, that forgetting is affected by the passage of time, he can say that forgetting is *dependent* upon time. If time is called an independent variable, then forgetting

dependent   can be called a(n) _____ variable.

39. The independent variable is the variable manipulated by the experimenter. The variable whose value may vary as a result of changes in the independent variable

dependent   is the _____ variable. In other words, the value of the dependent variable is dependent upon the value of the independent variable.

40. If we want to discover the effects of marihuana upon sexual behavior, marihuana

independent   is the _____ variable and sexual behavior is the dependent variable.

41. If we are concerned with the effect of age upon the accuracy of visual perception, age of the subject is the independent variable and the accuracy of per-

dependent   ception is the _____ variable.

42. If an experimenter varies the temperature in a classroom to determine its effect

independent   upon examination grades, the temperature level is the _____
variable and the examination grades of the students constitute the

dependent   _____ variable.

43. In a laboratory experiment the variable the experimenter manipulates, the

independent   _____ variable, can be varied with precision. Similarly, the
variable that is a consequence of the subject's behavior, the

dependent   _____ variable, can be carefully measured. Other variables that
the investigator does not want to influence the outcome of the experiment can
be *controlled.*

44. For example, if we want to study the effect of sleep loss upon learning ability, we can select subjects of the same age and intelligence, provide them with the same diet and living conditions, and then see how their performance on a learning task (such as memorizing a poem) varies with the amount of

sleep   _____ they are permitted. In this situation, variables that we
do not want to influence the results (such as age, intelligence, and diet) are

controlled   con_____. We can thus be fairly confident that differences in

dependent   scores on the learning task, the _____ variable, result from

independent   different amounts of sleep, the _____ variable.

control

independent

dependent

45. Laboratory experiments thus enable us to _____ variables that we do not wish to influence our results, as well as provide the means for careful manipulation of the _____ variable and precise measurement of the _____ variable.

46. But it is not possible to study all types of behavior in the laboratory. *Observation* in a natural setting is another method psychologists use to study behavior. Suppose we want to know how a child's aggressiveness on the school playground is related to his or her behavior at home. If the mother's answers to a questionnaire indicate that the child is quite "aggressive" at home, will the child also exhibit aggressive behavior on the playground? We cannot answer this question in the

controlled

observations

laboratory, where variables can be precisely _____. Instead we must determine how the ratings provided by the mother correspond to _____ made by trained observers who record notes on the child's behavior on the playground.

is not

47. The relationship between home behavior and playground behavior in this case (*is/is not*) determined by manipulating aggressive behavior at home and studying the results on the playground; instead we observe both variables as they occur in nature and then look for a *relationship* between them.

relationship

manipulate
(or control)

48. With observational methods we must find some method of determining the _____ between the two variables. The relationship between two variables in situations in which we cannot experimentally _____ the variables is determined by *correlation*.

cooperative

49. Suppose we want to know whether "cooperativeness" is a personality characteristic that persists throughout life. Will a child who exhibits cooperative behavior in nursery school be judged _____ as an adult?

correlation

cooperative

50. In this case we cannot use the experimental method to answer the question. Instead we use the method of cor_____ to determine the relationship between some measure of cooperative behavior in childhood and another measure of _____ behavior in adulthood.

cooperative

measure

51. As a measure of _____ behavior in childhood we might use judgments by nursery school teachers, who rate each child according to the degree he cooperates in play as opposed to being aggressive or withdrawn. As a _____ of cooperative behavior in adulthood we could look at the same individual when he is in college and note how his dormitory mates rate him on a scale of cooperativeness.

measures
(or variables)

cooperative

2

uncooperative

52. The figure on the next page shows the relationship between these two _____ for ten different young men. A rating of 1 indicates very uncooperative behavior, while a rating of 12 indicates extremely _____ behavior. Note that John received a rating of 2 in nursery school and the same rating of _____ in college. Thus we would say that John's behavior has been consistently (*cooperative/uncooperative*) over the years.

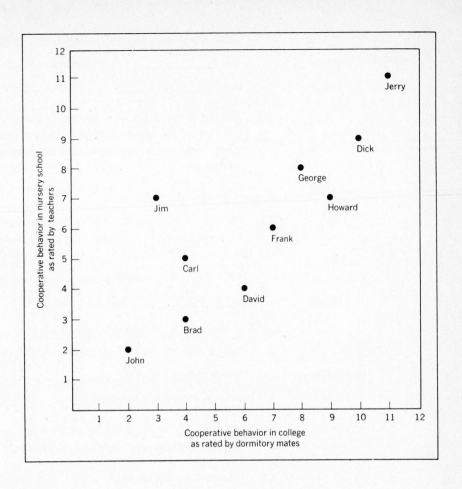

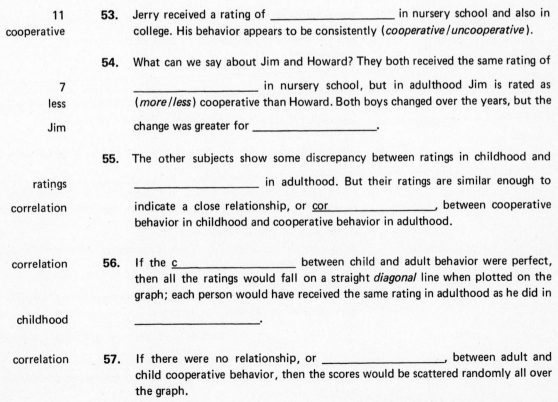

11
cooperative

53. Jerry received a rating of _____ in nursery school and also in college. His behavior appears to be consistently (*cooperative/uncooperative*).

7
less

Jim

54. What can we say about Jim and Howard? They both received the same rating of _____ in nursery school, but in adulthood Jim is rated as (*more/less*) cooperative than Howard. Both boys changed over the years, but the change was greater for _____.

ratings

correlation

55. The other subjects show some discrepancy between ratings in childhood and _____ in adulthood. But their ratings are similar enough to indicate a close relationship, or <u>cor</u>_____, between cooperative behavior in childhood and cooperative behavior in adulthood.

correlation

56. If the <u>c</u>_____ between child and adult behavior were perfect, then all the ratings would fall on a straight *diagonal* line when plotted on the graph; each person would have received the same rating in adulthood as he did in

childhood

_____.

correlation

57. If there were no relationship, or _____, between adult and child cooperative behavior, then the scores would be scattered randomly all over the graph.

58.

diagonal

correlation

Since the scores in this hypothetical experiment fall very close to a straight dia_____ line, we can conclude that there is a close relationship, a high _____, between child and adult behavior.

59.

coefficient

The actual measure in a correlational study is the *coefficient of correlation,* signified by the lower case letter *r,* which expresses the degree of relationship. If there had been a perfect correlation between cooperation in childhood and adulthood in the above study, then we would have a correlation coef_____ of $r = +1.00$.

60.

correlation

increase

The plus sign signifies that the relationship is *positive,* that a child who is cooperative will tend to be cooperative as an adult. A positive coefficient of _____, or *r,* indicates a positive relationship between the two variables; an increase in one variable is associated with an _____ in the other.

61.

correlation

variable

If, on the other hand, children who were cooperative in nursery school always turned out to be uncooperative adults, we would have a perfect *negative correlation.* A negative _____ of $r = -1.00$ indicates that one variable increases as the other _____ decreases.

62.

negative

Life expectancy decreases as the amount a person smokes increases. This is an example of a (*positive/negative*) correlation.

63.

positive

Life expectancy increases as the adequacy of one's diet increases. This is an example of a _____ correlation.

64.

positive

negative

A correlation of $+1.00$ signifies a perfect (*positive/negative*) relationship between two variables. A correlation of -1.00 indicates a perfect _____ relationship.

65.

coefficient

$r = .00$

A correlation coef_____ of $r = .00$ signifies no relationship at all. If we tried to determine the relationship between hair color and grades in college, we would expect a correlation of ($r = 1.00 / r = .00 / r = -1.00$).

66.

correlation

r

positive

is not

A correlation between $r = .00$ and either $+1.00$ or -1.00 indicates an imperfect relationship. The more closely the _____ approaches 1.00, either plus or minus, the greater the degree of relationship, either positive or negative. In our study on cooperativeness, for example, we might expect a correlation in the neighborhood of _____ $= +.86$ between childhood and adult behavior. There is a (*positive/negative*) relationship between the two variables, which (*is/is not*) perfect.

67.

independent

dependent

cannot

Cause-and-effect relationships cannot always be inferred from high negative or high positive correlations. In laboratory experiments we can manipulate the _____ variable and measure precisely its effect upon the _____ variable. In correlational studies we can only note that two variables vary together. We (*can/cannot*) say for certain that one variable *causes* the other.

68. For example, there is a high positive correlation between the softness of the asphalt in city streets during the summer and the infant mortality rate. We do not assume that some poisonous vapor from the soft asphalt causes infants to die. Instead we attribute the relationship to a third variable—probably

heat (or synonym)

_____.

69. Correlation implies the existence of a positive or negative relationship between

causes

two variables. It does not necessarily mean that one _____ the other.

70. Now let's review. Psychology is concerned with the study of behavior and mental activity. By behavior we refer to those activities of an organism that can

observed

be _____ by another person.

71. Mental activity includes internal events, such as emotions and memories, which

conscious

we are aware of and can report; these are called _____ proc-

unconscious

esses. Internal events of which we are not aware are called _____ processes.

activity

72. In studying behavior and mental _____ psychologists often measure quantities that are subject to change. Any quantity subject to change is

variable

called a _____.

73. The variable under the control of the experimenter is called the

independent

_____ variable; by manipulating this variable the experimenter

behavior

can observe its effects upon the b_____ of the subject.

74. The variable that the experimenter observes and that depends upon the value of

independent, dependent

the _____ variable is called the _____ variable.

75. In laboratory experiments we find careful manipulation of the

independent, measurement

_____ variable, precise _____ of the dependent variable, and _____ over variables that we do not wish to

control

influence the experiment.

76. In situations in which we cannot control the variables but simply make observa-

correlation

tions, we use the method of _____ to determine the relation-

variables

ship between the _____.

77. The coefficient of correlation, which is signified by the letter

r, relationship

_____, tells us whether there is a rel_____

positive

between the variables, and whether the relationship is _____ or

negative

_____. It does not necessarily imply that one variable

causes

_____ the other.

A reminder: This programmed unit is intended as an introduction to, not a substitute for, Chapter 1 of the text. If you have mastered the terms presented here, you will draw more meaning from the text itself. But you will find that the text presents more ideas, and goes deeper into the ideas presented here, than it is possible to do in this programmed unit.

TERMS AND CONCEPTS FOR IDENTIFICATION

behavior _____

_____

_____

_____

stimulus _____

_____

_____

_____

response _____

_____

_____

_____

cognition _____

_____

_____

_____

unconscious processes _____

_____

_____

_____

independent variable _____

_____

_____

dependent variable _____

_____

_____

observational method _____

_____

_____

_____

survey method _____

_____

_____

test method _____

_____

_____

longitudinal study _____

_____

_____

experimental group _____

_____

_____

control group _____

_____

_____

mean _____

_____

_____

correlation _____

_____

_____

_____ 1. Psychology has been defined by psychologists as
   a. the study of behavior
   b. the science that studies behavior and mental processes
   c. the study of mental activity
   d. all of the above

_____ 2. A plan to vary a single dependent.variable, while noting the effects on a single independent variable, is
   a. nonsense
   b. a simple "experimental design"
   c. likely to yield results which can be graphically represented as a curve
   d. both b and c

_____ 3. A correlation of +.90
   a. will always be statistically significant
   b. is twice as great as +.45
   c. is twice as great as +.30
   d. both a and c

_____ 4. A strict S-R psychologist would
   a. firmly oppose taking a "black box" approach
   b. not consider an individual's conscious experiences
   c. make inferences about mental activity from verbal reports of conscious experiences
   d. both a and c

_____ 5. The mean is
   a. the arithmetic average
   b. the sum of the measures divided by the number of measures
   c. the most common statistic used in psychology
   d. all of the above

_____ 6. A humanistic psychologist probably
   a. believes that people are driven by the same instincts as animals
   b. would be concerned primarily with an individual's subjective experience
   c. would see people as acted on by forces outside their control
   d. all of the above

_____ 7. In studying the influence of sleep on learning
   a. the amount of learning is the independent variable
   b. the amount of sleep is the dependent variable
   c. the amount of sleep is the independent variable
   d. sleep "is a function of" learning

_____ 8. To say that a difference between two numbers is statistically "significant" is to say that it is
   a. trustworthy
   b. important
   c. of practical significance
   d. all of the above

_____ 9. A neurobiological concept of man
   a. relates man's actions to events in his brain and nervous system
   b. is at present the best basis for understanding man's psychological make-up
   c. offers at present only a remote possibility of a comprehensive theory of man
   d. both a and c

_____ 10. Different methods in psychology serve different purposes. For example, the _____ method may be used prior to the experimental method, as an introduction to the problem.
   a. observational
   b. test
   c. case history
   d. longitudinal

_____ 11. In order to study experimentally the simultaneous effects of several variables, you would use
   a. graphical representation
   b. a multivariate design
   c. a coefficient of correlation
   d. the test method

_____ 12. In the early 1900s, John B. Watson
   a. introduced the "introspection" technique
   b. maintained that behaviorism was futile
   c. advanced a position later known as behaviorism
   d. advocated examining carefully a person's mental experiences and activities

13. Psychologists may be usefully categorized by
    a. the type of problems they are interested in
    b. their approach to problems that interest them
    c. the type of organization that employs them
    d. all of the above

14. A coefficient of correlation
    a. can be used only when experimental control is possible
    b. can be used with large masses of data
    c. is usually a good indication of cause-effect relationships
    d. all of the above

15. A psychoanalytic conception of people
    a. is somewhat pessimistic
    b. is widely accepted by psychologists
    c. is based on experimental studies
    d. emphasizes their differences from animals

16. The control group
    a. is a comparable group tested in a different experiment
    b. refers to the people running an experiment
    c. does not receive the variable being studied
    d. none of the above

17. The experimental method
    a. requires the use of a laboratory
    b. seeks orderly relationships among variables

c. requires precision apparatus
d. all of the above

18. Cognitive psychology
    a. argues that the mind is active rather than passive
    b. developed partly in reaction to S-R psychology
    c. can be considered analogous to an electronic computer
    d. all of the above

19. For controlling aggression, either a _____ or a _____ might suggest changing aspects of the environment.
    a. behaviorist, humanist
    b. psychoanalyst, humanist
    c. cognitive psychologist, neurobiologist
    d. neurobiologist, behaviorist

20. Would-be psychologists primarily concerned with satisfying their own curiosity should try to get into
    a. applied research
    b. the social sciences
    c. basic research
    d. Masters and Johnson's laboratory

KEY TO SELF-QUIZ

20. c	15. a	10. a	5. d
19. a	14. b	9. d	4. b
18. d	13. d	8. a	3. c
17. b	12. c	7. c	2. a
16. c	11. b	6. b	1. d

INDIVIDUAL EXERCISES

PSYCHOLOGICAL RESEARCH

One way to get an idea of what psychologists do is to look at their publications. Go to the library and ask where the psychological journals are located. They may be placed together in one area of the current periodical room, or they may be arranged alphabetically with the other periodicals. There are a large number of psychological journals published in the United States and in many other countries. Some like the *Journal of Experimental Psychology,* the *Journal of Comparative and Physiological Psychology,* and *Developmental Psychol-*

ogy publish primarily research reports. Others like the *Journal of Abnormal Psychology,* the *Journal of Personality and Social Psychology,* the *Journal of Applied Psychology,* and the *Journal of Educational Psychology* publish both theoretical and research papers. The *Psychological Review* presents original theoretical papers; the *Psychological Bulletin* publishes articles reviewing and evaluating areas of research. The *American Psychologist* publishes the official papers of the American Psychological Association, as well as articles of general interest to psychologists. *Contemporary Psychology* reviews current books in the field. These are some of the general research publications in psychology; many other publications are devoted to more specific interests—*Perception and Psychophysics* and *Psychotherapy: Theory, Research, and Practice* are examples. *Psychology Today* is a popular magazine with some articles written by psychologists.

Glancing at the index and scanning a few articles in several of these journals will give you an idea of the range of problems studied by psychologists as well as the way in which psychological research is conducted and reported.

THE SCIENTIFIC METHOD

Introduction

The status of psychology as a science depends on its use of the experimental method. An experiment involves observation of some aspect of behavior (dependent variable) while one factor (independent variable) is systematically changed under certain specified conditions (controlled variables). In the experimental method all the factors producing a given result, except the one whose effects are being examined, are held constant. Before an experiment is performed, the experimenter generally states a hypothesis describing the process that he believes underlies the behavior under investigation.

Although the experimental method provides the most reliable source of scientific information and is the preferred method of science, difficulties are encountered even in simple experiments. Many experiments appear to have satisfied the fundamental requirement of controlling relevant variables, but careful analysis of the procedures used sometimes reveals the presence of overlooked, uncontrolled variables that may invalidate the results.

This simple experiment will provide you with an opportunity to criticize procedure and to become somewhat more familiar with the scientific method.

Equipment Needed

None

Procedure

The results of a fictitious experimental study are given in Tables 1 and 2. Read carefully the experimental problem, the hypothesis, the procedures used, the results obtained, and the conclusions drawn. Then, using the concluding questions as an aid, make an analysis of the experiment.

1. EXPERIMENTAL PROBLEM: To investigate the effects of drinking coffee (which contains caffeine) on the achievement of college students on a final examination in general psychology.

2. HYPOTHESIS: Two cups of black coffee taken immediately before a task requiring mental exertion increase a student's academic efficiency.

3. PROCEDURE: Two groups of subjects were used. Group 1 consisted of 200 freshmen who were matched in age, intelligence, sex, and grade-point average with the 200 freshmen in group 2. Subjects in both groups were enrolled in the elementary course in psychology. All subjects in group 1 drank two cups of black coffee immediately before taking the final examination. All subjects in group 2 were instructed not to take any stimulants during the day the final examination was to be taken. For purposes of analysis, the grades of the students of both groups were converted into the following numerical equivalents (grade points): A = 4; B = 3; C = 2; D = 1; and F = 0. The average grade-point score for each of the two groups was then computed on this basis.

4. RESULTS: The results of the experiment are summarized in the tables. Table 1 indicates the number and percentage of students in each group obtaining each of the five letter grades on the final exam in general psychology. Table 2 gives the average grade-point scores of the two groups.

These results indicate that the students in group 1 did consistently better than the students in group 2.

TABLE 1				
	Group 1 (took coffee)		Group 2 (did not take coffee)	
Grade	Number	Percent	Number	Percent
A	30	15	14	7
B	46	23	24	12
C	80	40	112	56
D	36	18	40	20
F	8	4	10	5

TABLE 2	
Group	Average grade-point score
1 (coffee drinkers)	2.25
2 (noncoffee drinkers)	1.96

5. CONCLUSIONS: Comparison of the final examination grades earned in general psychology by two groups of college students (a stimulant-taking group and a non-stimulant-taking group) indicates that the taking of a mild stimulant, such as two cups of black coffee, immediately before an examination increases the academic efficiency and achievement of freshmen college students in a general psychology course.

Questions For Discussion

1. What is the dependent variable in this experiment?

2. What is the independent variable in this experiment?

3. What are the limitations of the experiment?

4. How would *you* design an experiment to test the hypothesis that taking a mild stimulant before an examination increases academic efficiency?

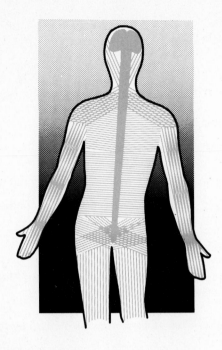

2 biological basis of psychology

LEARNING OBJECTIVES

Understand the structure of a neuron and how it transmits nervous impulses.

Outline the basic organization of the nervous system.

Identify the major parts of the brain and locate the projection areas of the cerebral cortex.

Describe how the major and minor hemispheres differ in function.

Describe the function of the two divisions of the autonomic nervous system and their relation to the endocrine system.

Understand how behavioral geneticists study hereditary influences on behavior.

PROGRAMMED UNIT

system

neurons

1. All behavior depends on the integration of bodily processes by the *nervous system.* The basic unit of the nervous _____ is the *neuron*, or nerve cell, which is diagrammed on the next page. The human nervous system contains many billions of these nerve cells, or _____.

body

2. The neuron has three main parts: the *cell body,* the *dendrites,* and the *axon.* As you can see from the diagram, the wide part of the neuron is its cell _____.

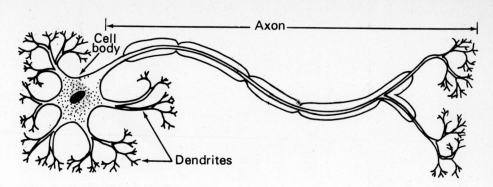

Cell body

Axon

Dendrites

3. The short, branching fibers at one end of the neuron are the *dendrites*. The

cell

dendrites and the _____ body receive impulses from the sense organs or from other neurons.

dendrites

4. A neuron receives impulses by way of its cell body or its _____. The nervous impulse travels across the cell body and out the *axon*. The axon transmits the nerve impulse to another neuron or to a muscle or gland.

5. Nerve impulses from sense organs or from other neurons are received by the cell

dendrites

body or the _____ of a neuron. The impulse is transmitted to

axon

other neurons, or to muscles and glands, by the _____.

receiving
transmitting

6. The dendrites are the (*receiving/transmitting*) end of the neuron and the axon is the (*receiving/transmitting*) end.

7. The dendrites and cell body receive impulses from the sense organs or from

neurons

other _____. The axon transmits the nerve impulse to another

gland

neuron or to a muscle or _____.

cell body

8. To review: The three main parts of the neuron are the _____

dendrites

_____; the _____, which receive(s) impulses;

axon

and the _____, which transmit(s) nerve impulses.

9. The junction between the axon of one neuron and the cell body or dendrites of

synapse

the next neuron is called a *synapse*. This junction, or _____, is not a direct connection. There is a slight gap across which the nervous impulse must be transmitted.

synapse

10. Neural transmission across this gap, or sy_____, is usually by means of a chemical intermediary. The axon of one neuron releases a chemical

neuron

into the synapse which stimulates the dendrites of the next _____.

11. Neural transmission at the synapse is in one direction only. The axon sends the impulse and the dendrites receive it. The impulse is transmitted across the

synapse, axon

_____ from the _____ of the first neuron to

dendrites

the _____ or cell body of the next neuron.

12. A *nerve* is a bundle of axons belonging to many neurons. The axons of hundreds

nerve   of neurons joined together form a _____.

nerves   **13.** Neuron axons, grouped together into bundles called _____, spread out to all parts of the body. Those nerves that carry information from the sense receptors and the internal organs to the spinal cord and brain are called *afferent* or sensory nerves.

afferent   **14.** Sensory information travels along <u>af</u>_____, or sensory, nerves. Nerves transmitting impulses from the brain and spinal cord to the muscles and organs are called *efferent,* or motor, nerves.

efferent   **15.** Messages instigating bodily action are transmitted along _____ nerves.

               16. Information from the external environment is carried to the brain by
afferent   _____ nerves. Signals to action are transmitted by
efferent   _____ nerves.

               17. A convenient way to remember the difference between *afferent* and *efferent*
efferent   nerves is to remember that the outgoing, or <u>ef</u>_____, nerves make connections with *ef*fectors, that is, with the muscles and glands that have an *ef*fect on the individual's response to the environment.

               18. The *central nervous system* is composed of the brain and the spinal cord. The spinal cord provides connections for simple reflexes (such as the knee jerk) and for the passage of nervous impulses to and from the brain. Together, the brain
central nervous   and spinal cord constitute the _____ _____
system   _____.

spinal   **19.** The central nervous system consists of the brain and the _____
cord   _____.

afferent   **20.** The incoming, or _____, nerves and the outgoing, or
efferent   _____, nerves form connections in the brain and spinal cord. Since these are the chief centers in which junctions between neurons occur, you might expect the brain and spinal cord to contain large numbers of such
synapses   junctions or <u>sy</u>_____.

               21. Nerves leading from the brain and spinal cord to other parts of the body form the *peripheral nervous system.* Some of these nerves carry incoming messages from the sense receptors, skeletal muscles, and body surface; they are
afferent   _____ nerves. Others carry impulses from the central
nervous   _____ system to other parts of the body where they initiate
efferent   action; these are _____ nerves. Some nerves, however, are mixed; they contain both afferent and efferent fibers.

22. Whether they are afferent or efferent, nerves connecting the brain and spinal cord with the sense receptors, skeletal muscles, and body surface are part of the peripheral nervous system; they form the *somatic division* of the peripheral

nervous _____ system.

peripheral **23.** Another part of the p_____ nervous system is the *autonomic system* which includes efferent nerves running to the *glands* and *smooth* muscles (those found in the stomach, intestines, and other internal organs). We would expect the efferent nerves leading to the salivary glands to be part of the

autonomic (*somatic/autonomic*) system.

peripheral **24.** The somatic and autonomic systems together make up the _____

nervous system _____ _____. The brain and the spinal

central nervous system cord form the _____ _____ _____.
The division into systems helps in anatomical discussions; in actuality, however, all parts of the nervous system function in a highly integrated manner.

brain **25.** Let's review. The central nervous system consists of the _____

spinal cord and the _____ _____. Nerves carrying messages to the central nervous system from other parts of the body are called

afferent _____ nerves; those carrying action messages out from the

efferent brain and spinal cord are _____ nerves. All nerves outside of

peripheral the brain and spinal cord are grouped into the _____ nervous

somatic system which has two divisions: the _____ division consists of nerves running to and from sense organs, skeletal muscles, and the body surface;

autonomic the _____ division consists of nerves running to the glands and smooth muscles.

26. Since the brain is the most important part of the nervous system, we will need to look at it in more detail. The illustration of the human brain on page 21 is an adaptation of the illustration you will find in the text. In this programmed unit you will begin to learn the names of the parts of the human brain. Note that the text illustration, in addition to listing the labels shown here, provides lists of the various functions of each part of the brain. (These functions are also described in the text.) You will not learn all these functions from this programmed unit, but you will get acquainted with some of them. (*Now look at the illustration and go on to the next frame. Refer to the illustration as necessary.*)

27. As the spinal cord enters the brain it enlarges to form the *brain stem* (*not labeled on the illustration*). The lower portion of the brain, connecting with the spinal

brain stem cord is the _____ _____.

28. An important structure within the brain stem is the *medulla.* The medulla regulates breathing and controls some of the reflexes that help us maintain an upright posture. Some very basic life processes are regulated by the

medulla _____.

29. Attached to the rear of the brain stem, just above the medulla, is a convoluted

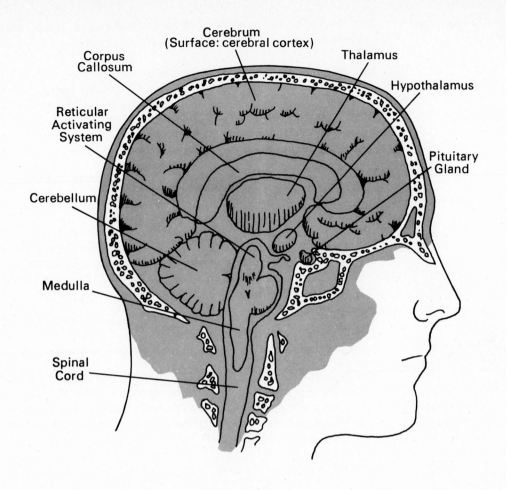

Cerebrum
(Surface: cerebral cortex)

Corpus
Callosum

Thalamus

Hypothalamus

Reticular
Activating
System

Pituitary
Gland

Cerebellum

Medulla

Spinal
Cord

structure known as the *cerebellum;* it regulates intricate motor coordination. The complex movements involved in such activities as walking, dancing, speaking, and playing a musical instrument are controlled by the _____.

cerebellum

30. Starting in the brain stem and extending upward is a system of neural circuits called the *reticular activating system.* The reticular _____ system controls our state of *arousal* or *alertness.* When we change from sleep to wakefulness, nerves in the _____ _____ system are involved.

activating

reticular activating

31. The reticular activating system controls our state of arousal or _____.

alertness

32. The convoluted structure to the rear of the brain stem that controls complex motor skills is the _____.

cerebellum

33. Now locate on the diagram a small but vital structure in the center of the brain called the *hypothalamus.* The hypothalamus plays an important role in *motivation* and *emotion.* It helps regulate hunger, thirst, and sex; it influences our feelings of pleasure, fear, and anger. When we experience pangs of hunger, the brain structure involved is the _____.

hypothalamus

motivation

34. The hypothalamus plays an important role in _____ and emotion.

35. By regulating hunger and thirst the hypothalamus attempts to maintain *homeo-stasis,* a level of functioning characteristic of the healthy organism. If blood-sugar level gets too low, the hypothalamus signals the organism to start eating. Ingested food raises the level of sugar in the blood thus restoring

homeostasis

homeo_____.

36. The hypothalamus attempts to maintain the body in a state of normalcy or

homeostasis

constancy. This optimal level of functioning is called _____.

37. When the concentration of salt and certain other chemicals in the blood becomes too great, the hypothalamus signals the organism to start drinking water. Water intake dilutes the blood chemicals to the proper concentration. This is another

homeostasis

example of _____.

38. The brain structure that maintains homeostasis and plays an important role in

hypothalamus

motivation and emotion is the _____.

39. Now locate another part of the brain stem, the *thalamus.* This portion serves as a sensory relay station for impulses coming up from the spinal cord and down from the higher brain centers. In any activity that requires the coordination of

thalamus

information from several receptors, the (*hypothalamus/thalamus*) is likely to be involved.

40. The thalamus is a sensory relay station for impulses coming up from the

spinal cord

_____ _____ and down from the higher brain centers.

41. For a review of the brain areas discussed so far, identify the structures involved in each of the following functions.

cerebellum

a. Controls body coordination as in walking or dancing. _____

b. Maintains homeostasis and plays important role in motivation and emotion.

hypothalamus

_____

thalamus

c. Serves as a sensory relay station. _____

reticular activating system

d. Controls state of arousal as from sleep to wakefulness. _____

_____ _____

e. Regulates basic body process such as breathing and postural reflexes.

medulla

_____

42. The large mass of brain tissue that surrounds the brain-stem structures is the *cerebrum*—the most highly developed portion of the human brain. The surface of the cerebrum is highly wrinkled, or convoluted. The fact that this surface, known as the *cerebral cortex,* has so many wrinkles or convolutions, means that

greater

the total surface area is much (*greater/smaller*) than it would be if the surface of the cerebrum were smooth.

43. Since the *cerebral cortex,* or surface, of the cerebrum is so large, it provides room for many interconnections of neurons. Thus the cerebral cortex makes it possible for us to learn, remember, think, and carry on many of the activities that distinguish us from the lower animals. You might expect the cerebral cortex of a fish to be (*more/less*) wrinkled, or convoluted, than that of a human being.

less

44. The _____, with its wrinkled surface, the _____ cortex, is the part of the human brain that makes possible thinking and reasoning.

cerebrum, cerebral

45. A top view of the brain, as distinguished from the side view shown here, would show that the *cerebrum* is divided into two halves, or hemispheres. (Your text will make this clear.) Now locate the *corpus callosum,* which contains fibers connecting the two cerebral hemispheres. The two cerebral hemispheres are connected by the _____ _____.

corpus callosum

46. Now locate the *pituitary* gland, a small structure below the hypothalamus. The pituitary gland is *not* a part of the nervous system; it is an important *ductless,* or *endocrine,* gland. Ductless, or _____ glands are glands that secrete their hormones directly into the blood stream.

endocrine

47. There are two kinds of glands: *duct* glands and *ductless* or _____ glands. *Duct* glands, such as the *tear* glands and the *salivary* glands, secrete their products on the surface of the body or into body cavities, but *not* directly into the blood stream.

endocrine

48. The pituitary, thyroid, and adrenal glands secrete their hormones directly into the blood stream and must therefore be _____ glands.

endocrine
(or ductless)

49. The tear glands and salivary glands are not endocrine glands because they secrete their products on the _____ of the body or into the body cavities rather than into the _____ stream.

surface

blood

50. Because the hormones of endocrine glands are secreted into the _____ _____, they have a widespread influence. They play an important part in many types of behavior and their functioning is complexly interrelated with that of the nervous system.

blood stream

51. The pituitary gland, which secretes its hormones directly into the blood stream and therefore must be a(n) _____ gland, is often called the *"master gland"* because it exerts a complex and pervasive influence on the other endocrine glands and on many aspects of bodily growth.

endocrine
(or ductless)

52. The _____ gland is often referred to as the "_____ gland" because it exerts a strong influence on the other _____ glands and on many aspects of bodily growth.

pituitary, master

endocrine
(or ductless)

53. Another important endocrine gland is the *adrenal* gland. One adrenal gland is located just above each kidney. The adrenal glands secrete their hormones into the _____ _____. Two important hormones secreted by the adrenal glands are *epinephrine* (also known as adrenalin) and *norepinephrine* (noradrenalin).

blood stream

adrenal

54. Epinephrine and norepinephrine are secreted by the _____
glands. They act in a number of ways to prepare the organism for an emergency.

55. We noted earlier that the autonomic nervous system consists of nerves running
to the smooth muscles (such as line the stomach and other internal organs) and

glands

the g_____. It should not be surprising to learn, therefore, that
there is a close interrelationship between the endocrine glands and the

autonomic nervous

_____ _____ system.

56. The secretion of the adrenal glands is regulated by the autonomic nervous
system. The autonomic nervous system controls many activities that are "autonomous" or "self-regulating." The process of digestion, for example, goes on
autonomously without any conscious willing on our part. Digestion is controlled

autonomic

by the (*autonomic/central*) nervous system.

57. The self-regulating activities controlled by the autonomic nervous system can go
on while a person is asleep or unconscious, that is, without his being

aware
(or conscious)

_____ of them.

58. The autonomic nervous system has two divisions: the *sympathetic* and the
parasympathetic divisions. These two divisions are often opposite, or *antagonis-*

smooth

tic, in their actions. Both divisions control the glands and the _____

antagonistic

muscles, but their actions are often an_____.

59. The sympathetic division of the autonomic nervous system operates to *dilate* the
blood vessels of the heart, while the parasympathetic division operates to
constrict these blood vessels. This is an illustration of the fact that the two

antagonistic

divisions are often opposite, or _____, in their action.

60. The sympathetic division tends to act as a *unit* in *excited* states, while the
parasympathetic division tends to act in a more *piecemeal* fashion and to be
more important in *quiescent* states, or those activities that conserve and protect
bodily resources. If you observe that a subject's heart rate has speeded up, that
he is perspiring profusely, and that his pupils are dilated, you might expect that

sympathetic

the _____ division of the autonomic nervous system was
playing a part in these responses.

61. Since the adrenal gland is dominant in excited states, it would be logical to

parasympathetic

conclude that the _____ division has no connection to
this gland.

sympathetic
parasympathetic
(either order)
sympathetic
parasympathetic

62. The two divisions of the autonomic nervous system are the _____
and the _____ divisions. The _____ divi-
sion tends to act as a unit in excited states, whereas the _____
division tends to act in a more piecemeal fashion in quiescent states.

autonomic

antagonistic

63. The _____ nervous system has two divisions, the sympathetic
and parasympathetic divisions, which are often _____ in their
action.

64. Let's review. The *autonomic nervous system* derives its name from the fact that
many of its activities are _____, or self-regulating, and occur
without our being _____ of them. It has two divisions that are
often _____ in their action: the _____
division and the _____ division.

The _____ division tends to act as a unit in exicted states,
whereas the _____ division tends to act in a more
piecemeal fashion in _____ states.

autonomous

aware

antagonistic, sympathetic

parasympathetic
(either order)
sympathetic

parasympathetic

quiescent

65. The autonomic nervous system is one division of the (*central/peripheral*) nervous
system. Its nerves are outside of the brain and spinal cord, which constitute the
(*central/peripheral*) nervous system. The other part of the peripheral nervous
system is the _____ system, whose nerves run to and from the
sense receptors, body surface and skeletal muscles. All of these systems coordi-
nate in complex fashion to provide for the smooth functioning of the organism.

peripheral

central

somatic

66. Many of our *physical characteristics* are inherited from our parents. *Genetics,*
the science of heredity, shows how physical ch_____ such as eye
and hair color are transmitted from one generation to the next. Psychological
characteristics—ability, temperament, and emotional stability—may also depend
to some extent on heredity. As you might guess, the branch of genetics that
studies the inheritance of psychological or behavioral characteristics is called
behavior g_____.

characteristics

genetics

67. Behavior genetics studies the degree to which psychological characteristics are
_____.

inherited

68. The *hereditary units* that an individual receives from his parents and transmits to
his offspring are carried by microscopic particles known as *chromosomes,* found
within each cell of the body. Each human body cell has 46 chromosomes. At
conception the human being receives 23 chromosomes from the father's sperm
and 23 ch_____ from the mother's ovum. These 46 chromo-
somes form 23 *pairs,* which are duplicated in every cell of the body as the
individual develops.

chromosomes

69. A fertilized ovum contains 46 _____, 23 of its own and
23 received from the sperm.

chromosomes

70. The chromosomes are duplicated in every cell of the body as the individual
develops. Thus every body cell contains _____ chromosomes
arranged in 23 _____.

46

pairs

71. The chromosomes carry the basic units of heredity, which are called *genes.* Each
chromosome carries many of these hereditary units, or _____.
Like chromosomes, the genes occur in pairs; one gene of each pair comes from
the sperm chromosome and one gene from the ovum _____.

genes

chromosome

72. Chromosomes occur in pairs, and each chromosome contains many pairs of

genes   _____.

73. In human beings each chromosome carries more than 1000 genes. Since the

23   fertilized ovum has _____ pairs of chromosomes, the number
of genes is high enough to make it extremely unlikely that any two persons
would have the same heredity. The exception would be individuals who develop
from the same ovum; such individuals are called *monozygotic twins.*

ovum   **74.** Monozygotic twins develop from the same _____. They are
also called identical twins; since they share the same heredity, they are alike in
many respects.

75. Fraternal or *dizygotic twins* develop from two separate ova fertilized by two

do not   separate sperm cells. Thus they (*do/do not*) share the same heredity and are no
more alike than ordinary siblings.

monozygotic   **76.** Because _____ twins have exactly the same heredity, differences between them are attributed largely to differences in environment.

77. Genetic studies frequently compare the similarities between monozygotic twins
and those between dizygotic twins to determine the extent to which a psychological characteristic is influenced by heredity. For example, monozygotic twins
are much more similar in intelligence test scores than dizygotic twins. This

heredity   finding suggests that (*heredity/environment*) influences intelligence.

78. If one monozygotic twin develops a mental illness called schizophrenia, there is a
60 percent chance that the other twin will be schizophrenic. Among dizygotic
twins there is only a 15 percent chance that if one twin is schizophrenic the

hereditary   other will be also. This indicates that there is a(n) _____
(or genetic)   component in the susceptibility to some forms of schizophrenia.

TERMS AND CONCEPTS FOR IDENTIFICATION

neuron _____

_____

_____

_____

dendrite _____

_____

_____

_____

axon _____

_____

_____

_____

glia cells _____

_____

_____

_____

synapse _____

_____

_____

_____

afferent nerves _____

_____

_____

_____

efferent nerves _____

_____

_____

_____

hypothalamus _____

_____

_____

_____

homeostasis _____

_____

_____

_____

reticular activating system _____

_____

_____

_____

limbic system _____

_____

_____

_____

cerebral cortex _____

_____

_____

_____

projection areas _____

_____

_____

_____

association areas _____

_____

_____

_____

autonomic nervous system _____

_____

_____

_____

endocrine glands _____

_____

_____

_____

epinephrine _____

_____

_____

_____

norepinephrine _____

_____

_____

_____

chromosome _____

_____

_____

_____

gene _____

_____

_____

monozygotic twins _____

_____

_____

dizygotic twins _____

_____

_____

_____

_____ 1. Homeostasis is maintained by the _____ which also plays an important role in emotion.
a. hypothalamus
b. thalamus
c. limbic system
d. reticular activating system (RAS)

_____ 2. In a test of a split-brain patient, if the name of an object is briefly flashed on the left half of the screen, he or she can
a. say what the object is
b. pick out the object from a pile of others
c. write down what the object is
d. all of the above

_____ 3. Each neuron in the nervous system consists of three main parts: the _____, the _____, and the _____.
a. glia, cell body, dendrites
b. axon, nerve, cell body
c. glia, axon, cell body
d. dendrites, cell body, axon

_____ 4. The _____ nervous system includes both the _____ system and the _____ system.
a. peripheral, central, autonomic
b. somatic, autonomic, peripheral
c. peripheral, autonomic, somatic
d. autonomic, somatic, peripheral

_____ 5. A normal male child has received
a. an X chromosome from his mother and a Y from his father
b. a Y chromosome from each parent
c. a Y chromosome from his mother and an X from his father
d. an X chromosome from each parent

_____ 6. Which of the following is _not_ one of the important types of cerebral cortex areas?
a. visual area
b. body-sense area
c. organization area
d. language area

_____ 7. The speech centers for left-handed people are
a. usually in the left hemisphere
b. usually in the right hemisphere
c. typically in both hemispheres
d. about evenly divided, with some left-handers having centers in the left hemisphere and some in the right hemisphere

_____ 8. A vivid memory can sometimes be elicited by electrical stimulation of a particular spot in a temporal lobe. When this particular spot is surgically removed,
a. the patient can no longer remember the event
b. the vivid memory can no longer be electrically elicited
c. the patient cannot remember having had the vivid memory
d. all of the above

_____ 9. The sympathetic and parasympathetic systems
a. typically act in an antagonistic fashion
b. are divisions of the autonomic nervous system
c. may be involved in the same behavior, via sequential action
d. all of the above

_____ 10. Damage to the _____ results in jerky, uncoordinated movements, because of its central role in coordinating complex motor activity.
a. cerebrum
b. cerebellum
c. medulla
d. limbic system

_____ 11. Myelinated fibers do _not_
a. utilize nodes
b. have a uniformly thick sheath
c. transmit impulses faster than unmyelinated ones
d. represent a recent evolutionary development

_____ 12. When release of a chemical transmitter at a synapse produces a potential shift in the receiving neuron that is in the same direction as the action potential, the synapse is
a. an excitatory one
b. an inhibitory one
c. becoming polarized
d. in a refractory phase

13. The many large areas of the cerebral cortex not directly concerned with sensorimotor processes have been called
   a. projection areas
   b. organization areas
   c. association areas
   d. thinking areas

14. The simplest reflex may involve
   a. an efferent neuron and a motor fiber
   b. a connector neuron
   c. only afferent and efferent neurons
   d. a three-neuron reflex arc

15. Synaptic transmission involves
   a. graded potentials
   b. a refractory phase
   c. an all-or-none principle
   d. all of the above

16. If you are a female with blue eyes, we know that
   a. your father had blue eyes
   b. one of your parents had blue eyes
   c. both of your parents had blue eyes
   d. none of the above

17. The human brain may be thought of as being composed of three concentric layers. Of these the _____ is on the outside, while the earlier evolutionary development, the _____, is concealed within it.
   a. limbic system, central core
   b. cerebrum, limbic system
   c. limbic system, cerebrum
   d. cerebral hemispheres, cerebrum

18. The _____ gland has been called the "master gland" because it _____
   a. pituitary, controls the secretion of several other glands
   b. adrenal, produces the largest number of hormones
   c. pituitary, produces epinephrine
   d. adrenal, controls the secretion of several other glands

19. When a rat is raised in an "enriched" environment,
   a. it weighs more
   b. its rate of neural conduction becomes faster
   c. it develops a large and complex cerebellum
   d. it develops a heavier cerebral cortex

20. In partialing out the effects of environment and heredity, one ideally should study
   a. monozygotic twins
   b. dizygotic twins
   c. both of the above
   d. neither of the above

KEY TO SELF-QUIZ

20. c	15. d	10. b	5. a
19. d	14. c	9. d	4. c
18. a	13. c	8. b	3. d
17. b	12. a	7. a	2. b
16. d	11. b	6. c	1. a

INDIVIDUAL EXERCISE

REACTION TIME

Introduction

Every voluntary motor act takes time, not only to perform, once movement begins, but to initiate. Because we do not easily sense small time increments, we normally assume that a movement occurs as soon as we think about it. While this is an acceptable approximation for ordinary daily activity, it is an oversimplification when movements are judged with respect to small time intervals. We typically encounter such intervals in relation to rapidly moving objects: tennis balls, hockey pucks, and other objects outside us, or automobiles and airplanes, with us inside them. As various organizations concerned with automotive safety often tell us, a major portion of the distance needed to stop a car is covered between the time the stimulus for stopping occurs and the time when the brakes are applied. Although your braking may seem "immediate" to you, the time needed to register the stimulus, interpret it, decide on action, signal that action, and operate the muscles allows your car to cover a substantial distance.

The time between the onset of a stimulus and the subject's response is called the *reaction time.* Obviously we cannot have our readers running down hapless pedestrians in demonstrations of their reaction time. This exercise, however, is designed to demonstrate a similar phenomenon: movement past you while you take time to react. It provides you with a scientific approach and, for the less inhibited among you, a party trick.

Equipment Needed

Ruler (preferably a yardstick)

Procedure

While this exercise can be attempted by one person, it is really necessary for one person to test another.

1. Have your subject stand and hold out either hand at right angles to the floor with the thumb about an inch in front of the index finger and the fingers set to quickly squeeze together (see photo). Hold the yardstick between the subject's fingers and thumb, and tell him to grasp the yardstick when you drop it. The subject is to watch your hand so that as soon as you release the yardstick, he is prepared to grasp it. Both of you may be surprised to see that it drops several inches no matter how quickly the subject tries to react.

2. Make your procedure more precise by specifying the subject's finger-to-thumb gap each time and by starting with one of the inch markers of the yardstick opposite his middle finger so that you can measure the distance it falls.

3. An even better technique is to stand your subject by a doorway, with his palm by the jamb and his fingertips curved loosely around the door jamb (see photo). Begin with the yardstick held flat against the jamb and the zero mark beneath the subject's middle finger. This helps assure a vertical fall of the yardstick and allows measurement directly from zero.

4. The number of inches the yardstick falls can be translated into seconds. For our purposes we can use the following equation for estimating the number of seconds it takes a falling body to move a certain distance:

$$\text{seconds} = \frac{\sqrt{\text{inches}}}{13.9}$$

A nine-inch fall thus represents a reaction time of

$$\frac{\sqrt{9}}{13.9} = \frac{3}{13.9} = .216 \text{ seconds}$$

Using the table below you can easily convert inches to reaction time in seconds.

INCHES		SECONDS
1	=	0.072
2	=	0.102
3	=	0.125
4	=	0.144
5	=	0.161
6	=	0.176
7	=	0.190
8	=	0.203
9	=	0.216
10	=	0.227

For greater precision, give five trials and use the average distance in calculating the reaction time.[1]

5. The basic procedure can now be used to study other variables. Some possibilities include comparing the reaction times of males and females, right hands and left hands, subjects suffering from lack of sleep and normal subjects, and so forth.

6. Other important variables that can be examined involve attention and expectation. You might try varying the cues: sometimes say "Get ready" and other times drop the yardstick without warning. Or allow the subject to get bored, while you explain at length the exceptional educational value of this procedure—then drop the yardstick without warning. To note the effects of distractions, use a confederate or take advantage of naturally occurring distractions; your distracted subject may feel he is paying attention, yet miss the yardstick completely.

7. A different demonstration based on the same principle does not yield measurements but is nonetheless dramatic and may serve to impress your friends—provided you do it right. Suggest that you are going to drop a dollar bill (or larger bill, for the high-rollers in the group) through your friends' fingers and that anyone who can catch it may keep it. Armed with your research data, you can arrange that no one is likely to do so. (If your subjects always took six inches or more to catch the yardstick and the bill is held halfway through your friends' fingers, you can see that you are pretty

[1] Reaction time data is usually presented in milliseconds (msec) rather than as fractions of a second (1000 msec = 1 sec); thus .216 seconds would be 216 msec.

safe.) If you want to be sure, control not only the finger gap and the length of bill left to catch, but also take advantage of the distraction effect. Under these circumstances you can use the same bill all evening.

Questions For Discussion

1. Why is it necessary that one person drop the ruler for another? Try catching the ruler yourself. Can you catch the ruler sooner than your subjects? Why? (Hint: your reflexes are *not* that fast!)

2. Is this a good test to compare reaction times for different individuals? Could the experimenter unintentionally bias the results? (Hint: if you wanted to make one person do better than another at the task, how could you use the variables noted earlier to ensure it?)

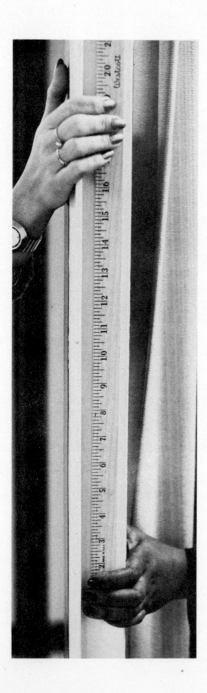
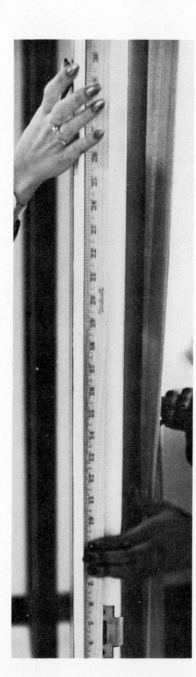
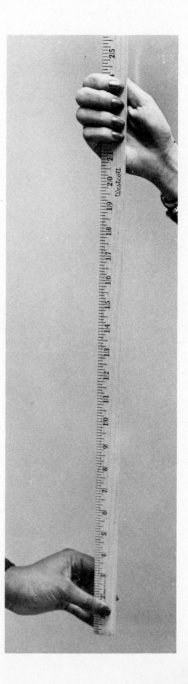

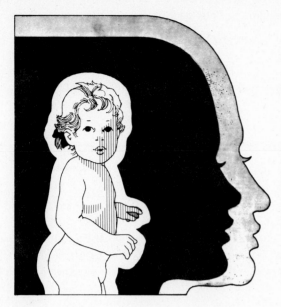

3 developmental psychology

LEARNING OBJECTIVES

Distinguish between the concepts of critical periods and stages.

Explain the principle of maturation, giving examples. Describe the interaction of maturation and environment in the development of the organism.

Discuss the effect of severe sensory deprivation or unusual stimulation on development; cite experimental evidence.

Describe Piaget's stages of cognitive development and Freud's psychosexual stages.

Describe the process of sex-role identification. List some of the variables that influence the process of identification.

Discuss some of the problems faced by adolescents. How real is the "generation gap"?

PROGRAMMED UNIT

1. An important concept in the study of development is *maturation.* Maturation refers to an innately determined sequence of physical growth that results in orderly changes in behavior relatively independent of learning or experience. If certain behavior appears in all members of the same species at about the same time, without special training, we may suspect that the behavior is largely the

   maturation   result of _____.

2. Some species of birds reared in isolation, so that they never hear the song

characteristic of their species, are still able to reproduce it properly at the appropriate stage of development. Thus we can reasonably say that singing in

maturation

these birds is controlled largely by _____ rather than by learning.

maturation

3. When behavior depends more upon physical *growth* processes than upon *learning,* the process controlling the behavior is said to be _____.

learning (or experience)

4. Maturation refers to growth processes that produce behavior changes that are relatively independent of _____. If the behavior change is due

learning

to training or experience, the process is called _____ rather than maturation.

5. The development of the fetus within the mother's body, which follows a fixed time schedule, provides a clear picture of what we mean by maturation. Fetal behavior, such as turning and kicking, follows an orderly sequence depending upon the growth stage of the fetus; fetal behavior is thus a result of

maturation

_____.

6. Growth, of course, is not complete at birth. The motor development of the infant after birth follows such an orderly sequence (rolling over, sitting, standing, walking) that this behavior appears to be the result of continuing

growth, maturation

_____ processes, or _____, rather than learning.

7. Maturation provides the readiness to learn, and most behavior depends upon both learning and maturation. Children will learn to talk only after they have

maturity (or synonym)

reached the proper stage of _____. The language they will

learning

speak is the one they hear, thus indicating the role of _____.

8. Behavior during the early developmental years frequently reflects an interaction

maturation, learning
(either order)

between _____ and _____.

9. Although the appearance of certain behavior may depend largely upon maturation, conditions of severe deprivation or unusual stimulation can influence the *rate of development.* Infants provided with a colorful mobile suspended above their crib will develop the eye-hand coordination necessary for reaching for an object earlier than infants who are kept in a bare crib with nothing to look at. Visually directed reaching is a response that develops in clearly specified maturational stages, but a more stimulating or enriched environment will ac-

rate

celerate the _____ of its development.

10. A deprived environment, on the other hand, can delay the rate of

development

_____. Three-month-old monkeys raised from birth in darkness show serious deficiencies in visual behavior when first exposed to light. For example, they do not follow a moving object with their eyes or blink when

deprivation

threatened with a blow toward the face. In this case severe <u>dep</u>_____

development

of visual stimulation resulted in delayed _____.

11. Once the visually deprived monkeys were exposed to light, they acquired the appropriate behavior in a much shorter time than newborn monkeys. This

maturation

finding points up the importance of _____ .

maturation, learn
12. Both _____ and the opportunity to _____ are necessary for the development of visual-motor behavior.

13. Research on the effects of early experience suggests that there may be *critical periods* in development, during which favorable or unfavorable experiences may have lasting effects upon behavior. For example, monkeys that are raised in isolation for the first six months of life show abnormal social behavior as adults; they rarely interact with other monkeys and are difficult to mate. Regardless of the amount of subsequent exposure to other monkeys, these early isolates never develop normal social behavior. For monkeys, then, the first six months of life

critical

may be a _____ period for the development of normal social behavior.

14. Some psychologists hypothesize that the first year of the human infant's life is critical for learning to trust other people. The infant who is cared for with warmth and affection learns that people are trustworthy; the infant who lacks affectionate care during this first year may grow up to distrust others. If this

critical

hypothesis is true, the first year of life may be a _____ period

trust

for the development of _____ in others.

period
15. The critical _____ concept assumes that at a given stage of development some kinds of influences are unusually important. If they are lacking, later development may be stunted; if they are favorable, there is a

critical

greater chance for optimal development. Failures at a _____ period of development can be made up, if at all, only with great difficulty.

16. Puppies isolated between five and seven weeks of age grow fearful of both dogs and people, while isolation earlier or later does not have much influence on their

critical

behavior. This example illustrates the concept of a _____

period

_____ .

17. Another way of looking at human development assumes that the individual passes through definable *stages* as he grows up. When we talk about infancy, childhood, adolescence, and adulthood, we are talking broadly about successive

stages

_____ in development.

periods
18. The concepts of stages and critical _____ are related but not identical. A failure in development at one stage need not be critical for future development.

19. For example, there is a period of time in the development of children when they are maturationally ready to learn to talk. (The time of most rapid language development is between ages two and four.) Suppose a child were raised by deaf-mutes during this period and exposed to language for the first time as a teen-ager. If he learned to talk as a teen-ager, even though with considerable difficulty, we would say that the two- to four-year period he had missed was

stage	a _____ of language development. If he never learned to talk despite intensive training, we would say that the period he had missed was a
critical	_____ period for language development.

20. The Swiss psychologist Piaget has proposed that children progress through a fixed sequence of stages in their *cognitive development*. The first stage, from

cognitive   birth to two years, is called the *sensorimotor stage* of _____

sensorimotor   development. During the <u>sensori</u>_____ stage children do not use language or symbols but explore the environment by means of the senses and motor activities. At first they can study objects only visually, but they soon learn to reach for and explore them with the fingers and mouth.

21. One of the many things the child learns during the sensorimotor

stage   _____ is that an *object* is *permanent;* that is, it continues to exist even when it is not present to the senses. The rattle does not disappear

object   forever when hidden by a blanket but is a permanent _____ that will reappear when the child lifts the blanket.

22. The concept of object permanence is achieved, according to Piaget, during the

sensorimotor   _____ stage of development, which occurs in the first

two   _____ years of life.

development **23.** A later stage in cognitive _____, called the *preoperational stage,* occurs between the ages of two and seven years. The child now possesses language and can begin to deal with problems by means of symbols and concepts. Objects become symbols that represent classes of things.

preoperational **24.** During the <u>pre</u>_____ stage, the child begins to use

symbols   <u>sym</u>_____ to conceptualize the environment. The preoperational

stage, seven   _____ covers the period from two to _____ years.

25. One of the concepts the child develops toward the end of the

preoperational   <u>pre</u>_____ stage is that of *conservation;* he learns that the amount of a substance does not change—that is, it is conserved—when the substance is divided into parts or placed in different-sized containers. If a four year old is shown two identical short jars containing what he acknowledges to be an equal amount of beans and watches while the contents of one jar are poured into a tall, cylindrical jar, he will say that the tall jar contains more beans. The four

has not   year old (*has/has not*) attained the concept of conservation.

26. A six- or seven-year-old child presented with the same situation will say that the contents of the short and tall jars are equal. He has attained the concept of

conservation   _____.

27. If a child says that a ball of clay contains the same amount of material when it is rolled into a sausage shape as when it is a sphere, he has achieved the concept of

conservation   _____.

28. The development of the concept of conservation occurs during the

preoperational, two

seven

_____ stage, which covers the ages of _____ to

_____. Later stages of cognitive development during which the child's thought processes gradually approach those of an adult are discussed in the text.

are not

29. Piaget's stages (*are/are not*) critical periods because, although cognitive processes usually develop in the sequence specified, behavior that fails to occur at a particular age owing to lack of appropriate stimulation can occur later.

cognitive

30. Piaget's stages are concerned with _____ development. Other theorists, such as Freud and Erikson, have proposed stage theories dealing with

personality

personality development. Freud proposed five stages of _____ development that have to do with deriving pleasure from different parts of the body at different ages. He called these *psychosexual* stages, using a very broad definition of sexuality.

psychosexual

31. The first of Freud's _____ stages is the *oral* stage, during which the infant derives pleasure from stimulation of the lips and mouth region, as in nursing or thumb-sucking. According to Freud, frustration during feeding may

oral

lead to *fixation* at the _____ stage. By "fixation" he meant that problems associated with unsatisfied needs at this stage might persist into later life.

32. If an adult who was severely frustrated as an infant during nursing shows a continual need for activities such as overeating, smoking, and gum-chewing,

fixated, oral

Freud would say the adult was fix_____ at the _____ stage of psychosexual development.

33. During the oral stage the child derives pleasure from stimulation of the

lips, mouth

psychosexual

_____ and _____ region. Subsequent stages

of psycho_____ development are the *anal* stage, during which the child secures pleasure from withholding and expelling feces; the *phallic* stage, in which gratification is obtained from fondling the sex organs; the *latent* stage, during which the elementary-school child turns his or her interests toward the environment so that sexual interests are no longer active; and the *genital* stage, at which point the sex organs are beginning to mature and the adolescent becomes interested in heterosexual relationships.

34. The second stage of psychosexual development, in which the child derives

anal

pleasure from withholding and expelling feces, is called the _____ stage.

35. As you might expect, the anal stage occurs during the second year of life while the parents are concerned with toilet training. According to Freud, a rigid and

fixation

harsh approach to toilet training may lead to fix_____ at the

anal, psychosexual

_____ stage of _____ development.

oral

anal

36. The first stage of psychosexual development is the _____ stage, the second is the _____ stage, and the third is the *phallic stage,* during which the child derives pleasure from fondling the genitals.

37. If the parents are overly upset and punitive when they discover their four year old masturbating, we might expect the child to have some problems during the

phallic, psychosexual

development

_____ stage of _____

_____ .

38. The first three psychosexual stages of development proposed by

Freud, oral, anal

_____ are the _____, _____,

phallic

and _____ stages. Following these stages in the preschool child, there is a *latent* stage during which the elementary-school youngster's sexual interests are said to be dormant, or latent, and his or her concerns are directed toward the environment and the acquisition of knowledge and skills.

latent

The _____ stage lasts until puberty, at which point hetero-sexual interests arise and the genital stage begins.

psychosexual

39. Freud's theory of _____ stages has had considerable influence upon theories of personality, but it is not accepted by most psychologists as a precise statement of development. Erikson, a later psychoanalyst, proposed a theory of *psychosocial* stages of development that is concerned with problems of

sexual

social development rather than _____ development.

psychosocial

40. Erikson's stages of _____ development are

social

concerned with the _____ problems encountered at different ages. For example, Erikson claims that during the first year of life infants learn to *trust or mistrust* other people, depending upon how well their needs are attended to at a period when they are helpless and totally dependent.

41. The infant's first social contact occurs while he is being fed. If the experience is a pleasant one and his needs are satisfied, he learns to associate his mother with

trust

satisfaction and relaxation. He learns that he can tr_____ other people to satisfy his needs.

42. If, on the other hand, the feeding situation is unpleasant and hurried, with the infant remaining hungry and uncomfortable much of the time, he may learn to

mistrust

mis_____ others as a source of satisfaction. We can see how these

first

experiences during the _____ year of life might well lead to a

trust, mistrust
(either order)

basic attitude of _____ or _____ toward people later in life.

43. During the second year of life children have their first real encounter with discipline and self-control in connection with toilet training and in learning what not to touch or investigate as they begin walking. According to Erikson the

psychosocial

psycho_____ problem at this stage is one of *autonomy* and *self-control* versus feelings of *shame* and *self-doubt.*

44. The psychosocial stage during the second year of life concerns autonomy and

self-control

_____-_____ versus feelings of shame and

self-doubt

_____-_____. If parental discipline is warm but firm, children learn pride in controlling their own impulses. If the parents try to discipline by shaming the child and making him feel that he does not live

shame

up to their expectations, he is likely to develop feelings of _____

doubt

and self-_____.

45. Erikson has proposed a number of later stages that are concerned with

psychosocial

_____ problems. Freud's stages, in contrast,

psychosexual

are concerned with _____ development, while

cognitive
(or intellectual)

Piaget's stages have to do with _____ development.

46. We noted that the child's first social contact occurs while he is being fed. It would be reasonable to assume that the child's close attachment to his mother

food (or milk)

during the early years occurs because she provides his _____. However, experiments with infant monkeys cast some doubt on this assumption. If a monkey is raised from birth in a cage containing two artificial "mothers," one constructed of wire but with a nipple providing milk and the other covered with soft terry cloth but with no milk supply, the monkey will spend most of its time clinging to the terry-cloth "mother."

47. The infant monkey will show greater attachment to the cuddly, terry-cloth

food (or milk)
is not

"mother" despite the fact that she is not a source of _____. These results indicate that attachment to the mother (_is/is not_) solely dependent upon the fact that she is a source of food.

48. In humans, attachment to the mother becomes most apparent at about the age of eight months. Before this time the infant will usually smile at anyone who smiles at him. But beginning at about eight months he will evidence fear at the appearance of a strange face and frequently cry when he is separated from his

eight

mother. _Fear of strangers_ thus appears at about the age of _____ months.

49. Prior to eight months the infant will smile indiscriminately at anyone. His responses during this time are not considered to be truly social. As he becomes able to discriminate between those who are familiar and those who are

strange

_____, he begins to restrict his social responses to those who are familiar.

50. Lisa's mother is proud of her happy, friendly baby who smiles and coos whenever friends come to admire her. But one day Lisa suddenly begins to cry when guests appear and frets whenever mother leaves the room. Lisa's mother wonders what is wrong with her child. She would be less concerned if she realized that her daughter's apparent personality change is a natural stage of fear

strangers

of _____, which occurs in most infants as they learn to

discriminate
eight

dis_____ between familiar and unfamiliar faces. We might guess that Lisa is (_five/eight_) months old.

51. **fear**
Although children soon outgrow the period of _____ of strangers, attachment to the parents and other members of the family remains close during the preschool years. Because the parents are the dominant figures in children's lives, they serve as models, or *identification figures,* for children to copy. When we say that children *identify* with their parents, we mean that they assume many of the parents' values and patterns of behavior as their own.

52. When Sarah bathes and diapers her doll using the same mannerisms and tone of voice that her mother uses in caring for her baby brother, we may assume that

identifies
she _____ with her mother.

53. When Tommy staggers around in his father's fishing boots casting an imaginary line into the bathtub, we may assume that Tommy's father serves as an

identification
_____ figure.

54. When we say that a person is identifying with another person, we mean that

like (or synonym)
whether he knows it or not, he is trying to become _____ the other person.

55. One of the major areas of behavior in which children identify with their parents

standards
is in the acquisition of *sex-role standards.* Sex-role _____ refer to the ways of behaving that a culture considers appropriate for men and women.

56. **sex-role, standards**
A child acquires his sex-_____ _____ by identifying with the parent of the same sex. If a culture expects aggressive

sex-role
behavior from its male members, then aggression is a _____-

standard
_____ _____ for men in that culture.

57. A girl acquires her sex-role standards by identifying with her mother; a boy

sex-role, standards
acquires his _____-_____ _____

identifying
by _____ with his father.

58. **same**
Sex-role identification develops as the child perceives himself as similar to the parent of the (*same/opposite*) sex.

59. If a girl's mother is aggressive and domineering and rejects the sex-role standards of her culture, we would expect the girl to have difficulty in developing the

identification
appropriate sex-role id_____.

60. Many personal qualities, however, are not sex-typed. A sense of humor, personal warmth, and many moral qualities are shared by both men and women. These

non-sex-role
are *personal* or *non-sex-role identifications.* Personal or _____-
_____-_____ identifications may be learned from either parent.

61. A girl may acquire her father's dry sense of humor, and a boy may learn considera-

non-sex-role
tion from his mother. These are _____-_____-
_____ identifications.

62. Characteristics and behavior that are not sex-typed and may be learned from either parent are called _____-_____-_____ identifications.

non-sex-role

Learning behavior that is appropriate to one's sex is called _____-_____ identification.

sex-role

63. *Adolescence,* the transitional period from childhood to adulthood, is a period of development marked by *changes.* The most striking ch_____ are the bodily changes in the *sex characteristics* and *rate of growth* that culminate in *puberty.*

changes

64. Mary is a typical twelve-year-old adolescent girl. We would expect her to experience striking bodily changes in _____ characteristics and in _____ of growth, culminating in _____.

sex

rate, puberty

65. Puberty, which is marked by menstruation in girls and the appearance of live sperm cells in the urine of boys, is reached at different ages by different youngsters. There is a wide variation in the age at which both boys and girls reach _____.

puberty
(or maturity)

66. In general, however, girls attain puberty two years earlier than boys. Thus, girls, on the average, mature (*earlier/later*) than boys.

earlier

67. Girls generally reach _____ before boys.

puberty

68. Boys and girls who mature markedly later than their classmates tend to have adjustment problems. Bob is a late maturer. He will probably have (*more/less*) difficulty in adjusting than his early-maturing classmates.

more

69. Emancipation from parental authority and from emotional dependence upon parents begins in childhood, but the process of emancipation is greatly accelerated during adolescence. Adolescents tend to be *ambivalent* about *independence.* They want the freedom to do as they please, but are not always willing to assume the responsibilities that go along with being independent. Mary plans a beach party without consulting her parents but expects them to provide the food and transportation. She is _____ in her attitude toward independence.

ambivalent

70. Adolescents tend to be ambivalent about _____.

independence

71. If parents insist upon close supervision and control of a youngster during adolescence, they are apt to produce an adolescent who continues his dependence and is unable to make his own decisions. A certain amount of freedom is thus necessary for the development of _____.

independence

72. Studies have shown that a "*democratic* family," in which the adolescent is allowed a fair degree of autonomy and is included in important decisions, produces a more capable and well-adjusted youngster than an "*authoritarian* family," in which rules are arbitrarily set and freedom of behavior is limited. Parents who wish to encourage the development of a well-adjusted adolescent, therefore, would seek to establish a(n) _____ family.

democratic

TERMS AND CONCEPTS FOR IDENTIFICATION

critical period _____   anal stage _____

_____   _____

_____   _____

_____   _____

maturation _____   psychosocial stages _____

_____   _____

_____   _____

_____   _____

principle of conservation _____   anxious attachment _____

_____   _____

_____   _____

_____   _____

formal operational stage _____   identification _____

_____   _____

_____   _____

_____   _____

psychosexual stages _____   sex-role standards _____

_____   _____

_____   _____

_____   _____

oral stage _____   puberty _____

_____   _____

_____   _____

_____   _____

____ 1. According to the psychoanalytic view, identification with a parent provides a child with
   a. a source for feelings of strength and adequacy
   b. self-control and a conscience
   c. a means of relieving separation anxiety
   d. all of the above

____ 2. When infant monkeys that had been raised with only brief exposure to diffuse light were first exposed to regular lighting, they
   a. could not track moving objects, but would blink in response to a threatened blow
   b. showed initial deficiencies in visual-motor behavior, but later acquired appropriate responses faster than younger monkeys
   c. were deficient in visual responses and never caught up to normal monkeys
   d. put out their arms when moved rapidly toward a wall

____ 3. Freud proposed a series of psychosexual stages. The chief ones, in sequence from birth, are
   a. oral, anal, phallic, latent, genital
   b. latent, anal, oral, phallic, genital
   c. oral, latent, anal, genital, phallic
   d. latent, oral, anal, phallic, genital

____ 4. Qualities such as personality, temperament, and attitudes toward work and play
   a. tend to come from the same-sex parent
   b. tend to come from the opposite-sex parent
   c. may come from either parent
   d. are most likely to come from peers

____ 5. According to Piaget, a child who can correctly predict that a ball of clay and a similar ball rolled out to a long sausage will balance on a scale must have achieved
   a. conservation of weight
   b. object permanence
   c. conservation of mass
   d. all of the above

____ 6. Recent research into the problems involved in the "generation gap" shows
   a. an increasing and nearly insurmountable gap between the views of parents and children in most countries
   b. some distance between parents and children but much less than implied by the mass media
   c. a rather large gap between parents and children in the United States but a much smaller gap in the more traditional society of Denmark
   d. substantial differences between the United States and Denmark in cultural values and in amount of parent-child estrangement

____ 7. The period during which children are most sensitive to peer pressures, as shown by the extent of conformity to such pressures, occurs in
   a. elementary school (ages 11 to 13)
   b. high school (ages 15 to 17)
   c. preschool (ages 3 to 5)
   d. primary school (ages 5 to 7)

____ 8. When mothers are insensitive or unresponsive to their babies during the first year, the babies
   a. come to depend more upon others
   b. cry less often and generally pay less attention to adults
   c. show anxious attachment in the "strange situation"
   d. show significantly different patterns of mother-child interaction in daily routines

____ 9. A study of the effects of early stimulation on human infants' visually-directed reaching showed that
   a. too much stimulation too soon may be upsetting
   b. the rate of development of this reaching response could not be significantly increased
   c. the enriched environment helped infants to discover their hands earlier than infants in a control group
   d. increasing the amount of handling was more effective than hanging elaborate ornaments over the cribs

____ 10. Maturation and environment are related, in that

a. environmental conditions can stimulate behavior only when the organism is maturationally ready

b. maturation can be accelerated by the environment

c. maturation can be impeded by the environment

d. all of the above

_____ 11. Which of the following is the most correct statement regarding early adolescent development?

a. while girls mature earlier than boys throughout childhood and are taller and heavier in each grade, this difference is most noticeable after puberty

b. beginning of growth of the secondary sex characteristics marks the onset of puberty

c. puberty takes place over about two years, the years of the adolescent growth spurt

d. on the average, boys experience their growth spurt two years later than girls

_____ 12. Piaget's concept of the _____ is demonstrated when a child systematically investigates the variables involved in the oscillation period of a pendulum.

a. formal operational stage

b. conservation of energy

c. sensorimotor stage

d. concrete operational stage

_____ 13. Studies show that an "authoritarian family" tends to produce an adolescent who is

a. childishly dependent and obedient

b. self-reliant and effective

c. independent but reserved

d. surface-compliant but rebellious underneath

_____ 14. Studies of sex-role indentification show that three-year-old boys

a. do not yet show sex stereotypes in their preference for toys

b. already prefer sex-appropriate toys

c. prefer neutral toys to sex-categorized ones

d. show a weak preference for feminine toys, although this is already beginning to reverse

_____ 15. One theory of social attachments proposes three stages in their development:

a. all people, selected people, mother

b. mother, family, other people

c. stimulation from the environment, people in general, family members

d. mother, father, peers

_____ 16. A critical period in sexual identification

a. has not yet been demonstrated

b. occurs between the ages of 9 and 12

c. is suggested by the problems of pseudo-hermaphrodites

d. begins at birth, since children of different sex are treated differently from then on

_____ 17. Child-rearing methods in the United States

a. differ little from those in other countries

b. differ from one social class to the next

c. have changed very little over the past 50 years

d. are now pretty much the same from one social class to the next

_____ 18. The data now available, while limited, seem to show a definite change in adolescents' sexual behavior; adolescents are

a. behaving more promiscuously

b. more open in their discussion of sex, although their actual behavior differs little from that of their predecessors

c. engaging in heterosexual activity at an earlier age than their parents

d. beginning to have sex at the same age as earlier generations, but doing so with more partners

_____ 19. When young monkeys were reared with access only to artificial "mothers,"

a. the females grew up to be unusually affectionate mothers

b. they preferred the terry-cloth "mothers"

c. they used the wire "mothers" for security when exploring strange objects

d. the females made poor mothers as adults, although their social relationships with peers were nearly normal

_____ 20. Which of the following summarizes best the problems of development over a lifetime?

a. developmental problems continue throughout life, but are different at the different stages of life

b. developmental problems are most severe for the adolescent and diminish thereafter, as people's lives become stable

c. biological problems get more severe as people age, even though psychological development has stopped

d. much of life has its problems, but middle adulthood is the smoothest period since vocational status is established, income is at its maximum, and family life is stabilized

INDIVIDUAL AND CLASS EXERCISE

BIRTH ORDER AND PERSONALITY CHARACTERISTICS

Introduction

Research has shown that some aspects of an individual's personality are related to order of birth. First-born or only children, in particular, tend to differ from other children. The text discusses several factors that make the first-born or only child's position in the family unique. This exercise will show whether personality differences among your acquaintances bear any relationship to birth order.

Equipment Needed

None

Procedure

Write the names of ten people of your own sex whom you know quite well in the spaces provided at the left of the data sheet (page 46). Now rate each person on the personality traits listed at the bottom of the data sheet. Note that a rating of 1 means that the person possesses the trait to only a slight degree, while a rating of 5 indicates that he possesses the trait to a high degree. For example, a rating of 5 on the trait of "aggression" indicates a very dominant, aggressive person; a rating of 1 would describe someone who was quite meek and unassertive. After deciding which number best describes the aggressive or nonaggressive nature of your first subject, enter this number in the first column next to his or her name. Now rate the subject according to the remaining three traits. Carry out the same procedure for each acquaintance. Try to avoid the common tendency of rating everyone toward the middle of the scale.

Treatment of Data

After you have rated each of your ten acquaintances on all four traits, find out their birth order (if you do not already know it) and turn to the data tabulation sheet on page 47. List the name of all first-born or only children in the appropriate column and enter their ratings for each trait. Do the same for those who were later born. Add the ratings for each trait and enter the total at the bottom of each column. Divide each total by the number of subjects in the column to find the average rating. Bring this sheet with you to class. Your instructor will tabulate the average ratings obtained by each class member for the four traits.

Questions For Discussion

1. Is there any difference in the average ratings for first-born or only children as compared to those for the later born? If so, which traits are most affected by birth order?

2. How do the circumstances of the study limit interpretation of the results? That is, might different results have been obtained if the subjects had been selected from the population at large rather than from a group of college students?

3. What are some of the factors relevant to the individual's position in the family that might explain the obtained results?

DATA SHEET

Name	Personality traits			
	Aggression	Conscientiousness	Intellectual ability	Sociability
1.				
2.				
3.				
4.				
5.				
6.				
7.				
8.				
9.				
10.				

Aggression

1. Very meek
2.
3. Moderately aggressive
4.
5. Very aggressive

Conscientiousness

1. Careless in attention to responsibilities
2.
3. Moderately conscientious
4.
5. Very conscientious

Intellectual ability

1. In lower 10% of class
2.
3. Average
4.
5. In upper 10% of class

Sociability

1. Withdrawn; a loner
2.
3. Moderately sociable
4.
5. Very outgoing and sociable

DATA TABULATION FOR BIRTH-ORDER STUDY

First-born or only child

Name	Aggression	Conscientiousness	Intellectual ability	Sociability
Total				
Average				

Later-born child

Name	Aggression	Conscientiousness	Intellectual ability	Sociability
Total				
Average				

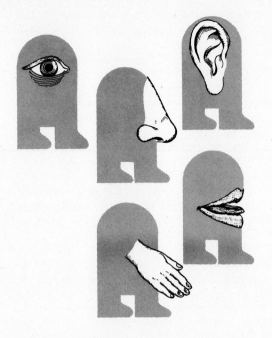

4
sensory processes

LEARNING OBJECTIVES

Define an absolute threshold and distinguish it from a difference threshold. Explain the formula for Weber's law.

Identify the main parts of the eye. Describe the functions of rods and cones and show how the process of dark adaptation provides evidence of two distinct mechanisms.

Understand the principles of color mixing with both lights and pigments. Be able to show on the color solid the interrelationships of hue, brightness, and saturation. Be familiar with the various types of color blindness.

Describe the mechanism of recurrent inhibition.

Know the physical properties of sound waves, how they are measured, and their psychological correlates. Identify the main parts of the ear.

Be familiar with the mechanisms involved in smell, taste, skin sensations, kinesthesis, and equilibrium.

PROGRAMMED UNIT

sense

1. All of our information about the world comes to us by way of stimuli impinging upon our *sense organs.* Without our eyes, ears, nose, and other _____ organs, we would know nothing about the people, objects, and events that make up our world.

2. We gain information about the world in which we live by way of our

sense organs   _____ _____. But a certain *minimum* of sense-organ *stimulation* is required before any sensory experience will be evoked. The minimum physical energy necessary to activate a given sensory system is called

absolute   the *absolute threshold.* To put it another way, the _____ threshold is the intensity at which a stimulus becomes effective.

3. A spot of light in a dark room must reach some measurable intensity before an individual can distinguish it from darkness. In other words, the degree of intensity necessary for the spot of light to be seen is its absolute

threshold   _____ for that individual.

4. Likewise, a sound emitted in a soundproof room must reach a certain intensity before it can be heard. The intensity at which it can be heard by someone is its

absolute   _____ threshold.

5. In both of the instances mentioned above, we see that a certain *minimum* of sense-organ stimulation is required before any sensory experience will be evoked.

absolute threshold   This minimum is called the _____ _____.

6. A pin prick cannot be felt unless the pressure of the pin on the skin reaches a certain intensity. The intensity of pressure necessary for the pin prick to be felt

absolute threshold   is its _____ _____.

7. We can see from these examples that whether the stimulus is light, sound, or

minimum, stimulation   touch, a certain _____ of sense-organ _____ is required before any sensory experience will be evoked. This minimum is called

absolute threshold   the _____ _____.

8. There must also be a certain magnitude of difference between two stimuli before one can be distinguished from the other. The minimum amount of difference necessary to tell two stimuli apart is known as the *difference threshold.* Thus two tones must differ to some degree before one is heard as higher than the

difference   other. The point at which they can be told apart is the _____ threshold.

9. The transition between no sensory experience and some sensory experience is

absolute   the _____ threshold; the transition between no difference and

difference   some difference in stimuli is the _____ threshold.

10. Thresholds *vary* from one person to the next and may even *fluctuate* over time within one individual. Therefore, we should think of a threshold measurement as a statistical average. If a psychologist was interested in measuring your

difference   dif_____ threshold for discriminating between two tones, he would probably not get identical results each time of testing. Likewise, your threshold for discriminating between the two tones would probably not be the same as someone else's threshold.

vary   11. Thresholds not only _____ from one individual to the next but may even *fluctuate* within one individual from time to time.

12. Threshold measurement should be thought of as a statistical average. That is, for

fluctuate

the same person thresholds may _____ from one time

individual
(or synonym)

to the next, and thresholds also vary from one _____ to another.

absolute

13. The two kinds of thresholds we have discussed are the _____ threshold, which is the transition between no sensory experience and some

difference

sensory experience, and the _____ threshold, which is the transition between no difference and some difference in stimuli.

sense

14. The human eye is one of the most complex _____ organs. Note the drawing of the human eye, and as you proceed consider the location and functions of its different parts. To begin, locate the *cornea,* where light *enters* the eye.

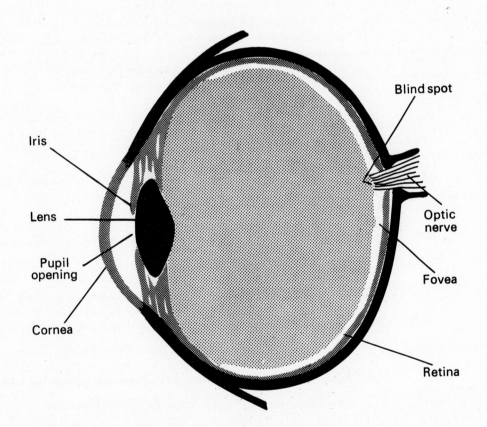

cornea

15. Light *enters* the eye through the _____, the amount of light being *regulated* by the size of the *pupil opening,* which is an opening in the *iris.*

enters

16. The cornea is the portion of the eye through which light _____; the amount of light entering the eye is regulated by the size of the

pupil

_____ opening.

cornea

17. After light has entered the eye through the _____ and its pupil opening

amount has been regulated by the _____ _____, the *lens* then *focuses* the light on the receptor surface, the *retina*.

18. The parts of the human eye we have identified thus far are the

cornea, pupil, iris

c_____, the p_____, the i_____, and the *lens,* which focuses light on the *retina.*

enters

regulated

focuses

19. Light _____ the eye through the cornea, the amount of light being _____ by the size of the pupil opening, which is an opening in the iris. The lens then _____ the light on the receptor surface, the retina.

lens

retina

20. The _____ focuses the light on the receptor surface, the

_____.

retina

21. The lens focuses the light on the _____, which is made up of a number of specialized cells. Two of these specialized types of cells (not shown in the drawing) are of particular interest. These are the rods and cones, which have different functions. (In the text you will find a diagram showing the rods and cones.)

22. *Rods* and *cones* are specialized cells with *different* functions and are found in

retina

the _____.

different

23. Rods and cones, which have _____ functions, are found in the receptor surface, the retina.

rods

cones (either order)

24. Two specialized types of cells in the retina are _____ and

_____.

25. *Cones* are active primarily in *daylight* vision and permit us to see both *achromatic* colors (white, black, and the intermediate grays) and *chromatic* colors (red, green, blue, and so on). The rods and cones are specialized cells with

different, retina

_____ functions and are found in the _____.

26. The cones of the retina permit us to see white, black, and the intermediate grays

chromatic

(the achromatic colors), and red, green, blue, and the other _____ colors.

27. The *rods,* in contrast to the cones, enable us to see only *achromatic* colors. The rods function mainly in vision under *reduced* illumination, as in twilight or *night*

achromatic, chromatic
(either order)

vision. Cones enable us to see both _____ and _____ colors.

28. The cones function in normal daylight vision, whereas the rods function under

reduced

_____ illumination, as in night vision.

achromatic	**29.** Rods enable us to see only _____ colors and function in vision
reduced	under _____ illumination.
daylight	**30.** Cones function in normal _____ vision, whereas the rods
night	function in _____ vision.
	31. When you enter a dark room your eyes gradually become more sensitive to light so that after a while you are able to see more than when you first entered. This experience is known as *dark adaptation.*
adaptation	**32.** The experience of dark _____ shows how the rods and cones differ in their functions. When you first enter a dark room the cones in your retina become more sensitive to light. Stated another way, their absolute
lowered	threshold is (*raised/lowered*).
	33. After about five minutes in the dark, the sensitivity of the cones has increased as much as it will. The rods, however, continue to adapt to the dark and become appreciably more sensitive for about a half an hour. You can see better after twenty minutes in the dark than after five minutes because of the functioning of
rods	the _____.
cone	**34.** The _____ cells no longer increase their sensitivity to light after a few minutes in a dark room because they function best in normal
daylight, achromatic,	_____ vision. Cones enable us to see both _____
chromatic (either order)	and _____ colors.
rod	**35.** The _____ cells function in night vision and enable us to see
achromatic	only _____ colors.
cones	**36.** In the experience of dark adaptation the _____ increase their
rods	sensitivity for the first few minutes, but the _____ become increasingly more sensitive over a longer period.
	37. The most sensitive portion of the eye in normal *daylight* vision is a small area of the retina called the *fovea,* on which is focused light that comes from the center
cone	of the visual field. The *fovea* must contain _____ cells because these function in normal daylight vision.
	38. The most sensitive portion of the eye in normal daylight vision is the
fovea	_____; it contains *only cone* cells, which are packed closely
Rod	together in a small area. _____ cells are found only *outside* the fovea.
rod	**39.** The portion of the retina outside the fovea contains *both* _____ and cone cells.
rod, cone (either order)	**40.** Outside the fovea are _____ and _____ cells.

cone

daylight

Within the fovea are only _____ cells, which are closely packed together and function best in _____ vision.

41. Not far from the fovea, on the surface of the retina, is an insensitive area, the *blind spot,* where nerve fibers from the retinal cells come together in a bundle to form the *optic nerve,* which carries impulses from the eye to the brain. The area

nerve

blind

where the optic _____ leaves the eye is called the _____ spot because it contains neither rods nor cones.

42. The most sensitive portion of the eye in normal daylight vision is the

fovea

blind

optic

_____, which contains only cone cells; the insensitive area is the _____ spot, where the nerve fibers from the cells of the retina come together in a bundle to form the _____ nerve.

43. Without looking at the earlier drawing you should be able to label the parts of the eye in the drawing presented here. Check your results with the labeled drawing of the eye. (*Rod and cone cells are not shown, but you should*

cone, fovea,

rod, cone

remember that _____ *cells are concentrated in the* _____, *whereas both* _____ *and* _____ *cells are found outside the fovea.*)

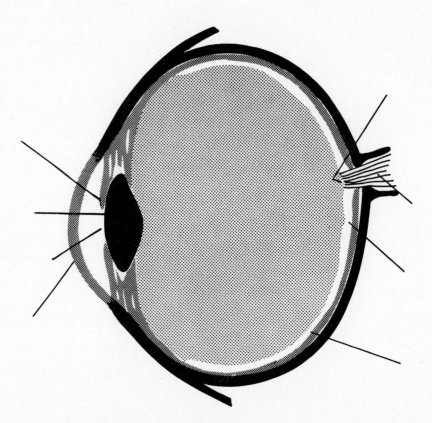

44. Let us now discuss color vision. You recall that red, blue, green, and so on, are

chromatic

_____ colors. We can produce the colors that are familiar to us in a *rainbow* by passing sunlight through a prism, which breaks it into a band of varicolored light.

45. When sunlight is passed through a prism, it breaks into a band of varicolored

rainbow   light that is familiar to us in the _____. The colors correspond
to *wavelengths,* the *red* end of the rainbow being produced by the *long* light
waves, the *violet* end by the *short* light waves.

46. Sunlight sent through a prism produces a rainbow effect. This band of varicolored light is called a *solar spectrum.* The colors correspond to

wavelengths   _____, the red end of the spectrum being produced by the

short   long light waves and the violet end by the _____ light waves.

47. The colors of the solar spectrum can be arranged in the form of a *color circle.*

solar   The _____ spectrum is bent back around itself to form a circle
as shown below. The break in the color circle between red and violet contains
colors that do not appear in the solar spectrum but can be produced by mixtures

color   of other colors. The colors *opposite* each other on the _____

circle   _____ are called *complementaries.* Note that blue and yellow,

complementaries   red and green are found opposite each other. They are _____.

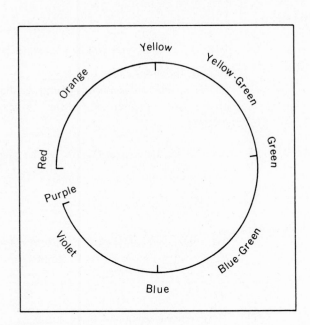

48. Blue and yellow, red and green are complementaries, since they appear

opposite   _____ each other on the color circle. When complementary
pairs of colors, such as yellow and blue, red and green, are mixed as *lights* (*not as
pigments*), they cancel each other and result in neutral *gray.* *Spectral colors* (the
colors of the solar spectrum) must be opposite each other on the

color circle   _____ _____ in order to be considered complementaries.

spectral   **49.** The _____ colors resemble a rainbow. When they are opposite

complementaries   each other on a color circle, they are called _____.

50. Blue-green and orange are a pair of complementary colors on a color circle. If mixed together as *lights,* the resulting color would be a neutral _____.

51. Complementaries are spectral colors that are opposite each other on a color circle; when mixed together as _____, they cancel each other and result in a neutral gray.

52. Some of the colors appear to be more elementary than others; that is, they appear to be composed of a single hue, which is a technical name for the quality of redness, blueness, greenness, and so on, that differentiates one color from another. These elementary colors are called *psychological primaries,* and usually four are named: *red, green, blue,* and *yellow.* Colors such as orange or purple are

not psychological _____, since their components can be recognized—for instance, both red and yellow can be identified in orange.

53. The _____ primaries are red, green, blue, and yellow.

54. The psychological primaries are _____, _____, _____, and _____.

55. Red, green, blue, and yellow appear to be more elementary than other colors and are therefore called _____ primaries. Another set of primaries is called *color-mixture primaries;* these are any three widely spaced colors on the spectrum that can be used to provide all the other colors by *additive mixture.*

56. Any three widely spaced colors on the spectrum can be used to provide all the other colors by additive mixture. These are called _____-_____ primaries.

57. Red, green, and blue are widely spaced colors on the spectrum that can be used to provide all the other colors by additive mixture. Therefore we call these colors _____-_____ primaries.

58. The psychological primaries are _____, _____, _____, and _____. The _____-_____ primaries are any three widely spaced colors on the spectrum that can be used to provide all the other colors by additive

_____.

59. The *negative afterimage* is an interesting phenomenon in color perception. If you stare at a red circle and then look at a plain gray surface, you will have the experience of seeing a green circle on it; that is, you experience a *negative afterimage.* The afterimage is called "negative" because green is the complementary color of red. You recall that blue and yellow are complementary colors. Were you to stare at a yellow circle and then look at a plain gray surface, you

blue

would have the experience of seeing a _____ circle on it.

60. If you stare at a green circle and then look at a plain gray surface, you are likely

red

to see a _____ circle on it; that is, you experience a

negative

_____ afterimage.

negative afterimage

61. A _____ _____ is so named because, after staring at a particular color, one usually sees its complementary color on a gray surface.

rods

62. The light sensitive receptors in the retina, the _____ and the

cones (either order)

_____, appear to be especially responsive to *changes in light intensity.* They will fire nervous impulses to the brain more rapidly when a light is turned on or turned off than they will in response to a steady light.

changes

63. The visual receptors are sensitive to _____ in light intensity.

64. If the eye is completely immobilized so that the light image impinging on the retina is unchanging, or *stabilized,* visual acuity decreases. This occurs because

intensity

the visual receptors respond primarily to changes in light _____.

65. Vision is, of course, only one of several human senses. In everyday language

five

most people speak of our having _____ senses: sight, hearing,

taste, smell
(either order)

_____, _____, and touch.

66. Students of psychology are expected to be more precise in defining the senses. As you will see shortly, the sense of touch is not one sensation but four. In addition, there are two special senses that provide information about body position and body movement and enable us to keep our balance. Therefore it is

senses

inaccurate to say that humans have only five _____. (Hearing and the senses dealing with body position and movement and balance are treated in the text.)

67. Taste, smell, and the skin sensations are important in everyday life, but they do not provide us with the rich patterns and organization that vision and audition do. Vision and audition are spoken of as the "higher senses"; taste, smell, and the

lower

skin sensations are therefore thought of as the "_____ senses."

68. Psychologists have identified four primary taste qualities: *sweet, sour, salt,* and *bitter.* But most taste experience is brought about by a fusion of these qualities with other sense experiences. As you might guess, the "taste" of strong cheese is

smell

considerably affected by our sense of _____.

taste

69. The four primary _____ qualities are *sweet, sour, salt,* and

bitter

_____. But taste is also affected by other senses. If you were blindfolded and your nostrils were pinched together so that you could not

smell

_____, you would have trouble distinguishing between the taste of an apple and a raw potato.

70. The four taste qualities are _____, _____, _____, and _____. Other _____ contribute to taste.

71. The sense of *smell* is from an evolutionary point of view one of the most

   primitive and most important of the _____. Smell has more direct neural pathways to the brain than any other sense.

72. The sense of _____ has more direct neural pathways to the brain than any other sense. It plays a more important role in the life of the lower animals than in humans.

73. There are four *skin* sensations. That is, the familiar sense of touch is not one sensation but at least four: *touch, pain, warm,* and *cold.* These sensations are felt

   through separate *sensitive spots* on the surface of the _____.

74. Touch is not one sensation but at least four: touch, _____, warm, and _____. These sensations are registered through separate _____ spots on the surface of the skin.

75. The sensations provided by sensitive spots on the surface of the skin include

   _____, _____, _____, and _____.

TERMS AND CONCEPTS FOR IDENTIFICATION

absolute threshold _____

_____

_____

_____

psychophysical function_____

_____

_____

difference threshold _____

_____

_____

just noticeable difference (j.n.d.)_____

_____

_____

Weber's law _____

_____

_____

rod _____

_____

_____

cone _____

_____

_____

fovea_____

_____

_____

dark adaptation_____

_____

_____

complementary colors _____

_____

_____

psychological primaries _____

_____

_____

color-mixture primaries _____

_____

_____

hue_____

_____

_____

brightness _____

_____

_____

saturation_____

_____

_____

trichromat_____

_____

_____

dichromat _____

_____

_____

monochromat _____

_____

_____

_____

negative afterimage _____

_____

_____

_____

recurrent inhibition _____

_____

_____

stabilized image _____

_____

_____

_____

pitch _____

_____

_____

_____

loudness _____

_____

_____

_____

decibel _____

_____

_____

kinesthesis _____

_____

_____

_____

equilibratory senses _____

_____

_____

SELF-QUIZ

_____ 1. After a few minutes in a dark room we can see better than when we first came in because the
   a. rods have adapted
   b. rods and cones have adapted
   c. cones have adapted
   d. bipolar cells have adapted

_____ 2. The most primitive and most important of the senses, from an evolutionary viewpoint, is the sense of
   a. smell
   b. touch
   c. vision
   d. taste

_____ 3. When we are at rest, our sense of our body's position is provided by the
   a. vestibular sacs
   b. otoliths
   c. hair cells
   d. all of the above

_____ 4. The _____ is the minimum physical energy necessary to activate a given sensory system.
   a. difference threshold
   b. absolute threshold
   c. psychophysical function
   d. stimulus intensity

_____ 5. Sound is a function of pressure changes in the air that can be represented as sine waves. In such a sine wave
   a. amplitude refers to the amount of compression and expansion of the air
   b. frequency is measured in the number of vibration cycles per minute
   c. amplitude is measured in Hertz
   d. frequency is shown by the amount by which the wave is displaced above or below the baseline

_____ 6. Of the several layers of the retina, the light-sensing cells (rods and cones) are
   a. closest to the front of the eye
   b. the second layer from the front of the eye
   c. the second layer from the back of the eye
   d. closest to the back of the eye

_____ 7. The person with normal color vision is called a
   a. quadrochromat
   b. trichromat
   c. dichromat
   d. monochromat

_____ 8. Feedback about the position of our body parts as we walk and climb is provided by the _____ sense.
   a. equilibratory
   b. vestibular
   c. kinesthetic
   d. otolithic

_____ 9. The _____ threshold is defined in terms of the crucial amount of change in the physical stimulus, i.e., the _____.
   a. absolute, crucial stimulus change (c.s.c)
   b. difference, barely detectable change (b.t.c.)
   c. absolute, minimal stimulus difference (m.s.d.)
   d. difference, just noticeable difference (j.n.d.)

_____ 10. If an image is projected onto the retina in such a way that the same cells continue to be stimulated, the image begins to
   a. seem unfamiliar
   b. quiver and oscillate in small movements
   c. fade and disappear
   d. change color

_____ 11. Our skin provides us with a sensation of "hot" when
   a. specific "hot" nerve-end structures in the skin are stimulated
   b. "warm" and "cold" skin receptors are stimulated simultaneously
   c. skin receptors for "warm" are stimulated beyond the intermediate threshold
   d. "warm" and "pain" skin receptors are stimulated simultaneously

_____ 12. The color solid helps us to understand the relationships between hue, saturation, and brightness. Which of the following is _not_ one of these relationships?
   a. hue is represented by points along the

radius

b. brightness ranges from white at the top to black at the bottom

c. hue is represented by points around the circumference

d. saturation varies from highly saturated on the outside to gray in the center

____ 13. Cones _____ while rods _____.

a. sense only chromatic colors, sense only achromatic colors

b. require more intense light, function under reduced light

c. function mainly at night, are active only in daylight

d. can be compared to black-and-white film, can be compared to color film

____ 14. The _____ represent(s) the final stage in the process by which the ear turns air pressure changes into neural impulses in the auditory nerves.

a. organ of Corti

b. basilar membrane

c. hair cells of the organ of Corti

d. cochlea

____ 15. Recurrent inhibition is important because it allows the organism to

a. process visual information from each eye separately

b. pay attention to the portions of the environment which are the most brightly lighted

c. utilize multiple receptor cells, as in the horseshoe crab

d. attend to the portions of the environment which are changing

____ 16. The dimensions of tone that correspond to hue, brightness, and saturation of colors are

a. pitch, loudness, and timbre

b. loudness, pitch, and overtone

c. timbre, pitch, and overtone

d. pitch, frequency, and loudness

____ 17. If a subject can detect a difference in temperature of $1°C$ at $20°C$, how small a difference can he detect at $60°C$, according to Weber's Law?

a. $1°$

b. $2°$

c. $3°$

d. $4°$

____ 18. The sense of taste is an interesting one, in that

a. some animals cannot taste sweet at all

b. the human taste receptors continuously reproduce themselves

c. even individual human taste cells vary in their responsiveness to sweet, salt, sour, and bitter

d. all of the above

____ 19. Colored lights that are complementary

a. fall adjacent to each other on the color circle

b. yield a neutral gray when mixed

c. are the same colors as complementary paint pigments

d. do not exist in the spectrum but can be produced by mixing wave lengths

____ 20. Some of the fibers from each eye cross over to the opposite brain hemisphere at the

a. optic chiasma

b. optic nerve

c. blind spot

d. fovea

KEY TO SELF-QUIZ

20. a	15. d	10. c	5. a
19. b	14. c	9. d	4. b
18. d	13. b	8. c	3. d
17. c	12. a	7. b	2. a
16. a	11. b	6. d	1. c

INDIVIDUAL EXERCISES

SEEING AND NOT SEEING

Introduction

There are several procedures that can help you experience aspects of your visual system not normally noticed. The text describes the eye in detail, but it is sometimes hard to relate that description to your own experience. Exercises such as those noted below, as well as those given in the text, can help you really "see" what is happening.

A. Phosphenes

First note that your eyes are sensitive to more than light. If you apply gentle pressure to them, with the lids closed, you will "see" patterns of color, called "phosphenes." These result when the eye translates pressure into a visual experience.

B. Fundus

Next, consider that light, the usual stimulus for the eyes, has to travel through a series of eye tissues before it is registered by the rods and cones. Normally you do not see the portions of the eye through which the light must pass, because they remain in a fixed location with respect to the retina. As noted in the text, recurrent inhibition ensures that anything not moving with respect to the retina is not seen. The network of blood vessels in the eye, however, can sometimes be noticed as a pattern of fine flickering movement when an exceptionally strong pulse causes the vessels to expand rhythmically.

This network, called the "fundus," can be seen more directly with the aid of a flashlight. Cover the end of the flashlight with a piece of aluminum foil and punch a 1/8" hole in it to provide a small beam of light. Go into a dark room and shine this beam into one eye at an angle, holding the flashlight directly under the eye just above the chin and aiming the beam toward the top of your head; you will probably have to experiment with the angle in order to get the proper result. Look straight ahead and move the flashlight around slightly. What you will see is a pattern of lines on a glowing reddish background, rather like the veining in a leaf; this is the fundus.

C. A Familiar Sight Not Usually Seen

Another portion of your anatomy, also rarely "seen," is much more obvious than the fundus. If you think about it as you read, you will discover that you can see not only this workbook but also a view of each side of your nose. Unlike the fundus, the invisibility of your nose is not based on recurrent inhibition, but on sensory adaptation or "attention." You are so used to these views of your nose accompanying every scene that you no longer notice them. (If you now have trouble *not* noticing them, don't worry about it; as you turn your attention to other activities, your nose will resume its customary place in the scheme of things.)

D. Seeing Color

Surprisingly, people often do not know that they are colorblind. We are not normally aware of how we learn to label colors or of how color constancy works to keep our perception of colors stable. A familiar object appears to be the same color regardless of the light conditions under which we view it. But it is possible to overcome the effects of constancy. Pick something you know the color of very well—your bike or car, some item of clothing, etc. Then look at it in various light conditions—from brilliant sun to as dark as you can still see at all. If you try to look at the object as if you and it were completely new to the world, you may be able to overcome the constancy effect and see how different its color appears under differing conditions. (Note that you will be able to observe these differences much more easily for a friend's object and vice versa, since the constancy will not be as strong for an unfamiliar object.)

You can also experiment with color constancy by wearing tinted glasses. One aspect of looking at the world through rose-colored glasses is that after a while it tends to look like the same old world. Try some of the brilliant lenses available in department stores—green, orange, violet, or even rose—the ones apparently designed more to be looked *at* than to look through. You will find that at first everything seems brighter and colors appear peculiar. But if you wear the glasses for a while, the world will seem more normal—as if you had been born with this particular kind of vision. You will still be able to name most colors appropriately, although a careful test will show some problems—just as it does with those who are colorblind from birth. One final experience awaits you, however. When you take the glasses off, the world will seem unusually drab for a time; your innate tendency to compensate for changes in visual stimulation will overcompensate when the lenses are first removed. Mercifully, your visual adaptation system will soon have things normal again.

E. The Importance of Vision

Finally, give a moment's thought to the extent to which sight dominates our lives. If you have never had a blind friend, imagine now that you do and think about trying to explain something to him. Whether your explanation concerns people, cars, clothes, school work, how to get somewhere, or whatever, you will be surprised to discover the extent to which you rely on vision and think in visual terms.

You may even wish to try the exercise, developed by sensory-awareness groups, of being "blind for a day" and being led about by someone as you concentrate on your other senses. (Remember if you attempt this exercise that you are still thinking in visual terms—something the congenitally blind cannot do.)

As a last way of noting the extent to which sight, when not blocked off, overrides the other senses, think about where the sound comes from in a movie or TV. Obviously, from the loudspeaker(s), which are often discriminably separated from the picture. But equally obviously, the sound seems to be located in the visually apparent source, e.g., the moving mouth on the screen. When some other sense conflicts with vision, it is almost always vision that prevails. The same phenomenon causes airplane pilots many problems because they tend to attempt to align the aircraft visually, even in the face of evidence and training to the contrary.

5
perception

LEARNING OBJECTIVES

Describe the four object constancies, providing an example of each. Give evidence for the role of learning in size and location constancy.

Discuss figure-ground organization as basic to stimulus patterning. Discuss reversible figures and visual illusions as illustrations of the role of perceptual hypotheses.

Describe two types of apparent motion. List the factors that influence the perception of real motion.

List the binocular and monocular cues to depth perception.

Explain how simple, complex, and hypercomplex cells in the visual cortex function to code information.

Discuss the nativist and empiricist viewpoints of perception, presenting evidence from several areas of research.

Describe some of the factors that determine which stimuli will gain our attention. Be familiar with the orienting reflex and the factors that affect it.

Define four types of ESP and describe how two of them are investigated in the laboratory.

PROGRAMMED UNIT

1. In our perception of the world around us, we respond not to isolated stimuli but to *patterns of stimuli* that are organized into a *meaningful whole.* When looking

at a painting of a landscape, you perceive not isolated daubs of paint but

patterns

_____ of stimuli that are organized in some meaningful way.

patterns

meaningful

2. In listening to a piece of music, you hear _____ of tones rather than isolated tones. The word "pattern" implies that the tones are organized in some m_____ way.

3. As you sit at your desk reading this unit, there are many stimuli impinging upon your sense organs, but what you actually perceive depends upon your *past experience* with patterns of _____.

stimuli

experience

4. When we say that perception depends upon past _____, we imply that at least some aspects of perception must be learned.

5. When you look at a silver dollar held at eye level, the pattern of

stimuli

_____ impinging on your eyes is quite different from the pattern produced by the same coin lying on a table. In both instances, however, you perceive the shape of the coin as round. In other words, the

shape

_____ of the coin is perceived as *constant* regardless of the viewing angle.

6. Similarly, we tend to perceive an object as having a *constant* color regardless of the degree of illumination on it. A tennis ball is perceived as white whether it is lying in bright sunlight or in the shade of a tree. That is, the tennis ball is

constant

perceived as having a _____ color.

7. The tendency to perceive objects as the same regardless of changes in the conditions of perception is called *object constancy*. We recognize a tin can as being cylindrical regardless of its position. This is an example of

object

_____ constancy.

8. The fact that we perceive an object as being one particular color even when the

object

constancy

illumination is changed is another illustration of _____

_____.

9. A closed door is rectangular in shape, but as it swings toward you its shape goes through a series of distortions. When the door is partially open, it is actually a trapezoid, in terms of the pattern of stimulation on the retina. When it is completely open, we see only a vertical line the thickness of the door. Although we can easily distinguish these changes, what we perceive is an unchanging door swinging on its hinges. The fact that you perceive the door as a rectangle

object

constancy

regardless of its position is an illustration of _____

_____.

10. Psychologists distinguish among several kinds of object constancy. For example, the tendency to perceive objects as the same *shape,* regardless of the viewing

shape

angle, is known as _____ constancy.

11. When we see a person close to us, we may recognize that he is about 6 feet tall. If we perceive this same person at a distance of 100 yards, the image on the retina is much smaller than it was when he was right next to us. Still we perceive him as being approximately the same *size*, 6 feet tall. This is an example of

size   _____ constancy.

12. We perceive a tin can as being cylindrical, regardless of its position, because of

shape   _____ constancy.

13. We perceive a fence post at the end of the block as being as tall as the one next

size constancy   to us because of _____ _____ .

14. The fact that an orange flag is perceived as orange even when the conditions of

color   illumination change is an example of c_____ constancy.

constancy   15. Another kind of object _____ is *location* constancy. Even though the stimuli impinging upon our senses change rapidly as we move about, we perceive objects as maintaining a fixed location.

16. The tendency to perceive objects as being in a fixed location, regardless of

location constancy   continual changes in stimulation, is known as _____ _____ .

17. When we speak of object constancy, then, we are speaking about the tendency

constant   to perceive objects as _____ regardless of alterations in illumi-
(or the same)   nation, viewing angle, distance, or other conditions of perception.

18. The general name given to the tendency to perceive objects as the same regardless

object   of changes in the conditions of perception is _____

constancy   _____ .

location, color   19. We have examined four kinds of object constancy: _____ ,
size, shape   _____ , _____ , and _____
(any order)   constancy.

20. The perceptual constancies suggest that our perceptions are organized in some way. If you look around, you will notice that certain objects seem bolder and better defined than others. Writing upon a blackboard stands out against the background of the blackboard. We call what stands out the *figure* and the background the *ground*. The perceptual organization of figure and ground—in

figure   the above example, white against black—constitutes the _____-
ground relationship.

21. When we look at a picture of a woman standing on a beach with the ocean

figure   behind her, the woman is the _____ and the ocean is the

ground   _____ .

22. An object standing out against a uniform background is an example of a

figure-ground   _____-_____ relationship.

23. Another example of organization within perception is the tendency, called *perceptual grouping,* to *group* stimuli into some sort of pattern or structure. In the top figure below, you tend to perceive three pairs of straight lines with an

right extra line on the _____. In the bottom figure, the addition of extensions to the same lines makes you perceive three broken squares and an

left extra line on the _____.

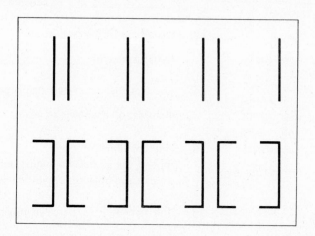

24. The tendency to group stimuli according to a pattern of some sort is called

grouping perceptual _____.

figure-ground 25. Two examples of organization within perception are _____-

perceptual grouping _____ relationships and _____ _____.

26. Many problems in perception are still not well understood. One of these is *visual illusions.* You are probably familiar with geometrical illusions like those below.

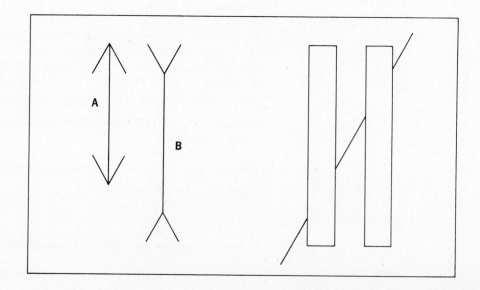

For the figure on the left, line segment B looks longer than line segment A, though both are actually the same length; this is an example of a visual

illusion
_____. For the figure on the right, the line that projects through the two rectangles is actually straight, though it appears staggered. This

visual illusion
is another example of a _____ _____.

27. Another type of illusion is *apparent motion,* the illusion of motion when there is no real movement of the object. If you stare at a fixed spot of light in a dark room, after a few seconds the light will appear to move about in an erratic manner. This phenomenon, called the *autokinetic effect,* is an example of

motion
apparent _____.

illusion
28. Apparent motion is the _____ of motion when there is no real movement.

29. One example of apparent motion, the movement of a fixed spot of light in a

autokinetic
dark room, is the _____ effect.

motion
30. Another example of apparent _____, familiar to you as the basis of "motion pictures," is called *stroboscopic motion.* If a series of pictures (each picture slightly different from the preceding one) is presented rapidly enough, the pictures blend into smooth motion.

31. The illusion of motion created when separated stimuli, not in motion, are

stroboscopic
presented rapidly in succession is called _____ motion.

motion
32. Stroboscopic _____ and the autokinetic effect are both exam-

apparent
ples of _____ motion. Apparent motion, as you recall, is one

illusion
form of visual _____.

33. The perception of depth is another problem in the study of perception. The

three
surface of the retina has only two dimensions, yet we perceive in _____ dimensions.

three
34. The process by which we perceive in _____ dimensions is similar to the effect produced by the old-fashioned stereoscope. The stereoscope is a device by means of which two flat pictures, one presented to each eye, combine to yield an experience of depth. The pictures appear to be identical but are actually photographed from slightly different *angles.*

35. Since our eyes are separated in our head, each views the world from a slightly

angle
different _____. The combination of these two scenes provides

depth
the experience of _____.

36. The perception of depth that results from the overlapping visual fields of the two eyes is called *stereoscopic vision.* Stereoscopic vision depends upon the fact

different
that each of our eyes sees a slightly _____ picture.

37. Having two eyes helps us to perceive depth and distance by means of

stereoscopic vision

_____ _____. But a person with only one

eye can still use many cues to determine the distance or depth of an object. Cues

one (or a single)

that require the use of only _____ eye are called *monocular distance cues.*

38. If one object cuts off the view of another, we assume that the first object is

nearer. Since we can make this observation with only one eye, it is a

monocular

_____ distance cue.

39. Another monocular cue is the fact that parallel lines appear to converge in the

distance. When you look down a railroad track, the rails appear to come together

monocular

at the horizon. This is a _____ cue to distance.

40. The fact that objects appear to decrease in size with distance is another cue that

distance

a person with only one eye could use to estimate dis_____.

41. Thus we see that there are many cues that can be utilized to judge the depth or

distance of an object. Some of these require the use of only one eye. These are

monocular

called _____ distance cues. Others require the use of both

eyes; these are *binocular* cues.

42. When we judge the distance of an object, we generally depend upon both

monocular, binocular
(either order)

_____ and _____ cues.

binocular

43. Stereoscopic vision is a _____ cue, while the fact that objects

monocular

appear to decrease in size with increasing distance is a _____

cue.

44. As adults, we know that we are capable of certain kinds of visual perception. But

disagreements remain over whether our abilities to perceive the spatial aspects of

our environment are learned or whether we are born with them. Those who

support the role of *learning* are called *empiricists.* Those who maintain that we

are born with the ability to perceive the way we do are called *nativists.* If one

argues that the perceptual constancies must be learned, he is supporting the

empiricists

viewpoint of the _____.

empiricists

45. The _____ feel that we have to learn to perceive the world in

nativists

the way that we do. The _____, on the other hand, argue that

this ability is innate.

46. Most psychologists today agree that practice and experience play a vital role in

determining what we perceive. In other words, they emphasize the importance

learning

of _____ in perception. This is the position of the

empiricists

_____. The question that remains is whether we are born with

some ability to perceive the world or whether it is all learned.

47. When by the removal of cataracts vision is given to a person who has been blind

all of his life, he cannot distinguish a square from a triangle or tell which of two sticks is longer without feeling them. This evidence supports the role of

learning _____ in perception.

48. On the other hand, as you will see in the text, there is evidence for some innate

nativist basis for what we perceive. Thus, the _____ viewpoint is not completely wrong.

49. Perception is selective. We pay attention to only a few of the many stimuli that surround us. The question naturally arises, What determines the stimuli to which we will attend? Some of the variables are internal, such as the *needs* and *expectations* of the individual. Those stimuli that are pertinent to one's needs

expectations and _____ are those most likely to attract attention.

50. When we are hungry, we are more likely to notice the smell of cooking bacon

need than when we are not. Our attention is determined by our _____ for food. A person awaiting an important letter is likely to pick out the

expectation mailman's step amid many other sounds. His _____ influences his attention.

needs, expectations 51. Thus, internal variables such as _____ and
(either order) _____ can influence our perception. The characteristics of stimuli are also important. Intensity, size, contrast, and move-ment are some of the *physical properties of the stimulus* that help to gain our

more attention. A large, bright red neon sign that flashes on and off is (*more/less*) likely to attract our attention than a small gray poster.

stimulus 52. Physical characteristics of the _____ are external variables that

needs, expectations affect our perception, while _____ and _____
(either order) are internal variables.

53. When something attracts our attention, we usually perform certain body move-ments to enhance our reception of the stimulation—such as turning our eyes in the direction of a visual stimulus or cupping our hands behind our ears so as to hear a faint sound. These body movements in response to changes in the environment are accompanied by a pattern of physiological reactions called the

reflex *orienting reflex.* The orienting _____ occurs in response to even slight changes in the environment. It includes such physiological changes as constriction of the peripheral blood vessels and changes in muscle tone, heart rate, and respiration.

orienting 54. These physiological accompaniments of attention, called the _____
reflex _____, *facilitate the reception of stimulation* and prepare the organism to respond quickly in case action is needed.

55. A loud tone arouses the orienting reflex in a laboratory subject. He now reports that he can see a light that was too faint to be detected before the tone sounded.

facilitates This demonstrates the fact that the orienting reflex _____ the
(or synonym) reception of stimuli.

56.

changes

If the same stimulus is repeated a number of times, the orienting reflex gradually diminishes. A *change* in the stimulus or the introduction of a new stimulus will reactivate the orienting reflex in its original strength. Thus the orienting reflex is responsive to ch_____s in the environment. Such a reflex has important survival value for the organism.

57.

senses

When we discuss perception, we are usually speaking of *sensory perception* or, in other words, perception that takes place through the _____. It has been suggested that there may be perceptions that do not require any sense-organ stimulation. These phenomena have been called *extrasensory perception* (ESP).

58.

extrasensory

Research on extrasensory perception has been carried on for a number of years. Although some psychologists believe that the evidence for the existence of certain forms of _____ perception is indisputable, most remain unconvinced.

59.

telepathy

There are several different phenomena classified as ESP. *Telepathy* means the transference of thought from one person to another. In more familiar terms, _____ is the word for "mind-reading."

60.

telepathy

A person who claims to be able to transmit thoughts across a distance to another person is maintaining that _____ exists. Of course, one who claims to be able to receive such thoughts also supports the existence of this phenomenon.

61.

clairvoyance

telepathy

clairvoyance

telepathy

One of the most common kinds of research in ESP is based on experiments in card-guessing. The experimenter may ask the subject to guess the symbol on a card that is in a sealed envelope. No one knows what card it is. The ability of the subject to perceive the card is called clairvoyance. The perception of objects or events that are not influencing the senses is known as _____.

At times, one may not be sure whether _____ or clairvoyance is at work. If someone else knows, for instance, what the card is, then the subject might be perceiving the card directly (_____) or might be reading the thoughts of the person who knows (_____).

62.

precognition

Another kind of ESP is *precognition,* or the perception of a future event. For a man who bets on horse races, _____ would seem to be the most valuable kind of ESP.

63.

telepathy

precognition

clairvoyance

The phenomena of ESP are discussed under a number of classifications:
a. Thought transference from one person to another, or _____.
b. The perception of a future event, or _____.
c. The perception of an object or event that is not influencing the senses, or

_____.

64. A related phenomenon has to do with the influence of a mental operation over a material body or an energy system—for example, the idea that wishing for a given number affects the number that will come up in a throw of dice. This is called *psychokinesis.* If you can move a vase on your desk by merely willing it to

psychokinesis

move, you are demonstrating the operation of _____.

65. A person who feels that he is a better roulette player than others is (unless he is

psychokinesis

cheating) operating with some belief in _____.

TERMS AND CONCEPTS FOR IDENTIFICATION

color constancy _____

_____

_____

_____

shape constancy _____

_____

_____

size constancy _____

_____

_____

location constancy _____

_____

_____

figure-ground organization _____

_____

_____

autokinetic effect _____

_____

_____

stroboscopic motion _____

_____

_____

phi phenomenon _____

_____

_____

stereoscopic vision _____

_____

_____

retinal disparity _____

_____

_____

feature detectors _____

_____

_____

nativist theory of perception _____

_____

_____

empiricist theory of perception _____

_____

_____

orienting reflex _____

_____

_____

extrasensory perception _____

_____

_____

telepathy _____

_____

_____

clairvoyance _____

_____

_____

precognition _____   psychokinesis _____
_____   _____
_____   _____
_____   _____

_____ 1. Laboratory studies of the orienting reflex show that
   a. after the orienting reflex has habituated, any change in the stimulus will reactivate it
   b. arousal of the reflex by a loud tone increases auditory sensitivity at the expense of the other senses
   c. a new stimulus is much more effective in reestablishing a habituated orienting reflex than a change in the old one
   d. all of the above

_____ 2. A person with vision in only one eye *cannot* see
   a. spatial relationships
   b. three-dimensional configurations
   c. well in dim light conditions
   d. with stereoscopic vision

_____ 3. Proponents of Gestalt psychology might be expected to approach questions of perception with one of their favorite phrases:
   a. "the whole is only the sum of its parts"
   b. "the parts of an object together create the whole"
   c. "the whole is different from the sum of its parts"
   d. "the whole is an integration of all its parts"

_____ 4. In research investigating the effects of experience on visual development, kittens were raised with visual exposure only to bright dots. Subsequent testing showed that the kittens'
   a. retinas had deteriorated
   b. visual cortex contained neurons unusually responsive to spots of light
   c. ability to discriminate forms was very poor
   d. vision was essentially normal

_____ 5. The Necker cube is a classic
   a. apparatus for testing children's vision
   b. size constancy illusion
   c. reversible figure
   d. test of shape constancy

_____ 6. While the full explanations for geometrical illusions remain uncertain, it seems that
   a. some illusions are based on relative size in contrast with surroundings
   b. some illusions are based on a tendency to see flat figures as if they were representations of three dimensions
   c. some illusions depend for their full effect on our learning to use linear perspective cues
   d. all of the above

_____ 7. Researchers studying the visual system with microelectrodes have described simple and complex cells, which function in such a way that
   a. a complex cell responds to a shape, such as a square, while a simple cell responds to a straight line
   b. a complex cell responds to a shape, such as a square, by integrating the information from simple cells which respond to the sides of the square
   c. a complex cell responds to a line with a particular orientation anywhere in the visual field by integrating information from a number of simple cells
   d. a complex cell responds to a line at any angle in the visual field by integrating information from a number of simple cells

_____ 8. Most psychologists remain skeptical about ESP because
   a. improved methods fail to yield better results than crude methods
   b. no statistically significant results have been obtained
   c. they reject the legitimacy of the basic inquiries
   d. all of the above

_____ 9. The perceptual constancies (e.g., size, shape, and location constancy) suggest that perception
   a. is oriented toward constant sensory features
   b. is oriented toward things rather than sensory features
   c. is based on one constancy per sensory feature
   d. provides constant-feature inputs that must be further integrated

10. Monocular cues that an artist may use to give depth to a picture include
   a. placing distant objects higher in the picture
   b. making the "grain," or texture gradient, finer as distance decreases
   c. making nearer objects smaller
   d. all of the above

11. When we judge the color of an object we do so on the basis of
   a. wavelength of the light being reflected
   b. information about the color of surrounding objects
   c. information about the nature of the illuminating light
   d. all of the above

12. Persons blind from birth because of cataracts *cannot*, soon after the cataracts are removed,
   a. distinguish a triangle from a square
   b. distinguish figure from ground
   c. fixate a figure
   d. follow moving objects with their eyes

13. Studies with the "visual cliff" show that
   a. depth perception is present at birth for most species
   b. very young animals sometimes step off on the deep side, while older ones do not
   c. animals freeze in a state of immobility when placed on the deep side
   d. stereoscopic depth cues are necessary to perceive the danger of the deep side

14. If one could influence the numbers turning up on dice by thinking about them, this would be an example of
   a. clairvoyance
   b. psychokinesis
   c. telepathy
   d. precognition

15. The ability to focus on stimuli in which we are interested while resisting distracting stimuli is called
   a. concentrated attending
   b. stimulus focusing
   c. structured perceiving
   d. selective attention

16. When we look at a distant object, we usually judge its size by
   a. object size
   b. perspective size
   c. a compromise between object size and perspective size
   d. retinal size

17. Subjects attending to two different spoken messages, one in each ear,
   a. can listen to either one at will
   b. can repeat aloud one of the messages
   c. will know if their name is mentioned, even while attending to the message in the other ear
   d. all of the above

18. The apparent movement that occurs when you stare at a single spot of light in a dark room is called
   a. induced movement
   b. the autokinetic effect
   c. stroboscopic motion
   d. the phi phenomenon

19. The view that we are born with the ability to perceive the way we do is held by
   a. sensory psychologists
   b. nativists
   c. empiricists
   d. most contemporary psychologists

20. The phenomenon of induced movement is involved in
   a. the apparent movement of the moon when viewed through moving clouds
   b. the apparent movement of a single spot of light in a dark room
   c. the apparent movement of a spot of light when several lights are turned on and off in sequence
   d. a motion picture

KEY TO SELF-QUIZ

20. a	15. d	10. a	5. c
19. b	14. b	9. b	4. b
18. b	13. c	8. a	3. c
17. d	12. a	7. c	2. d
16. c	11. d	6. d	1. a

CLASS EXERCISE

EXTRASENSORY PERCEPTION

Introduction

Extrasensory perception is a controversial topic in psychology. Many psychologists doubt that it is possible to transfer thoughts from one person to another without any physical intermediary. Others claim that thought transference—a form of ESP known as telepathy—has been adequately demonstrated in the laboratory. This exercise is similar to some laboratory experiments that have been conducted to demonstrate the existence of telepathy. The procedure has been simplified, however, to avoid the necessity of elaborate statistical analysis.

Equipment Needed

An Indian-head nickel and a screen to shield the "sender" from view of the class.

Procedure

The instructor will select from the class someone who feels that he or she might be a good "sender of thoughts." The sender will sit behind a screen and toss a nickel for ten separate trials, each time concentrating on the side of the coin that faces up (either buffalo or Indian head) and trying to transfer this image to the class, which will act as subjects. One student will observe the sender and record the results of each toss. It is best if the sender shakes the coin in a glass or cup and then inverts the container to deposit the coin on a flat surface.

The instructor will start each trial by saying the word "now"; the sender will toss the coin and concentrate upon the upturned image; the instructor will say "receive" and the students will try to concentrate upon the image being sent; when the instructor says "record"

students will write by the proper trial number the word "buffalo" or "Indian head," depending upon the image they feel they have received.

Treatment of Data

On the basis of chance we would expect five Indian heads and five buffalos from ten coin tosses. And if subjects' guesses were based on chance alone, rather than ESP, we would expect them to be correct on five out of ten guesses—or 50 percent of the time. With only ten trials we would expect considerable chance variation from the 50/50 results. Many more trials would be required before chance effects would become insignificant. But our experiment should give us a rough approximation.

The instructor will read the results of the ten trials so that you can score your guesses. He or she will then determine by a show of hands the number of students obtaining one correct guess, two correct guesses, and so on. How many students had results that were below chance level? How many above chance level? How many exactly at chance level? What do you think the results demonstrate concerning the possibility of ESP?

The instructor will now select the three students with the lowest number of correct guesses and the three with the highest number and repeat the experiment with the same sender and these students.

Questions For Discussion

1. Are the students who were good receivers in the first part of the experiment still scoring above chance for the second ten trials? Are the students who were initially poor receivers still poor?

2. How do these results affect your interpretation of the findings from the first experiment?

3. What additional controls would you want to see enforced to make this a better ESP experiment?

INDIVIDUAL EXERCISES

A. THE PHI PHENOMENON

This drawing illustrates the phi phenomenon. Hold the hand in either position and alternately close the right and left eyes. While actually seen in a stationary posi-

tion, the finger appears to move. Thus you get a perception of motion without a moving stimulus.

Why does this occur? Can you think of an industry that depends on this same phenomenon?

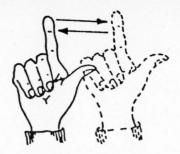

B. THE AFTEREFFECTS OF MOTION

Cut out the spiral disk on page 79 and paste it on a piece of cardboard. Attach it with a thumb tack to the end of a pencil. Spin the disk slowly and stare steadily at it as it moves. Stop the disk and notice what happens. Does it seem to be turning in the opposite direction? If you were turning the disk so that the spiral was expanding, it will seem to contract when stopped, and vice versa. When the spiral is turning steadily, our visual system tends to suppress the perceived motion, apparently by generating some sort of opposing process. When the actual movement stops, the opposing process continues for a while, and you see it as apparent motion in the opposite direction.

Now look at the spiral again as it spins slowly, then turn to look at a blank wall or a picture. The opposing process will make even the wall or picture appear to move in the opposite direction to the direction of the spiral's movement. The process apparently is not limited to spirals but applies to anything in the visual field.[1]

You may have noticed a similar effect in nature. If you look steadily at a waterfall or a flowing river for a while and then transfer your gaze to the rocks beside the falls or the river bank, whatever you are looking at appears to move in the opposite direction from the flow of water.

[1] Courtesy of Dr. Cornsweet.

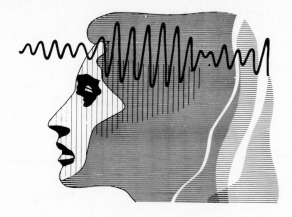

6

states of consciousness

LEARNING OBJECTIVES

Be familiar with some of the modifications of waking consciousness, both normal and abnormal.

Describe the stages of sleep and their relationship to dreaming.

Discuss Freud's theory of dreams and some objections to it.

Know the characteristics of the hypnotic state, the method of measuring hypnotic susceptibility, and the theories of hypnosis.

Be familiar with some of the techniques for inducing meditation.

Describe the three classes of psychoactive drugs, noting examples of each and their effects on behavior. Know the five major patterns of drug use.

PROGRAMMED UNIT

1. There are various states of awareness, or *consciousness.* Even the familiar, *normal waking consciousness,* in which we can report what is happening around us, is not a simple state. While we are listening to a friend describing a play she attended, we may explain to her why we could not attend and at the same time be thinking of the examination scheduled for the next hour. It is clear that

complex   normal waking consciousness is (*simple/complex*).

2. Not all of our waking states are *alert;* we may find ourselves staring blankly into space, neither examining anything nor thinking of anything in particular. This

alert

state in which we are less a_____ contrasts with a state of mental activity or alertness that is sometimes called *vigilance.*

vigilance

3. The squirming, pencil-chewing, and finger-tapping one does while studying are methods of keeping oneself alert, or in a state of _____.

vigilance
(or alertness)

4. As you might expect, studies show that loss of sleep results in poor performance on tasks that require sustained _____.

consciousness

5. Besides the normal waking c_____, in which we can report accurately what is happening around us, there are other states of waking awareness in which consciousness is altered, such as excessive fatigue, delirium, intoxication, and ecstasy.

altered (or distorted)

6. Some *altered* or *distorted* states of consciousness are caused by disease or by drugs. An example is *delirium,* a state of _____ consciousness most often associated with alcoholism, but which may also accompany high fever. In delirium the person is confused, agitated, and may experience the distortions of reality known as *hallucinations* and *delusions.*

reality

7. An hallucination is a distortion of _____; it is a *senselike perception* that has a minimum of support from external stimuli. If a young woman hears her mother reprimanding her when in reality the mother has been

hallucination

dead for five years, she must be experiencing an _____.

hallucinations

8. False sensory perceptions that have a minimum of support from external stimuli are called _____.

9. *Delusions* are *faulty thought systems* in which sense perceptions may be accurate but *events misinterpreted.* for example, a mental patient believes that creatures from another planet are trying to gain control of his thoughts by sending impulses through the electrical outlets of his room. He sees a nurse plug in a lamp and believes that she is in league with his persecutors. The patient's sense

misinterprets

perceptions are accurate, but he mis_____ the events he perceives.

delusions

He is experiencing _____.

10. The same patient also sees green spiders crawling out of the electrical outlets when actually there are no spiders in his room. He is experiencing

hallucinations

_____ in addition to his delusions.

11. Both hallucinations and delusions may occur during the altered state of waking

delirium

consciousness that is called _____.

12. The state that is most commonly contrasted with waking consciousness is *sleep.*

sleep

We might think of _____ as a state of *lessened awareness* and activity.

13. Sleep is *not* altogether unconscious, since we can recall many of our dreams.

Sleep does not come about simply because the bodily processes resulting from waking activities require it, since, to a degree, a person can choose either to sleep or to remain awake regardless of the condition of the body. Sleep is *not* entirely quiescent, because some people toss and turn in their sleep and some even

awareness

sleepwalk. Therefore we think of sleep as a state of lessened _____ rather than a state of complete unawareness.

Sleep

14. _____ is a state of lessened awareness. Because it differs from the normal conscious state, we think of it as an altered state of consciousness.

15. Scientists have discovered *five stages* of sleep. They have done this by using the *electroencephalogram* (abbreviated EEG), a method of studying the electrical action of the brain, and have found changes in the brain waves with deepening of sleep. They have also observed that *rapid eye movements* (abbreviated REMs) tend to occur during *dreams.* If subjects are awakened during a period of rapid eye movements, you would expect them to report that they have just had a

dream

_____.

16. We can measure the electrical action of the brain with the electroencephalogram

EEG

(abbreviated _____), and we can tell whether a person is

REMs

dreaming because there will be rapid eye movements (abbreviated _____) accompanying dreaming.

five

17. There are _____ (number) stages of sleep. Stages 1 through 4 represent a scale of increasing depth of sleep, with Stage 1 the lightest sleep and Stage 4 the deepest.

easier

18. You would expect it to be (*easier/more difficult*) to arouse a person from Stage 1 sleep than from Stage 4.

19. It is in the fifth stage of sleep that rapid eye movements (REMs) occur. You

dreaming

recall that REMs are associated with _____. Stage 5 sleep is called REM sleep, while the other four stages are known as non-REM (or NREM)

eye movements

because rapid _____ _____ are *not* likely to occur.

REM

20. Stage 5, or _____ sleep, shows an EEG pattern similar to Stage 1 sleep. You recall that the electroencephalogram or EEG is a method of

brain

studying the electrical activity of the _____. The EEG pattern during REM sleep indicates that it should be easy to arouse the person since it is

1

similar to Stage _____ which is light sleep. But actually it is as difficult to arouse a person from REM sleep as it is from Stage 4 NREM sleep.

difficult

21. When a person is in REM sleep there is a *decrease in muscle tone* of some of the striate muscles. This may be one reason why it is (*easy/difficult*) to awaken someone from REM sleep.

22. The stage of sleep during which dreams occur can be distinguished from the

eye movements	other four stages by two measures: rapid _____ _____
muscle	and decrease in _____ tone. REM sleep occurs in cycles during the night. The average adult spends about 25 percent of his sleeping time in REM sleep.

23. Does everyone dream? If we accept REM sleep as evidence, then it is true that *everyone* dreams, though some people recall very few dreams. Thus we can say

everyone
that (*everyone/not everyone*) dreams.

24. Another interesting question is, "Can the sleeper react to stimuli from the environment without awakening?" During REM sleep, if stimuli such as spoken names are presented while the person is dreaming, the subject is not likely to awaken but instead will *incorporate* the external stimuli into his dreams in some manner. Thus, if John is in REM sleep and he hears the name "Mary" (the name

incorporate
of his girl friend) spoken to him, he is likely to _____ her name into his dream in some manner.

25. The answer to the question "Can the sleeper react to the environment without

yes
awakening?" is (*yes/no*).

26. Both *sleeptalking* and *sleepwalking* occur primarily during NREM sleep and

REM
probably not in relation to dreaming, which occurs during _____ sleep.

sleepwalking

27. Occurring primarily in NREM sleep are two phenomena, sleep_____

sleeptalking
(either order)
and sleep_____.

28. The most influential theory of dreams within the last half-century has been that of Freud. He believed that *unconscious* impulses were responsible for the dream, and that the aim of the dream was the *gratification* of some *drive*. Jane, who has been married two years, dreams that she is single. According to Freud, Jane has

unconscious
a(n) _____ wish that she were single.

unconscious
gratification

29. According to Freud, dreams express _____ impulses and provide the _____ of some drive.

30. According to Freud's analysis, the *remembered* aspects of a dream constitute the *manifest content* of the dream. However, the *real meaning* of the same dream, or the *latent content,* is not directly expressed but is instead dramatized in disguised form; even the dreamer cannot readily discern its hidden meaning. If Bob recalls that he dreamed last night that he was flying over the campus

manifest
grounds, this would be the dream's _____ content, since it is the remembered content of the dream.

31. The real meaning of Bob's dream is incomprehensible to him; it is the

latent
_____ content of the dream.

32. Freud believed that dreams are highly *symbolic* and basically *wish-fulfilling.*

gratification
(or fulfillment)
That is, the dream is directed toward the _____ of some drive,
or unconscious wish.

33. Dreams are difficult to interpret, even for the dreamer, because they are highly

symbolic,
unconscious

_____. They express the _____ impulses of the dreamer.

34. Sexual tensions may be reduced by erotic dreams. In this case the dream may

unconscious

satisfy some of the un_____ impulses of the dreamer, thus its

wish

function is _____-fulfilling.

35. Freud believed that dreams are the _guardian of sleep._ In dreams unfulfilled

symbolic

impulses appear in disguised or sym_____ form; thus the dreams prevent the sleeper from being awakened by the disturbing impulses. In this

guard

sense dreams serve to g_____ sleep.

36. Experimental studies, however, cast doubts on Freud's notion that dreams are

sleep

the guardian of _____. The prevalence of REM states in newborn infants and in lower animals makes it unlikely that the purpose of REM

wishes, drives, impulses

sleep is to discharge unfulfilled _____.

37. Another altered state of consciousness, which was once believed to be similar to sleep, is _hypnosis._ Evidence indicates, however, that hypnosis differs from sleep; EEG measures taken during hypnosis are like those of waking rather than any of

stages

the five _____ of sleep.

is not

38. We can thus say with assurance that hypnosis (_is/is not_) like ordinary sleep.

39. An individual in a _hypnotic state_ does not initiate activity but waits for the hypnotist to tell him what to do. Thus we may say that one characteristic of the

hypnotic

_____ state is a decrease in the _planning function._

40. Another characteristic of the hypnotic state, in addition to a decrease in the

planning

_____ function, is a _reduction in reality testing._ A hypnotized individual will readily accept reality distortion or hallucinated experiences (for example, petting an imaginary rabbit that he has been told is sitting on his lap). The same person in the normal waking state would usually reject such a

reality

distortion of _____.

41. The hypnotic state thus differs from the normal waking state in (1) a decrease in

planning function

the _____ _____ and (2) a reduction in

reality

_____ testing.

testing

42. Closely related to the reduction in reality _____ under hypnosis is an increase in _suggestibility._ The hypnotized person will readily accept suggestions. If the hypnotist says, "You are very warm," the subject may begin to perspire. If the hypnotist says, "You are angry," the subject may show signs of irritability.

suggestibility

43. Another characteristic of the hypnotic state is increased sug_____.

44. Let's review. Hypnosis (*is/is not*) similar to sleep. Hypnosis also differs from the normal waking state. A hypnotized person usually shows a decrease in the _____ _____, a reduction in _____ testing, and increased _____.

is not

planning function
reality,
suggestibility

45. Hypnosis is an altered state of c_____ usually induced by another person, the h_____tist. It is possible, however, for a person to induce an altered _____ of consciousness on his own through a kind of *self-hypnosis* or *controlled meditation*.

consciousness

hypnotist

state

46. Both the Hindu system of *yoga* and the Buddhist system of *Zen* stress a kind of self-hypnosis or _____ meditation in which one strives to exclude all extraneous thoughts and stimuli.

controlled

47. The kind of meditation achieved by those who practice yoga or _____ frequently results in an altered state of _____.

Zen

consciousness

48. Two methods for altering waking consciousness are _____ and controlled _____. It is also possible to produce profound changes in conscious experience by means of drugs.

hypnosis

meditation

49. Drugs that affect *behavior* and *conscious experience* are called *psychoactive drugs*. *Tranquilizers* reduce anxiety and make a person feel more serene; they are one kind of psycho_____ drug.

psychoactive

50. Tranquilizers, alcohol, barbituates, and narcotics such as heroin form one group of _____ drugs that are called *depressants*. They vary in their effects, but all slow down the activity of the central nervous system.

psychoactive

51. Alcohol in small quantities may make a person more talkative and sociable, because it inhibits some of the restraints on social behavior. But several drinks produce slowed reaction times and drowsiness. Therefore, alcohol is classed as a _____.

depressant

52. Another group of psycho_____ drugs are called *stimulants* because they speed up the activity of the central _____.

psychoactive

nervous system

53. Amphetamines increase alertness and wakefulness. They are classed as _____.

stimulants

54. Two classes of psychoactive drugs are _____ and _____.

depressants,
stimulants
(either order)

behavior experience (or awareness)	**55.** Psychoactive drugs are drugs that affect a person's _____ and conscious _____.
	56. A third class of psychoactive drugs are called *hallucinogens* or *psychedelic drugs* because they produce profound alterations in one's perceptions and conscious experience. LSD may produce serious distortions of consciousness, including
psychedelic	hallucinations; it is therefore classed as a hallucinogen or _____ drug.
	57. Marihuana, while much milder in its effects than LSD, tends to distort one's
hallucinogen	time sense. Consequently, it is also classed as an _____gen.
psychoactive, depressants stimulants, hallucinogens (or psychedelic drugs) (any order)	**58.** To recapitulate: drugs that affect behavior and conscious experience are called _____ drugs. They fall into three classes: _____, _____, and _____. (The text discusses a number of patterns of drug use and the risks each entails.)

TERMS AND CONCEPTS FOR IDENTIFICATION

delusion _____

_____

_____

_____

hallucination _____

_____

_____

_____

fugue state _____

_____

_____

_____

multiple personality _____

_____

_____

_____

circadian rhythm _____

_____

_____

_____

EEG _____

_____

_____

_____

REM sleep _____

_____

_____

_____

latent content of a dream _____

_____

_____

_____

manifest content of a dream _____

_____

_____

_____

posthypnotic amnesia _____

_____

_____

_____

transcendental meditation _____

_____

_____

_____

biofeedback _____

_____

_____

_____

psychoactive drugs _____

_____

_____

_____

amphetamines _____

_____

_____

_____

LSD _____

_____

_____

_____

_____ 1. The National Commission on Marihuana and Drug Abuse has suggested that the word addiction, because of its many connotations, be replaced with the more neutral term, drug
   a. reliance
   b. usage
   c. responsiveness
   d. dependency

_____ 2. Studies of sleep stages have found that
   a. Stage 1 is characterized by delta waves
   b. a familiar name can often arouse a person from deep sleep
   c. dreaming is marked by the fading of alpha waves from the EEG
   d. eye movements during NREM sleep show when dreaming occurs

_____ 3. The more dramatic altered states of consciousness arise under a variety of circumstances; such circumstances include
   a. extreme enhancement of external stimulation
   b. subjective practices to heighten alertness and mental involvement
   c. sensory deprivation
   d. all of the above

_____ 4. REM sleep occurs in cycles that appear to be
   a. randomly determined
   b. dependent upon external disturbances
   c. uninfluenced by interruptions of NREM sleep
   d. controlled by some internal pacemaker

_____ 5. "Seeing" a person in a darkened room when the stimulus is actually a coat on a rack, could be classified as a(n) _____; "seeing" and talking to a nonexistent person in daylight would be considered a(n) _____.
   a. illusion, delusion
   b. delusion, hallucination
   c. illusion, hallucination
   d. hallucination, delirium

_____ 6. In addition to the "pleasurable" sensations experienced, people are said to use dangerous drugs like heroin for several reasons. Which of the following was not given as such a reason by the text? People
   a. like to experience danger
   b. are influenced by social factors
   c. don't believe the addiction and mortality statistics apply to them
   d. often have a hidden death wish

_____ 7. According to Freud's theory of dreams,
   a. the manifest content derives from day residues
   b. the latent content is directly expressed in the dream action
   c. condensation refers to the reduction of the whole dream to the lesser version that we remember the next day
   d. the latent content derives from day residues

_____ 8. In an experiment on vigilance where subjects were asked to report double jumps of a clock's second hand, errors increased after half an hour at the task. These errors could be reduced by
   a. reminding subjects before the experiment to be especially vigilant
   b. calling subjects on the phone during the experiment and asking them to do better
   c. offering subjects more pay for maintaining a high level of vigilance
   d. all of the above

_____ 9. In testing whether sleepers can react to the environment without awakening, it has been found that subjects
   a. can learn simple auditory material using sleep-learning techniques during REM sleep
   b. sometimes incorporate auditory signals given during REM sleep into their dreams
   c. can discriminate auditory signals better during REM sleep than during Stages 1 and 2
   d. all of the above

_____ 10. It has been shown that subjects can learn to control the alpha wave component of the EEG. One important limitation, however, is that they usually do this by

a. techniques that cause unpleasant side-effects, such as headaches
b. using special equipment not commercially available
c. learning to turn alpha off, not on
d. changing the temperature of their bodies through blood-flow changes

_____ 11. Careful studies of LSD have shown that
a. effects differ depending on drug dosage and the personality characteristics of the user
b. difficulty in concentrating is common
c. those who have better control of themselves in general maintain that control under the drug
d. all of the above

_____ 12. Studies of sleepwalking and sleeptalking have shown that
a. people can be taught to talk about their dreams while they are happening, without awakening
b. sleeptalking is primarily associated with REM sleep, although 20-25 percent is associated with NREM
c. sleepwalkers believe they are dreaming, since their reports of dreams match what they were doing while sleepwalking
d. sleepwalking is associated with REM sleep

_____ 13. Which of the following is *not* a characteristic of the hypnotic state?
a. the subject loses the sense of his own identity
b. attention is redistributed
c. the subject ceases to make his own plans
d. reality testing is reduced

_____ 14. If one regularly used amphetamines when studying for exams, but not otherwise, this pattern of drug use would fall into the category of
a. intensified drug use
b. social-recreational use
c. circumstantial-situational use
d. compulsive drug use

_____ 15. A ten-year study of why people who are not alcoholics drink alcohol found that a prominent motive was to
a. overcome a sense of weakness

b. forget one's troubles
c. lose social inhibitions
d. all of the above

_____ 16. In studying who can be hypnotized, it has been found that
a. anyone can be hypnotized if enough attempts are made
b. childhood experiences can be important in determining whether a person can be hypnotized
c. studies of twins show no evidence of a hereditary factor in susceptibility
d. measures of susceptibility are useful when given, but the results cease to be meaningful as the subjects grow older

_____ 17. When a person engages in uncharacteristic activities over an extended period of time and then denies them because they have been forgotten, we characterize the episode as a(n)
a. fugue state
b. alternating personality state
c. multiple personality state
d. memory-gap episode

_____ 18. The modern induction of hypnosis often involves
a. convincing subjects that they are going to sleep
b. authoritarian commands by the hypnotist
c. asking a subject to concentrate on a visual target
d. hypnotizing an uncooperative subject

_____ 19. When a subject engaged in experimental meditation by concentrating on a blue vase, the most common effects did *not* include
a. an altered, more intense perception of the vase
b. an apparent lengthening of the time, so that hours seemed to pass
c. conflicting perceptions of the vase, e.g., filling and not filling the visual field
d. a pleasurable state, reported to be valuable and rewarding

_____ 20. Studies of the effects on performance of "jet lag" and loss of sleep have shown that
a. students who flew to Germany and back

recovered fully in about 5 days

b. the time needed to recover from jet lag is somewhat longer when the flight is east to west than when it is west to east

c. the effects of jet lag are due to interference with normal bodily rhythm rather than to loss of sleep

d. the effects of jet lag are due primarily to the loss of sleep

INDIVIDUAL OR CLASS EXERCISE

BEHAVIOR MODIFICATION
WITHOUT AWARENESS

Introduction

As you have seen from this chapter, there are varying states of awareness. At times we are perfectly aware of what we are doing and seem to know why we are doing it. At other times we may do something and not know the cause. For example, sometimes we hear ourselves whistling a tune but have no idea how we came to choose this particular song until we become aware of someone else humming it. This exercise is set up to show that we can be influenced by stimuli and not know that our behavior has been changed, much less what has changed it.

A fair amount of research data indicates that a person's verbal behavior can be influenced through subtle reinforcement. In this exercise the attempt will be made to cause a subject to give one kind of response rather than another kind, while keeping him unaware of the fact that he is being influenced. This type of study demonstrates the fact that some influences on behavior occur below the level of awareness.

Equipment Needed

A stopwatch or watch with a second hand. Small notebook or pad and pencil.

Procedure

This exercise may be done in class, with the instructor supplying the subject. Or you may try it yourself on your own subject. Tell your subject that you are inter-

ested in investigating word associations, and that you want him to recite as many different nouns as he can think of and to continue to do so until told to stop. For the first minute you the experimenter should do nothing. For the second minute you should say "um-hmm," or "okay," or nod your head after each plural noun but should do nothing after singular nouns. You should vary the type of reinforcement ("um-hmm," "okay," or nod) in a random order and should make your responses seem as natural as possible. If the experiment is done in class, a third person can be used to unobtrusively record the number of plural nouns given in each of the one-minute intervals. If you are conducting the experiment on your own, you can jot down marks in your notebook as the subject talks, using one kind of symbol for plural nouns (just the letter P will do) and a different symbol for singular nouns. The percentage of plural nouns should increase from the first to the second minute due to the reinforcing effect of your responses.

Now select a different subject and reverse the sequence, reinforcing plural nouns during the first minute and doing nothing during the second. The percentage of plural nouns should decrease from the first to the second minute. In both instances ask the subject at the end of the procedure what he noticed about the experimenter's behavior and what he thought the procedure was all about. If he comments on the experimenter's responses, ask whether he felt that they had any effect on his behavior. You can also ask him whether he thought the percentage of singular or plural nouns changed as he went on. Usually the subject will not be aware that his verbal behavior has changed, nor will he be aware of the influence of the experimenter's responses.

This experiment can also be done using other parts of speech. For example, you could ask the subject to say as many "words" as he can think of and reinforce adjectives or pronouns or words beginning with an "s" sound, and so forth.

INDIVIDUAL EXERCISES

A. EXPERIMENTAL MEDITATION

There are a number of ways of attaining a sense of detachment or meditation. Try both of the following techniques to see which helps you best to free your mind from extraneous thoughts while expanding your awareness. For either procedure you should choose a time when you are not sleepy; sit relaxed in a comfortable chair or on the floor supported by pillows. For the first procedure put an object such as a vase or a bowl on a table about eight feet in front of you, keeping the background as simple as possible. Now concentrate all your attention on the object, excluding all other thoughts or feelings or body sensations. Do not try to analyze the object or associate ideas with it; simply concentrate on it as it is. After a few minutes you will find that it will be difficult to keep your eyes in proper focus. Do not try to retain a sharp focus; let your eyes unfocus but continue to concentrate on the object for at least five minutes.

How did you feel? Were you able to avoid being distracted by events going on around you? Did you have a feeling of detachment, of being able to step aside and watch your feelings and ideas flow by without getting involved in them? Were there any perceptual distortions of the object being viewed? Did you have a feeling of more intense perception of the object? Was the state a pleasurable one?

Now try the second technique and see if you get the same results. Again sit in a comfortable position but do not be so relaxed that you will go to sleep. Breathe naturally and focus your attention on your breathing: the movements of your chest and stomach, not the sensations in your nose and throat. Try to avoid being distracted by extraneous thoughts or stimuli. Keep your attention on your breathing, turning aside all other thoughts.

What are your feelings? Are they similar to or different from those elicited by the first technique? How do the sensations in both cases differ from those you experience while drowsy or in a half-asleep state?

After you have tried these two meditation techniques, reread the section in the text entitled "Meditation and self-induced alterations of consciousness" (Chapter 6, pages 177–79). How do your experiences compare with the findings described in the text?

B. RECORDING DREAMS

Keep a notebook in which you record your dreams as soon as you wake up in the morning. With practice you will find that you remember more of your dreams than you thought possible. Keep a record for several weeks. Are there recurring themes in your dreams? Can you trace events in your dreams to things that happened during the day? Do you dream in color? (Women tend to more than men.) Are your dreams populated by familiar people or by strangers? Do members of the opposite sex appear in your dreams more frequently than members of the same sex? Do you see yourself in your dreams? Do certain strong emotions permeate all your dreams?

The intention of this exercise is not to psychoanalyze yourself by means of dream analysis but to find out as much as you can about your dreams and what factors you think influence them. It might be interesting to compare your dream experiences with those of a classmate.

7
conditioning and learning

LEARNING OBJECTIVES

Describe the processes of classical conditioning and operant conditioning, giving several examples of each. Know the technical terms used in each procedure. Describe the stages of classical conditioning (e.g., acquisition, extinction, generalization, and discrimination).

Distinguish between operant and respondent behavior. Know how operant strength is portrayed by the cumulative curve and how partial reinforcement affects learning. Understand the principle of secondary reinforcement and the use of operant-conditioning techniques in shaping behavior.

Discuss the principle of reinforcement as related to both classical and operant conditioning, the effect on learning of such variables as amount and delay of reinforcement.

Be able to plot a learning curve for a sensorimotor skill.

Understand the distinction between associative learning and learning as a cognitive process. Explain how Köhler's experiments, Tolman's notion of sign learning, and experiments on latent learning relate to this distinction. State Tolman's distinction between learning and performance.

PROGRAMMED UNIT

1. *Learning* is a *relatively permanent change* in *behavior* that occurs as the result of

learning   *prior experience.* Not all changes in behavior can be called l_____; thus the definition must be qualified.

permanent

2. Learning is a relatively _____ change in behavior. This specification excludes changes in behavior resulting from such temporary conditions as fatigue or adaptation.

experience

3. Learning occurs as a result of prior _____. By this statement we exclude from the definition of learning behavioral changes due to maturation, disease, or physical injury.

change

behavior, prior

experience

4. Therefore we say that learning is a relatively permanent _____ in _____ that occurs as the result of _____ _____.

learning

5. Learning is one of the most basic problems in psychology. There are various explanations of learning, but we shall concentrate on two important interpretations of _____.

learning

6. Some psychologists interpret learning as an *associative process.* By this they mean that one learns a particular behavior by *associating* a stimulus with a response. This process, then, is referred to as associative l_____.

associative

associate

7. Learning to respond with a certain name when we perceive a stimulus object is an example of _____ learning. For example, we learn to say "pen" when we ask for an ink-filled writing instrument. We _____ the word with the object.

stimulus, response

8. Many habits involve associating a *stimulus* with a *response.* If a smoker lights a cigarette whenever he begins to sip a cup of coffee, he has associated the _____ of coffee-drinking with the _____ of smoking.

associative

9. Some habits consist of the association of several stimuli with a particular response. If a smoker always lights a cigarette when he sees another person smoking (as well as when he begins to sip coffee), then he has connected more than one stimulus with the smoking response through the process of _____ learning.

understanding

10. Some psychologists argue that stimulus-response associations cannot adequately explain all learning, especially in humans. They agree that one can learn a poem by learning a connection between each word as a stimulus and the next word as a response, but they say that a person who also *understands* the meaning of the poem is no longer operating on the basis of associative learning alone. They regard u_____ing as a significant part of the learning process.

processes

relationships

11. This second group of psychologists argues that *cognitive processes,* the processes of *perceiving* and *inferring* the *relationships* among events, are necessary for many types of learning. By cognitive _____ we refer to the perceptions and inferences that the learner makes about the rel_____ among events in his environment.

12. Thus the two groups of psychologists differ in their interpretations of learning.

associations   One thinks of learning in terms of the build-up of _____ between stimuli and responses. The other feels that often learning is not an

cognitive   associative process but rather a _____ process. Cognitive processes enable the learner to make inferences about events in the world; future behavior is governed by these inferences rather than by an automatic sequence of stimulus-response associations. (We will return to the distinction between associative learning and cognitive processes toward the end of the programmed unit.)

13. In the study of associative learning, a particular experimental arrangement has often been used. A dog is placed in a harness and apparatus is set up in such a way that the dog's salivary flow can be accurately measured. Then some meat powder is placed on the dog's tongue, and the dog will secrete a copious amount of saliva. Since this response of salivating will take place even if the dog has never before been exposed to meat powder, it is an *unlearned response.* Such a

response   response. Thus we can call it a(n) _____ response.

14. We find that blinking an eye to a puff of air aimed at the eye is also an unlearned

unconditioned   response. Thus we can call it a(n) _____ response.

15. If putting a bottle into the mouth of a newborn infant gives rise, the first time,

unconditioned   to sucking, we would call the sucking a(n) _____

response   _____.

16. Any response to a stimulus that is an unlearned response can be called an

response   unconditioned _____.

17. If a response that is unlearned is called an *unconditioned response,* then it seems logical to call the stimulus that gave rise to that response an

unconditioned   _____ *stimulus.*

18. In the case of the salivation mentioned above, the meat powder that gave rise to

stimulus   the salivation is called an unconditioned _____.

19. Suppose now, in the dog experiment mentioned above, we ring a bell just before the meat powder is delivered to the dog. If this is done often enough, the bell

response   will eventually give rise to the _____ of salivation even if the meat powder is not presented.

20. The bell becomes the stimulus for the response of salivation. However, since the bell would not elicit salivation before it was associated with the meat powder, the connection between the bell and the salivation had to be

learned   l_____.

21. Thus the bell is a learned stimulus, and we call that sound a conditioned

stimulus   _____.

22. A *conditioned stimulus* is a stimulus that would not by itself give rise to the desired response but that gains the power to do so by being associated with an

unconditioned   un_____ stimulus.

23. If putting a bottle into the mouth of an infant gives rise to sucking, this illustrates an unconditioned stimulus (bottle in mouth) that elicits an unconditioned response (sucking). If, later on, the child begins to suck at the *sight* of the bottle, then this stimulus (sight of bottle) would be called a(n)

conditioned   _____ stimulus.

24. A stimulus that gives rise to a response the first time the stimulus is offered is

unconditioned   called a(n) _____ stimulus and the response a(n)

unconditioned   _____ response.

25. If we have to associate a stimulus with an unconditioned stimulus in order to

conditioned   evoke a response, the learned stimulus is called a(n) _____ stimulus.

26. If the response to an unconditioned stimulus is called an unconditioned response, then the response to a conditioned stimulus will be called a(n)

conditioned   _____ response.

27. The connection between a conditioned stimulus and a conditioned response

learned   must be _____ .

28. The connection between an unconditioned stimulus and an unconditioned

unlearned   response is _____ .
(or innate)

29. *Classical conditioning* is the name given to the method by which organisms acquire (learn) connections between stimuli and responses through associative learning. It can be defined as the formation of an association between a

conditioned   conditioned stimulus and a c_____ response through repeated presentation of the conditioned stimulus in a controlled relationship with the unconditioned stimulus until the conditioned stimulus alone produces the response originally elicited by the unconditioned stimulus.

30. The experiment described above, in which the dog learns to salivate to the sound

classical   of a bell, is an example of _____ conditioning.

31. The more times we present the conditioned stimulus with the unconditioned

conditioned   stimulus, the stronger will be the response to the _____ stimulus.

32. In other words, the more often the conditioned stimulus is associated with the unconditioned stimulus, the better the animal will learn the association. The

unconditioned   pairing of the conditioned stimulus with the u_____ stimulus is called *reinforcement,* because the pairing makes the conditioned response stronger.

33. If we pair the bell (conditioned stimulus) with the meat powder (unconditioned stimulus) twenty times, the salivation to the bell will be stronger than if we only pair them ten times. The association between the bell and the salivation is stronger in the former case because the association has been

reinforced   re_____ more often.

34. The paired presentation of the conditioned stimulus and the unconditioned stimulus, which strengthens the conditioned response, is called

reinforcement   _____.

35. However, if we set up in a dog the response of salivating to a bell (the conditioned stimulus) and then continually ring the bell without giving any meat

unconditioned   powder (the _____ stimulus), eventually the dog will stop salivating to the bell.

36. In other words, if we pair the conditioned and unconditioned stimuli until the dog responds with salivation to the conditioned stimulus, and then continually

reinforcement   present only the conditioned stimulus, so that there is no re_____, gradually the dog will stop salivating to the stimulus.

37. Repetition of the conditioned stimulus without reinforcement is called *extinction*. The association between the bell and the meat powder is weakened by presenting one without the other. In *extinction* we repeatedly present the

conditioned   _____ stimulus without the unconditioned stimulus.

38. When we present the conditioned stimulus without the unconditioned stimulus,

reinforced   the conditioned response is weakened because it is not being re_____.

39. Suppose we condition a dog to respond with salivation to a touch on the back near the hindquarters. To do this we touch the dog on the back and, a second later, put meat powder on its tongue. Let us call the touch near the hindquarters

conditioned   (which is the _____ stimulus) stimulus 1 (S_1).

40. Once this conditioning has been established, if we touch the dog on another spot on its back (S_2), we find that the dog will make the response of salivation to this stimulus as well, although it has never been reinforced for this stimulus. There-

S_1 fore S_2 has substituted for _____.

41. Responding to S_2 with the response that was conditioned to S_1, even though S_2 has not been established as a conditioned stimulus, is called *generalization*. The more similar S_2 is to S_1, the stronger will be the tendency to generalize. In

generalization   _____ the organism makes the *same* response to a new stimulus that it learned to make to an old stimulus; it does so because the new stimulus is similar in some way to the old stimulus.

42. Generalization consists of the following sequence: (1) a stimulus is conditioned to a response; (2) the organism is presented with a new stimulus that is similar to, but not identical with, the conditioned stimulus; (3) the organism responds

same
to the new stimulus as though it were the _____ as the old
one.

43. When an organism makes the same response to a new stimulus (S_2) that it has
learned to make to a different stimulus (S_1), we note the operation of the

generalization
principle of _____.

44. Let us suppose that, in the experiment described above, every time we touch the
dog near the hindquarters (S_1) we put meat powder on its tongue and we never
put meat powder on its tongue after touching the dog on the other spot (S_2).
Eventually the dog will no longer respond to S_2, although it will continue to

respond
_____ to S_1. The animal has learned to tell the two stimuli
apart (to react to them differentially).

45. In the situation just described, the dog has learned to *discriminate* between the

same
(or conditioned)
two stimuli and thus does not make the _____ response to
both of them.

46. When the organism learns *not* to make the same response to both of the
stimuli—that is, when it distinguishes between them—we call the process *dis-crimination*. When there are two stimuli, one of which is *always* reinforced and

discriminate
(or distinguish)
the other *never* reinforced, the organism will in time _____

between them and respond to the former and not to the latter.

47. If we condition a dog to salivate to a tone of 1000 cycles, reinforcing the tone
with food, and then present a 500-cycle (lower) tone, the dog will probably
salivate in response to both tones. However, if we never reinforce the 500-cycle
tone with food but always reinforce the 1000-cycle tone, the dog will eventually
stop salivating in response to the 500-cycle tone but will continue to salivate to

discrimination
the 1000-cycle tone. This is an example of the process of _____.

48. In classical conditioning the stimulus in some way forces the response. Thus the

salivation
meat powder gives rise to _____ as an involuntary response;

involuntary
the air puff gives rise to blinking as a(n) _____, not as a
voluntary, response.

49. There are other kinds of behavior in which the stimulus leads to the response but
does not force it. For example, the stimulus of someone's ringing your doorbell
will usually lead to your going to the door to open it; however, the stimulus

does not
(*does/does not*) force you to do so.

50. In the example in the preceding frame, if you don't want to open the door, you
don't have to. The response of opening the door is called an *operant* response

response
because such a _____ usually "operates" on the environment.

51. If we put a hungry rat in a maze that contains food, it will make certain
responses to get to the place where the food is; if we cover the food, the rat will

operant
learn to turn over the cover. These are _____ responses.

52. Whenever an organism acts in order to get something from the environment (when it does something to operate on the environment), we may call this an

operant   _____ response.

53. *Operant conditioning* differs in certain ways from classical conditioning. In the classical-conditioning situations we discussed, the animal was passive; it did not have to do anything in order to receive the unconditioned stimulus (the reinforcement). When we were teaching the animal to salivate to a bell, we rang the

unconditioned   bell and then delivered the meat powder (the _____ stimulus) regardless of what the animal did.

operant   **54.** In op_____ conditioning, however, the animal must make some kind of response in order to get the reinforcement.

55. In classical conditioning the animal can be passive and still be reinforced; in

operant   _____ conditioning the animal must be active in order to be reinforced.

56. Operant conditioning refers to increasing the probability of a response by

reinforcement   following the response with _____.

57. For example, we want Mary to develop the habit of working hard in school. To do this we give her extra spending money for each high grade she receives. Since the extra money strengthens the response of working hard in school, it consti-

reinforcement   tutes a _____ of the response of working hard in school.

58. Jimmy continually comes home late for dinner. His mother wants to strengthen the response of mealtime promptness, so she gives Jimmy a special dessert

reinforcement   whenever he is on time. The dessert constitutes a _____ of the response of promptness.

59. We have been assuming that every time an organism did something we would reinforce it. Thus every time a rat ran to the end of the maze, we would give it food. Suppose, however, we gave the rat reinforcement only every other time it performed the act that led to reinforcement. This procedure is called *partial reinforcement*. When we reinforce an organism only part of the time, we are

partial
reinforcement   using _____ _____.

60. Since a child's mother is not always present to reinforce a desired response,

partial   _____ reinforcement is the state of affairs that is most prevalent in children's lives.

61. One of the characteristics of partial reinforcement is that it makes the behavior more resistant to extinction than the behavior that is subject to 100 percent

partially   reinforcement. Thus when a child is _____ly reinforced for a given behavior, this behavior tends to persist against many nonreinforcements.

62. When Jimmy cleans his room his mother notices his efforts only 40 percent of the time. She rewards him each time that she notices. With this reinforcement

longer than   schedule, Jimmy's behavior of cleaning the room will last (*longer than/not as long as*) it would if 100 percent reinforcement were used.

63. As in classical conditioning, an operant response can be extinguished. If we suddenly stop giving Mary extra spending money for making good grades, we run the risk that Mary will eventually stop working hard (if money was her only reason for working). We would be producing *extinction* of the response of

reinforcement

working hard by withdrawing _____.

64. If a rat has learned to press a bar to receive food and the delivery of food no longer follows a bar press, we say that the operant response of bar-pressing is

extinction

undergoing _____.

65. Classical conditioning and operant conditioning are two important but clearly different forms of learning. In classical conditioning, learning depends upon the experimenter's pairing of the unconditioned stimulus with the conditioned

passive

stimulus; in this sense the learning is (*active/passive*), since the organism cannot determine when the pairing will occur. In operant conditioning, the organism acts upon the environment in order to obtain reinforcement. The strength of the organism's response increases whenever the response is followed by

reinforcement

_____.

66. So far we have discussed classical and operant conditioning: two simple forms of learning that can be viewed as *associative learning.* When more complex forms of learning are analyzed (such as mastering calculus, finding your way about a new city, or memorizing the lines of a play), it is doubtful that S-R associations alone can explain what takes place. Learning in these situations undoubtedly involves

stimulus-response
(or S-R)

more than simple _____-_____ associations; it requires perceiving and understanding the relationships among events occurring in the environment. The process of perceiving and, in turn, understanding

cognitive

the relationships among events are what earlier we called cog_____

processes

_____.

67. Often we learn to solve a puzzle by *suddenly* perceiving a relationship, previously not seen, between parts of the puzzle. This type of problem-solving

sudden

through _____ perception of a relationship is called *insight* learning.

68. Since insight requires perceiving new relationships among parts of a problem, it

cognitive processes

reflects the operation of _____ _____ rather than simple associative learning.

Note: Much of our behavior is governed by the laws of classical and operant conditioning. To say that we are creatures of our habits is to describe at least part of our behavior accurately. At the same time, associative learning alone is not enough to account for some of the complex forms of learning and problem-solving that we will encounter in later chapters. In these cases learning depends on our ability to perceive and infer relationships among objects and events in our environment. These processes of perception and inference are what psychologists refer to as cognitive processes. They represent a higher form of learning that permits us to be more than an organism that responds automatically to each stimulus input. To understand learning, one needs both to understand the laws that govern classical and operant conditioning and to take account of the role of cognition.

TERMS AND CONCEPTS FOR IDENTIFICATION

learning _____

_____

_____

_____

classical conditioning _____

_____

_____

_____

operant conditioning _____

_____

_____

_____

conditioned response _____

_____

_____

_____

unconditioned response _____

_____

_____

_____

conditioned stimulus _____

_____

_____

_____

unconditioned stimulus _____

_____

_____

_____

reinforcement _____

_____

_____

_____

extinction _____

_____

_____

_____

_____

gradient of generalization _____

_____

_____

conditioned discrimination _____

_____

_____

respondent behavior _____

_____

_____

operant behavior _____

_____

_____

cumulative curve _____

_____

_____

partial reinforcement _____

_____

_____

secondary reinforcer _____

_____

_____

shaping behavior _____

_____

_____

paired-associate learning _____

_____

_____

_____

cognitive processes _____

_____

_____

_____

sign learning _____

_____

_____

_____

latent learning _____

_____

_____

_____

_____ 1. If we wish to regulate the variables affecting reinforcement so as to produce the optimum conditions for learning, we provide
   a. the largest amount of reinforcement available, presented immediately after the behavior
   b. a moderate amount of reinforcement, presented immediately after the behavior
   c. the largest amount of reinforcement available, presented with a 1- to 5-second delay after the behavior
   d. the smallest amount of reinforcement which is functional, presented with a 2-second delay after the behavior

_____ 2. Secondary reinforcement has important practical implications because it
   a. can strengthen responses other than the one used in its establishment
   b. can function with drives other than the one operating when it was originally established
   c. greatly increases the range of possible conditioning
   d. all of the above

_____ 3. In Pavlov's experiments with dogs, the CR was _____ while the UR was _____.
   a. meat powder, salivation
   b. salivation, salivation
   c. a light, meat powder
   d. salivation, a light

_____ 4. The learning curve typical of sensorimotor skills is one of
   a. less gain per trial as the subject learns
   b. the same gain per trial as the subject learns
   c. more gain per trial as the subject learns
   d. more gain per trial as the subject first learns, reversing to less gain per trial later on

_____ 5. Which of the following is *not* a true statement regarding reinforcement by brain stimulation?
   a. human patients reported that it made them feel relief from anxiety
   b. it follows the same rules as learning with food reinforcement
   c. while brief stimulation in some areas is reinforcing, prolonged stimulation is aversive
   d. hungry rats will endure more shock for it than they will for food

_____ 6. Generalization and the complementary process of _____ operate to produce specific appropriate behavior, such as a child saying "bow-wow" only in response to dogs.
   a. conditioning
   b. reinforcement
   c. discrimination
   d. extinction

_____ 7. In comparing the value of S-R and cognitive theories, the text points out that
   a. it is possible to view them as complementary
   b. the S-R approach has proved most satisfactory for complex human learning
   c. the cognitive approach in itself provides a complete explanation
   d. all of the above

_____ 8. _____ may be defined as an acquired expectation that one stimulus will be followed by another in a particular context.
   a. Latent learning
   b. Probability learning
   c. Expectation learning
   d. Sign learning

_____ 9. One crucial difference between the two major types of conditioning is that in classical conditioning reinforcement _____ the response, while in operant conditioning reinforcement _____ the response.
   a. maintains, produces
   b. elicits, follows
   c. precedes, produces
   d. produces, elicits

_____ 10. Tolman's view of learning as sign learning differs from an S-R view in that Tolman wishes to distinguish between
   a. learning and expectation
   b. knowledge and learning

c. learning and performance

d. response probability and behavior

_____ 11. Rote memorization
a. is one form of sensorimotor learning
b. uses the pursuit rotor to pace the memorization
c. includes serial memorization
d. shows a learning curve of increasing gains

_____ 12. A person who has been trained to respond with salivation to the word "good" by pairing it with food is found to salivate also to the sentence "Leningrad is a wonderful city"; this illustrates
a. classical conditioning
b. generalization
c. semantic conditioning
d. all of the above

_____ 13. The _____ viewpoint argues that the dogs in Pavlov's experiments were not forming S-R associations but were learning to anticipate food.
a. insight
b. cognitive
c. encoding
d. mixture theory

_____ 14. When an experimenter specifically rewards a particular behavior, the reinforcement is "contingent" upon that behavior, and therefore strengthens it. When reinforcement is "noncontingent," however,
a. the behavior is weakened
b. there is no change in behavior
c. some random behavior is strengthened
d. the organism becomes frustrated

_____ 15. Rats exposed to a bright light while being injected with insulin eventually produce an insulin shock reaction to the injection of saline solution in the presence of the bright light. In this experiment, _____ is the CS, while insulin shock is the UR.
a. bright light
b. insulin shock
c. saline solution
d. insulin

_____ 16. "A relatively permanent change in behavior that occurs as the result of prior experience" is a formal definition of
a. classical conditioning
b. operant conditioning
c. learning
d. conditioning

_____ 17. Operant-conditioning principles were used in one case to modify the shy withdrawn behavior of a three-year-old girl. Which of the following is *not* a true statement regarding that study?
a. when her behavior was indistinguishable from that of the other children, the experimenters reversed the reinforcement procedure
b. the experimenters reinforced the girl by giving her candy when she stood up and participated in social interactions
c. it took only two weeks to drastically modify her behavior
d. the experimenters used a double reversal of her behavior to demonstrate that the reinforcement schedule was the causative factor

_____ 18. Extinction of a classically conditioned response is likely to occur when
a. there is only partial or intermittent reinforcement
b. the conditioned response generalizes to other stimuli
c. the unconditioned stimulus is presented continually without the conditioned stimulus
d. the conditioned stimulus is presented continually without the unconditioned stimulus

_____ 19. Which of the following is *not* true of insight?
a. insight depends upon a gradual process of trial and error
b. once the solution occurs, it can be repeated promptly
c. the solution achieved with insight can be applied to new situations
d. insight depends upon the arrangement of the problem situation

20. When a phone rings, we usually answer it. In Skinner's terms, the ringing is a _____, which tells you to answer but does not force you to.
a. conditioned stimulus
b. operant stimulus
c. respondent stimulus
d. discriminative stimulus

CLASS EXERCISE

THE PROCESS OF LEARNING

Introduction

Learning so pervades human activity that any curiosity about the nature of people and their behavior sooner or later leads to inquiry about how habits are formed, how skills are acquired, how preferences and tastes develop, how knowledge is obtained and put to use. But what exactly is "learning"? Although there are many varied definitions of this process, it might be defined as the modification of behavior through experience. This exercise will enable you to study the process of learning that goes on in modifying previously acquired behavior.

Equipment Needed

Red pencil or pen with red ink. A stopwatch or watch with a second hand.

Procedure

Tear out page 106, which you are to use for this experiment. When the instructor says "Go," write the letters of the alphabet backward in a vertical column from top to bottom. *Do not sacrifice accuracy for speed.* Your instructor will allow you twenty seconds to write as many letters as you can for each trial. If you complete the alphabet, start over again. As soon as the instructor says "Stop," fold the paper along the vertical line for each trial. This procedure will be continued for fifteen trials. Start with Trial 1 when the signal is given.

Treatment of Data

1. At the end of the fifteenth trial, count the number of correct letters on each trial and record these numbers at the bottom of page 106 in the space provided.

2. Copy the number of correct letters for each trial under "Score" in the following table.

Trial	Score	Trial	Score	Trial	Score
1		6		11	
2		7		12	
3		8		13	
4		9		14	
5		10		15	

3. Your instructor will ask you to record on a slip of paper the number of letters you got correct on each trial so that the average number of correct letters per trial for the class as a whole can be ascertained. When your instructor reads these group averages for each trial aloud, enter them in the space in the following table.

Trial	Group average	Trial	Group average	Trial	Group average
1		6		11	
2		7		12	
3		8		13	
4		9		14	
5		10		15	

4. Now plot your learning curve and the learning curve of the class as a whole on the graph on page 107. Use a pencil for your curve, and a red pencil or red ink for the class curve.

Questions For Discussion

1. Are there differences between the shape of your learning curve and that of the class? How do you account for the difference?

2. Does your progress from trial to trial indicate gradual learning?

3. Were there uncontrolled variables in this particular learning experiment?

4. How would you test for the permanence of learning to write the alphabet backward?

Trials

	1	2	3	4	5	6	7	8	9	10	11	12	13	14	15

NUMBER
CORRECT

Trial
number

1	2	3	4	5	6	7	8	9	10	11	12	13	14	15

LEARNING CURVE

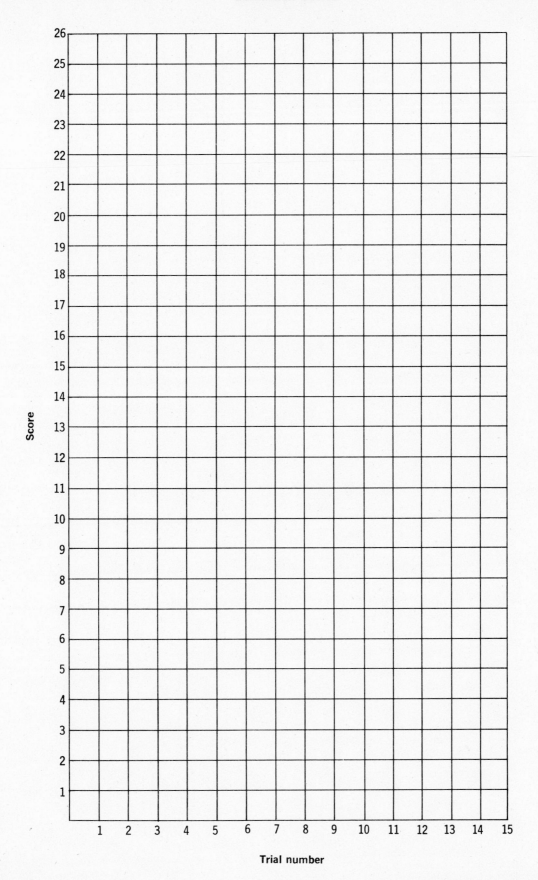

8
memory and forgetting

LEARNING OBJECTIVES

Describe three methods for measuring memory. Know the three traditional explanations of forgetting and the evidence for and against each. Be able to draw the paradigms for testing retroactive and proactive inhibition.

Understand the distinction between trace-dependent and cue-dependent forgetting. Relate the results of Penfield's studies on electrical stimulation of the brain to the hypothesis that memories are permanent.

Discuss the two-process theory of memory and its relationship to the traditional theories of forgetting. Understand how the behavior of patients with hippocampal lesions relates to the notion of STM and LTM.

Discuss some of the techniques for improving retention.

PROGRAMMED UNIT

1. There are several ways in which we can show that we remember something. One kind of *remembering* is called *redintegration,* which refers to remembering the *whole* of an earlier experience on the basis of *partial cues.* Redintegration is one

remembering

of several kinds of _____.

2. To redintegrate means to reestablish an earlier experience on the basis of partial

cues

_____. In sorting through a box of souvenirs you discover a seashell you picked up on the beach while vacationing with friends several years ago. The shell brings back vivid memories of the spot where you found it and the

redintegration

people you were with. This kind of remembering is called _____.

3. In this example of redintegration, the seashell that evokes other memories is a

partial

_____ cue.

4. While cleaning out a desk drawer Mrs. M. comes across the theater program of a play she and her husband attended the night they became engaged. The program, which evokes happy memories of that evening, is a partial cue for the process of

redintegration

_____.

5. When partial cues reestablish an earlier experience, we speak of redintegrative

memory
(or remembering)

_____.

6. Redintegration may also occur in remembering factual information. If you are trying to remember all you know about the battle of Gettysburg and one or two

cues

facts, or partial _____, lead you to gradually retrieve from

redintegration

memory all your knowledge on the topic, then this is a form of _____.

7. Another kind of remembering is *recall,* which differs from redintegration in that the material is remembered pretty much in its entirety without having to be pieced together, and the circumstances under which the learning took place may

recall

not be remembered. For instance, you may _____ a poem by reciting it in its entirety, even though you may not be able to remember when you learned it or who taught it to you.

remembering
(or synonym)

8. Recall is an easier kind of _____ to measure than redintegration and is therefore the kind of remembering commonly studied in the laboratory.

9. When we ask a laboratory subject to memorize a series of letters, and then to

recall

reproduce them, we are measuring _____. The percentage correct is the recall score. This kind of remembering is easier to study than

redintegration

_____, which involves the reestablishment of a past event and its surrounding circumstances.

recall

10. Of the two kinds of remembering mentioned thus far, _____ is the kind more likely to be studied in the laboratory.

recall
redintegration
(either order)

11. Still another kind of remembering is *recognition.* Two other ways of remembering are _____ and _____.

12. *Recognition* merely requires the acknowledgment of something or someone as *familiar.* To measure recognition we might have a subject look through a series of cards containing words (or pictures). We then mix this series with an equal number of new words (or pictures) and ask the subject to indicate which ones he has seen before and which are new. Since the subject is asked merely to pick out

recognition

the items that look familiar to him, this would be a test of _____.

recognition

13. Police use the kind of remembering called _____ for the identification of suspected criminals. The suspect is sandwiched in among a group of people, and a witness is asked to pick out the suspect merely on the basis of familiarity.

14. Recognition is one kind of remembering; it differs from recall and redintegration

familiar

in requiring only that something or someone be recognized as _____.

15. Another way to show that something is remembered from past experience is to measure *relearning*. Material that you think you have completely forgotten may be easier to relearn because it was once learned in the past. For example, suppose in high school you memorized Lincoln's Gettysburg Address so that you could recite it without an error. It took you one hour to accomplish one perfect recitation. In college, not having seen or practiced the speech in the meantime, you are sure you have forgotten it completely. But you find that you can now learn the speech to the same *criterion of mastery* in less than a quarter of an hour. Something must have been remembered from the original learning that was

relearning

evidenced by the test of re_____.

16. To test for relearning in the laboratory, we have the subject learn a list of word pairs well enough to achieve a certain standard of performance or criterion of

mastery

criterion

_____. Being able to go through the list once without any errors would be one _____ of mastery.

17. Four months later the subject relearns the same list to the same criterion of

mastery

_____. If the second learning requires fewer trials than the first, then we assume that there has been some *saving* due to prior learning.

saving

Retention of earlier learning is measured by the s_____ in relearning.

18. Study the formula given below, which expresses the saving due to prior

learning

_____ in the form of a *percentage*.

$$\text{Saving score} = \left[\frac{\text{Original trials - Relearning trials}}{\text{Original trials}} \right] \times 100$$

saving

19. The _____ score is expressed in the form of a percentage.

20. If a subject initially required twenty trials to learn a list of word pairs and four months later required twenty trials to relearn the same list, the saving score

0, no

would be _____. In this case there is (*good/no*) evidence of retention.

21. If initially you required twenty trials to learn a list and four months later required ten trials to learn the same list, your saving score would be

50

_____ percent.

22. Peg learned a list of 100 Russian words in fifty trials. A year later she learned the

60

same list in twenty trials. Her saving score would be _____ percent.

23. To obtain a saving score you subtract the number of relearning trials from the original trials, divide by the number of (*original/relearning*) trials, and then _____ by 100.

24. A saving score is an indication of how well the subject *retains* the learned material. The effects of intervals of *no* practice after initial learning, as shown by tests introduced at set periods following learning, can be plotted on a curve called a *retention curve*. Retention of learning, expressed as a saving score

percentage

p_____, is plotted against the intervals of time since initial learning.

25. Study the curve in the graph below. As the label on the vertical axis indicates, it

retention

is a _____ curve.

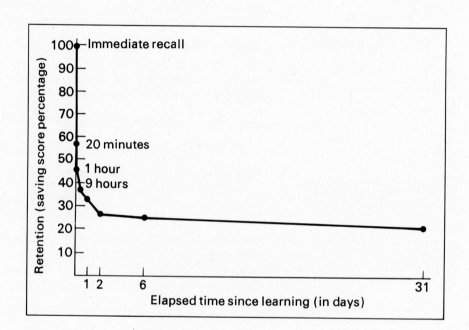

26. A saving score is an indication of how well the subject retains the material. The

retention curve

effects of time on retention of learning can be plotted on a _____

_____. Note that a typical retention curve falls *rapidly* at first and then gradually tapers off.

rapidly

27. Though the curve of retention generally falls _____ at first and then gradually tapers off, the rate at which forgetting occurs will vary greatly with the materials used and with the circumstances under which learning takes place.

28. Let's review. We have discussed four kinds of remembering. These are

redintegration,
recall, recognition,
relearning (any order)

_____, _____, _____, and

_____.

29. Of these kinds of memory only three can be readily studied in the laboratory.

recognition, recall
relearning (any order)

These three are _____, _____, and

_____.

30. Sometimes you may not be able to recall a certain piece of information but can show by recognition or ease in relearning that you have some memory of it. Thus, recognition and relearning are more sensitive measures of memory than

recall

_____.

31. To remember something requires three different cognitive operations: *encoding, storage,* and *retrieval.* To encode a piece of information means to change it into a form that can be stored in memory. When we want to retrieve that information, we must locate it in memory. Sometimes information may be encoded and

memory

stored but we have trouble retrieving it, or locating it in _____.

32. For example, sometimes you may feel quite sure you know a certain word or name but can't recall it immediately. The correct word is on the tip of your tongue, and eventually you do hit upon it, but the process takes some time. In this case the word is apparently stored in memory but you have difficulty

retrieving

_____ it.

33. There are three traditional theories of *forgetting.* One of them, the theory of *decay* through disuse, assumes that learning leaves a "trace" in the brain; this *memory trace* involves some sort of physical change that was not present prior to learning. Some theorists believe that forgetting occurs because the

memory

_____ traces fade or decay with the passage of time, so that traces of material once learned gradually disintegrate and eventually disappear altogether.

34. As you look at a picture, it may reveal a wealth of detail, but after a period of time you forget many of the details of the picture. This lends credence to the

decay

view that forgetting is due to de_____ of the memory trace.

decay

35. One theory, then, attributes forgetting to _____ of the

memory

_____ trace.

36. There are arguments, however, against the theory that the memory trace decays with the passage of time. Some old people can vividly recall events of their youth, whereas they can barely remember the events of the day. This fact

decay

suggests that memories do not simply _____.

37. A second theory assumes that it is not the passage of time that determines the course of forgetting but what we do in the interval between learning and recall. New learning may *interfere* with material that we have previously learned. Thus

interference

inter_____ rather than decay is the crucial factor.

38. The interference theory attributes forgetting to *retroactive* and *proactive inhibition. Retroactive inhibition* emphasizes that *new* learning interferes with *old* learning and thus causes forgetting of what was learned earlier. Assume that two hours ago you learned a list of twenty words. Now you learn a new list of

old	twenty words. The *new* learning should interfere with the _____
retroactive	list you learned two hours ago. Forgetting in this instance is caused by _____ inhibition.

39. The theory that new learning may interfere with the retention of the old is

inhibition   known as retroactive _____.

40. An experimental group learns list A, then learns list B, and after an interval tries to recall list A. The control group learns list A, rests, and then tries to recall list A. If the control group does much better in recalling list A than the experi-

retroactive   mental   group,   we   attribute   the   difference   to   _____

inhibition   _____.

41.
Experimental group	Learn A	Learn B	Recall A
Control group	Learn A	Rest	Recall A

retroactive   The above is an arrangement for testing _____ inhibition.

42. A certain amount of retroactive inhibition occurs as the result of *normal waking activity.* Two groups of subjects learn a list of words. The subjects in one group go about their usual activities for three hours and are then tested for recall of the word list. The other group is tested at the same time but spends the intervening three hours sleeping. The latter group shows better retention of the word list. We conclude that some amount of retroactive inhibition occurs as the result of

waking   normal _____ activity.

43. The notion that studying for an exam just before going to bed yields a better test performance than studying earlier in the day for the same amount of time, is

retroactive inhibition   based on the theory of _____ _____.

44. A companion interference theory, based on the same principles as retroactive inhibition and known as *proactive inhibition,* maintains that *prior* learning can also interfere with the learning and recall of *new* material. Note how the experimental arrangement below differs from that for testing retroactive inhibi-

inhibition   tion. It is a method for testing *proactive* _____.

Experimental group	Learn A	Learn B	Recall B
Control group	Rest	Learn B	Recall B

45. When *prior* learning interferes with the learning and recall of *new* material,

proactive   _____ inhibition is demonstrated.

new	**46.** Retroactive inhibition emphasizes that _____ learning inter-
old (or prior)	feres with _____ learning. Proactive inhibition, on the other
prior (or synonym)	hand, emphasizes that _____ learning interferes with
new	_____ learning.

47.
Experimental group	Learn A	Learn B	Recall A
Control group	Learn A	Rest	Recall A

retroactive

The above arrangement is for testing _____ inhibition.

Experimental group	Learn A	Learn B	Recall B
Control group	Rest	Learn B	Recall B

proactive

The above arrangement is for testing _____ inhibition.

forgetting

48. The theories of _____ discussed above emphasize the *decay* of memory traces through *disuse,* and the *interference* that *new* learning and *prior* learning exert on retention.

49. Thus far we have discussed two theories of forgetting. The first emphasizes the

decay, disuse

_____ of memory traces through _____; the

prior (or synonym)

second emphasizes the interference that new learning and _____ learning exert on retention.

50. A third theory of forgetting is that of *motivated forgetting.* That is, some memories are forgotten and cannot be recalled because their recall would activate feelings of shame, anxiety, or guilt. Amnesia is a dramatic example of

motivated

_____ forgetting, since in amnesia certain personal memories are inaccessible to recall but impersonal memories remain intact.

51. The concept of *motivated forgetting* is based on the principle of *repression.* In repression, individuals forget certain memories because of the way they relate to personal problems; their recall would produce shame, anxiety, or guilt. If an individual cannot consciously remember an act of which he is ashamed, many

repressed

psychologists would say that the memory is _____ed.

motivated

52. A third theory of forgetting is that of _____ forgetting, whereby a person cannot consciously recall certain memories that would produce too much guilt, shame, or anxiety if recalled. Through the process of

repression

_____ these unacceptable memories are denied conscious expression.

53. If you committed an act that made you feel very guilty, ashamed, or anxious, the memory of that act may become inaccessible to conscious awareness through

repression

the process of _____. When repression accounts for the loss of

motivated

certain memories, we speak of _____ forgetting.

54. Motivated forgetting refers to the fact that memories are sometimes repressed from conscious awareness if recalling them would activate a person's feelings of

guilt, anxiety
(either order)

shame, _____, or _____.

55. The theory of motivated forgetting proposes that repressed memories are *not permanently lost;* they are just inaccessible to awareness. The fact that a person may become aware of repressed memories during psychotherapy or while under

permanently

hypnosis indicates that such memories are not _____

lost

_____.

memory

trace

retroactive
proactive
(either order)

decay
motivated

two-process

LTM

STM

rehearsed

STM

buffer

STM

rehearsed

56. The theory that attributes forgetting to decay of the _____ _____, however, implies that memories are permanently lost.

57. We have discussed three traditional theories of forgetting. The interference theory postulates two kinds of interference with learned material, _____ and _____ inhibition. Of the remaining two theories, one stresses _____ of the memory trace through disuse, while the other considers _____ forgetting, based on the principle of repression.

58. Because no single one of these theories gives an adequate account of forgetting, a number of theorists have argued for a *two-process* theory of memory. They propose that one type of storage mechanism is involved in remembering events just recently perceived and a different type is involved in the recall of material that has been repeatedly practiced. A _____-_____ theory, then, postulates that there are two different storage mechanisms, one for *short*-term memory (STM) and the other for *long*-term memory (LTM).

59. A two-process theory of memory postulates that there are different storage mechanisms for STM and for _____.

60. Your own telephone number, which you have used repeatedly, is a relatively permanent memory and would be stored in LTM. The telephone number that you have just looked up in the directory will remain with you only momentarily in _____. Unless you make a conscious effort to focus attention on the new number by repeating, or *rehearsing*, it to yourself, it is quickly lost from memory.

61. Incoming material enters the STM mechanism and, while there, can be recalled as long as it is *rehearsed.* If the information is not rehearsed, it will fade rapidly. Once an item ceases to be _____, its trace in STM begins to decay.

62. Information can be maintained in _____ as long as it is rehearsed, but only a limited number of items of information can be rehearsed at the same time. The set of items being maintained in STM at any one time is called the *rehearsal buffer.*

63. The rehearsal _____ is the set of items, or memory traces, being maintained in _____ at any point in time.

64. The rehearsal buffer has a limited capacity because only a certain number of items can be _____ at the same time. When new information enters STM the person must decide whether to include this item among those currently being rehearsed or permit it to decay.

65. Information remains in the rehearsal buffer until new, incoming information replaces it or until it is coded and transferred to LTM. If an item in the rehearsal buffer is replaced by new information before it is transferred to

LTM

_____, it decays and is permanently lost.

66. In contrast to STM, the LTM mechanism has a virtually unlimited storage

LTM

capacity. Theoretically, once material is transferred to _____, it should never be forgotten.

67. Actually, we know that this is not true. There are cases in which material we knew very well is not available to us. Forgetting may occur because the *cues* needed to retrieve the material are incomplete. For instance, an exam question may not contain the relevant cues to allow the retrieval of the appropriate

cues

information. If the _____ needed to retrieve the material are not complete, it will appear that the material has been forgotten.

68. It is also possible that initially only part of the desired information was coded

STM

into LTM and the rest decayed and was lost from _____. In this case complete retrieval would not be possible—the information would not be available.

69. Forgetting may also occur when memories stored in LTM would make us feel ashamed or anxious. Repressed memories are permanently stored but are inac-

motivated

cessible for retrieval. This is an example of _____ forgetting.

two-process

70. A _____-_____ theory of memory postulates

short, long
(either order)

two storage mechanisms. One deals with _____-term memory and one with _____-term memory.

71. Incoming material enters STM and is maintained there for a brief period in the

rehearsal buffer

_____ _____. Rehearsal prevents the mem-

decaying

ory trace from _____. Information in the rehearsal buffer may

LTM

be coded and transferred to _____. Information not trans-

decay

ferred to LTM will rapidly _____. Information that is transferred will be stored permanently in LTM, from which it may be retrieved unless

cues

the _____ needed for retrieval are incomplete.

72. Now that we have discussed the theories of remembering and forgetting, a logical question is, How can we improve recall? One useful technique in memorizing a poem or a series of words is to form a *mental image* of the items. For example, to memorize a set of chemicals that form a certain compound one might visualize the chemicals as they appeared in labeled beakers upon a table. This

recall

mental picture would facilitate re_____ of the chemicals.

73. If we learn a series of unrelated word pairs, such as *dog-bicycle* or *bird-sweater,* by visualizing a dog wearing a silly hat riding on a bicycle or a shivering bird

mental

dressed in a sweater, we would be using _____ images to facilitate recall.

74. The *organization* of material in some meaningful fashion is another technique to improve memory. Thus a long list of minerals could be remembered more readily if the items were organized into categories (such as precious and nonprecious stones, rare and common metals) than if they were simply learned in random

Organization   order. Org_____ aids memory.

75. If one wants to remember the names of the original thirteen colonies, it would

organize   help to _____ them according to geographic location or to

image   form a mental _____ of them as portrayed on a map.

76. A third technique to aid in memorizing is *self-recitation.* Studies have shown

reciting   that re_____ material to yourself increases retention better than simply reading and rereading the material. If you have two hours to devote to the study of an assignment that you can read in thirty minutes, you could reread the assignment four times or you could read it once and spend three-fourths of your time asking yourself questions about the material you have read. Active

self-recitation   recall, or self-_____ would be the better of the two methods.

77. The three techniques to improve recall that we have mentioned so far are

mental images,   forming _____ _____, _____,

organization   and _____-_____.

self-recitation

78. If you wish to retain something over a long period of time, should you learn it to the point of bare recall or should you *overlearn* it? By *overlearning* we mean learning something well beyond the point of bare recall. Experimental evidence shows that a moderate amount of overlearning aids retention. Therefore, if you wish to retain new learning over a considerable period of time, you would be

overlearn   wise to _____ the material *beyond bare mastery* of it.

overlearning   **79.** A moderate amount of _____ aids retention. Therefore, you learn something you wish to retain for an extended period of time beyond

bare   _____ mastery of it.

80. Let's review. There are three traditional theories of forgetting. These are

trace   (1) decay of the memory _____ through disuse; (2) the

interference   _____ of new learning with old learning, which is known as

retroactive   _____ inhibition, or of prior learning with new learning, which

proactive   is known as _____ inhibition; and, finally, (3)

motivated   _____ forgetting, which utilizes the process of

repression   _____, whereby unacceptable memories become inaccessible to conscious awareness.

81. Since no one of these theories can adequately explain forgetting, some psychol-

two-process   ogists have proposed a _____-_____ theory

short, long
(either order)

of memory, which distinguishes between _____-term and _____-term memory.

images, organize

82. We can improve our memories in several ways. We can make use of mental _____ to help in recall; we can _____ the material in some meaningful fashion; and we can make use of self-

recitation

_____ to increase retention. It is also desirable to

overlearn

_____ material beyond the point of bare mastery.

TERMS AND CONCEPTS FOR IDENTIFICATION

redintegrative memory _____

_____

_____

_____

recall _____

_____

_____

_____

recognition _____

_____

_____

_____

relearning _____

_____

_____

_____

criterion of mastery _____

_____

_____

_____

saving score _____

_____

_____

_____

retention curve _____

_____

_____

_____

tip-of-the-tongue phenomenon _____

_____

_____

_____

memory trace _____

_____

_____

retroactive inhibition _____

_____

_____

_____

proactive inhibition _____

_____

_____

_____

repression _____

_____

_____

_____

trace-dependent forgetting _____

_____

_____

_____

cue-dependent forgetting _____

_____

_____

_____

STM _____

_____

_____

_____

LTM _____

_____

_____

_____

rehearsal buffer _____

_____

_____

_____

method of loci _____

_____

_____

_____ 1. Research on the use of visual imagery to aid the learning of verbal material shows that
a. information may be encoded verbally or nonverbally
b. in the absence of specific instructions to visualize, subjects rely primarily on verbal coding
c. nonverbal encoding is best for representing concrete-spatial events and objects
d. all of the above

_____ 2. The kind of forgetting in which memories become inaccessible because of the way in which they relate to our personal problems is
a. retroactive inhibition
b. interference effect
c. repression
d. decay through disuse

_____ 3. At which point in the memory process are we _least_ likely to effect an improvement in memory?
a. encoding
b. storage
c. retention
d. retrieval

_____ 4. One major reason why skills learned in childhood are retained, even after years of disuse, is that
a. they are overlearned
b. sensorimotor learning tends to be retained much longer than learned information
c. they are learned during a critical period of motor development
d. children can concentrate more on motor skills than adults, who overintellectualize

_____ 5. When you reconstruct the memory of your high-school prom or seek out information about Cleopatra, you are using the form of memory called
a. recall
b. recognition
c. redintegration
d. relearning

_____ 6. Which of the following is not considered to be true by theorists who argue for a two-process memory system?
a. LTM is characterized by trace-dependent forgetting
b. information is permanently recorded in LTM
c. information can be maintained in STM by rehearsal
d. STM is viewed as a rapidly decaying system

_____ 7. A subject in the TOT state who cannot recall the target word _symposium_ would be more likely to guess
a. conference
b. simple
c. moratorium
d. cymbidium

_____ 8. Trace-dependent forgetting
a. occurs when the information is stored but we are unable to retrieve it
b. implies the actual decay of the memory trace
c. is most clearly illustrated in the TOT state
d. is supported by the theory of motivated forgetting

_____ 9. The memory technique of taking an imaginary walk and locating images of objects to be remembered along the route, is called the
a. mental-walk system
b. method of imagery
c. image-organization technique
d. method of loci

_____ 10. In a semantic network of the type proposed by Collins and Quillian
a. a sentence is considered true if the number of nodes is the same as the number of pointers
b. the connections in the network are called nodes
c. information about a class of things is stored at the level of hierarchy for that class
d. all of the above

_____ 11. If you originally required 10 trials to learn the information involved in this set of

questions but when studying for the final require only 2 trials, your saving score is
a. 10 percent
b. 50 percent
c. 80 percent
d. 100 percent

____ 12. Direct electrical stimulation of exposed human brains is done in the course of "mapping" prior to surgery. The results of such stimulation tell us something about memory, i.e.,
a. many memories remain intact long after the ability to recall them has disappeared
b. surgical removal of the area from which a memory has been evoked destroys the memory of that event
c. directly evoked memories are vague and hazy ones
d. experiences so evoked are more hallucination than real memory

____ 13. A cognitive view of memory divides it into three stages:
a. organization, storage, and retrieval
b. encoding, processing, and organization
c. storage, retrieval, and processing
d. encoding, storage, and retrieval

____ 14. One way to study is to ask yourself questions about what you have read—not unlike what you are now doing. This technique
a. is useful, but only for a limited amount of time, perhaps 25 percent or less of your study time
b. has proved to be an effective way to spend more than half of your study time
c. is less useful than spending the same time rereading the material
d. works best if done as the last step in studying

____ 15. A two-process theory of memory says that long-term recall may fail because
a. information was never transferred from STM to LTM
b. not enough cues may be available at the time of attempted recall to locate information in STM
c. the trace in LTM has decayed
d. all of the above

____ 16. The decay-through-disuse theory of forgetting

a. is dubious or at least incomplete
b. is becoming more accepted as experimental evidence builds up in its favor
c. accounts for a substantial percentage of forgetting
d. accounts for most forgetting

____ 17. If asked to name all the people you met at a large party, you are likely to remember more of the names learned at the beginning and at the end of the party. The _____ illustrates the _____.
a. increase for the end names, primacy effect
b. dip for the middle names, interference effect
c. increase for the beginning names, recency effect
d. increase for the end names, recency effect

____ 18. Retroactive inhibition is demonstrated by an experiment in which the following sequence is used:
a. learn A, test A, learn B, test B
b. learn A, learn B, test A
c. learn A, learn B, test B
d. learn A, learn B, learn C, test C

____ 19. Individuals suffering from lesions of the hippocampus
a. probably cannot remember their name
b. have deficiencies in STM
c. will be unable to remember the names of people they have just met
d. are unlikely to be able to do complicated mental arithmetic

____ 20. Proactive and retroactive inhibition are examples of which theory of forgetting?
a. decay through disuse
b. interference effects
c. motivated forgetting
d. amnesia

KEY TO SELF-QUIZ

1. d	6. a	11. c	16. a
2. c	7. d	12. a	17. d
3. c	8. b	13. d	18. b
4. a	9. d	14. b	19. c
5. c	10. c	15. a	20. b

INDIVIDUAL EXERCISES

A. EPISODIC MEMORY AND EMOTION

Some experiences remain vividly in our memories, while others are quickly forgotten. Think back over your earlier years, say, the period from age five through the first year of high school, and list in the space below your ten most vivid memories. Just jot down a few words to remind you of each episode. Do this before reading further.

1. _____
2. _____
3. _____
4. _____
5. _____
6. _____
7. _____
8. _____
9. _____
10. _____

Now examine each episode and rate it according to whether it was pleasant or unpleasant. Mark + beside a pleasant experience, 0 if the episode was essentially neutral, and − for an unpleasant memory. Count the number of positive, negative, and neutral experiences. In general, did you recall more pleasant or more unpleasant experiences? Why do you think this is so? Ask several of your friends to follow the same procedure. How did their memories compare with yours on the pleasant-unpleasant dimension?

If the entire class does this exercise, record your results on a slip of paper and give them to the instructor to tabulate.

B. ORGANIZATION AS AN AID TO MEMORY

Introduction

Organization of material to be learned is one factor that aids retention. This exercise will demonstrate that it is easier to remember a list of related words (words that can be grouped into categories) than a list of words that has no such organization. It will also demonstrate the primacy and recency effects—that is, the tendency to recall more items at the beginning and end of a list than in the middle.

Equipment Needed

Stopwatch or watch with a second hand.

Procedure

Select a subject and tell him that you want him to memorize a list of 20 words. Explain that you will read each word aloud until you have completed the list (on page 124). (Time your reading of the list, allowing approximately three seconds per word. You should practice reading and timing the list before trying it out on your subject.) Immediately upon completion of the list, hand the subject paper and pencil and ask him to write in a single column as many words as he can recall, in any order. Give him exactly two minutes to write the words he can recall.

Repeat this procedure with a second subject.

Treatment of Data

You will notice that ten of the words have no obvious relationship to one another, five belong to the category of "furniture," and five can be classed as "parts of the body." Check each subject's list and record in the table below the number of words recalled that are categorized words (that is, belong to the categories "furniture" and "body parts") and the number that do not belong to a category. Also note any intrusions (words that are not in the original list) and mark whether they are related to either of the two categories.

	Category words	Non-category words	Intrusions
Subject 1	_____	_____	_____
Subject 2	_____	_____	_____
Total	_____	_____	_____

To demonstrate the primacy and recency effects it is necessary to construct a serial position curve for your two subjects. First go through each subject's recall list and mark each word with the number at which it appears in the original list. In the table below tabulate for the first subject how many of the first four words in the study list were recalled correctly, how many of the second four words, and so on for each of the five segments. Do the same for the second subject, add the results for both subjects in the row marked "total," and plot these numbers on the graph provided on page 124. Connect the data points by a line to show the serial position curve.

	Presentation order in word list				
	1–4	**5–8**	**9–12**	**13–16**	**17–20**
Subject 1					
Subject 2					
Total					

There are eight possible correct responses for each point on the curve. In our hypothetical curve the subjects recalled most of the words in the first four positions. This tendency to remember the first words in a list is known as the *primary effect*. Note that the curve is depressed for words in the middle of the list but rises again toward the end. The tendency to recall words toward the end of the list is called the *recency effect.*

Questions For Discussion

1. Were more categorized words recalled than words that do not fall into a category? If so, what are the implications for learning?

2. Did the subject's responses tend to cluster in categories? That is, when he recalled one word in the furniture category did it tend to be followed by another word in the same category?

3. Judging from the responses of your two subjects, are there individual differences in the total number of words recalled? In the type of words recalled?

4. Were the intrusion words, if any, related to either of the two categories?

5. What does your serial position curve indicate? Is it similar to the hypothetical one? Do your subjects show a primacy effect? A recency effect? Which is greater?

WORD LIST

* 1. finger   8. ruby   15. mountain
  2. rabbit   * 9. arm   *16. foot
** 3. table   10. house   **17. sofa
  4. fire   11. flower   18. bicycle
  5. teacher   **12. desk   19. ring
** 6. chair   **13. bed   *20. toe
* 7. hand   14. paper

*category of "body parts"
**category of "furniture"

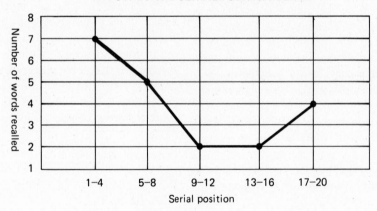

HYPOTHETICAL SERIAL POSITION CURVE

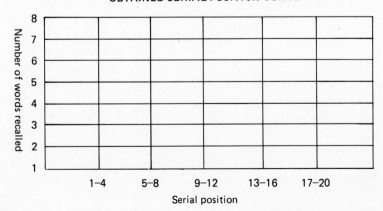

OBTAINED SERIAL POSITION CURVE

9 optimizing learning

LEARNING OBJECTIVES

Understand how programmed instruction is carried out by computer and by textbook. Distinguish between linear and branching programs. Discuss the learning principles illustrated by programmed instruction.

Give examples of negative and positive transfer of learning. Discuss some of the factors that affect transfer and their application to education.

Discuss the distinction between intrinsic and extrinsic rewards, the effects of punishment on learning, and the relationship between anxiety and learning.

PROGRAMMED UNIT

1. One of the methods of organizing material to be learned, based on the principles of learning theory, is called *programmed learning.* You should be familiar with this method, since much of this study guide is presented in the form of

programmed

_____ learning.

2. In programmed learning, the material is arranged so that students can learn it on their own with a minimum number of errors. Each item, called a *frame,* builds

frame

on the preceding fr_____ in such a way that there is little conceptual distance between them.

3. In other words, each frame tries to convey only a small amount of new information—the *steps* between frames are very small. The size of a

step

s_____ is important; the smaller the step size, the fewer will be the *errors* made.

4. Small steps are necessary to ensure a minimum number of

errors

_____. The idea is for the student to make a correct response

incorrect

to each frame and rarely, if ever, make an _____ response.

5. Because programmed material is set up so that the students can learn on their own without a teacher or tutor, they can proceed at their *own rates.* Some students can go through a program twice as rapidly as others and still learn as

rate

much. Their _____ of learning is rapid.

6. If we start 100 students on a given set of programmed material, some will finish in a week while others may take two weeks or more. This is possible because

own rates

students proceed at their _____ _____.

7. If students must make an *active response* to some kind of stimulus (for example, writing a response to a frame), their learning is likely to be better than if they merely sit and listen to the same material given in lecture form. Since in making

active

a response the students are *active* in some way, we call this _____ learning.

8. There is evidence that active learning is more efficient than passive learning. Thus, in programming, the fact that the students must make an active

response

_____ to the material is considered an advantage over merely listening to a lecture.

9. In programmed learning students find out whether they are right or wrong *immediately* after they make a response. This type of *feedback* permits immediate correction of an error, and the knowledge that the answer is correct serves as

response

immediate *reinforcement* of the correct _____. Students get

feedback

immediate fe_____ of results, which aids efficient learning.

10. In programmed learning, then, immediate feedback of results leads to immediate

reinforcement

_____ of the correct response. Also, learners cannot be passive in the learning process; they must be _____.

active

11. Once you had written your response in the previous frame, you were able to get immediate feedback of results. If you responded with the words "reinforce-

reinforcement

ment" and "active," you received immediate _____

correct (or right)

by learning that your response was _____.

12. To recapitulate: In programmed learning the material is arranged in small

steps

_____ so that students can proceed at their

own rates

_____ _____ without the aid of a teacher or the limitations of a class schedule.

responses	**13.** Also, the students must make active _____, which are then
feedback	reinforced by immediate _____ of results.
	14. Some instructional programs follow a straight sequence of questions and answers; after answering each item the student moves on to the next regardless of whether the response was correct. These are called *linear programs.* Linear
programs	_____ can be presented in book form, as in this study guide.
	15. More complicated programs, called *branching programs,* provide alternative answers from which the student can select. If the student chooses a wrong answer, the error is pointed out, and he may be *branched* to additional material
branching	that will help him avoid that error again. A br_____ program
linear	thus provides a more *individualized* type of instruction than a _____ program.
	16. In a branching program a student who has done well on a number of questions may be given a chance to jump ahead to more complicated material. Branching
individualized (or individual)	programs thus provide more _____ instruction than linear programs.
	17. Either type of program allows students to proceed at their own
rates, branching	_____. But only a _____ program permits them to skip ahead or go back for additional remedial material.
	18. Branching programs are usually too complicated to present in textbook form and must be presented by means of a *computer.* Programmed material presented
computer	by a _____ is called computer-assisted instruction (CAI).
assisted	**19.** In computer-_____ instruction the computer keeps track of the student's progress and decides from one moment to the next what material to present. Computer-assisted instruction thus provides a highly
individualized	_____ type of instruction.
	20. Let's review. When students progress from one frame to the next regardless of
linear	whether their responses were correct, they are using a _____ program.
	21. If the students are given alternative answers from which to select and the frame that is presented next depends upon the answer chosen, they are using a
branching	_____ program.
do not	**22.** Linear programs (*do/do not*) need to be presented by a computer. Programs that
branching	may require computer assistance are called _____ programs.
	23. The most highly individualized type of instruction is provided by a
branching, computer	_____ program presented by a _____.

24. An important problem in the efficiency of learning procedures is the extent to which the learning of one thing helps in the learning of something else. A boy who has learned to shoot at a target with an air rifle may find it *easier* to hit the target when he begins to practice with a 22-caliber rifle than if he had had no

easier   practice at all. His learning with the air rifle has made it _____ to learn to handle the 22-caliber rifle.

25. The air-rifle learning makes the 22-caliber learning easier because the handling of both rifles requires similar skills. Psychologists believe that in such situations

learning   aspects of the earlier _____ are *transferred* to the new learning.

26. In learning to shoot an air rifle, a boy should learn, among other things, to hold the gun steady, to line up the front and rear sights on the target, and to squeeze the trigger slowly rather than with a quick jerk. All of these acquired skills can

transferred   usefully be _____ when he learns to shoot the 22-caliber rifle, thus making the new learning easier. We call this *positive transfer.*

27. When having learned one thing makes it easier to learn something else, we say

positive   that the learning has been transferred. We call this _____ transfer.

28. John takes a bookkeeping job in a firm that has its books set up in a manner that John has never seen. Yet, his previous training as a bookkeeper enables him to

positive   master this new system. This is an example of _____ transfer.

29. Sometimes having learned one task makes it more *difficult* to learn a new task. For example, if you have learned to drive using a car with an automatic shift, it may be more difficult to learn to drive a car with a stick shift than it would be if you had never learned to drive at all. This example illustrates *negative*

transfer   tr_____.

30. *Transfer of learning* refers to the effect of past learning on subsequent learning.

easier   In other words, if previous learning makes it either _____ or

harder (either order)   _____ to learn something else, transfer has occurred.

31. Negative transfer occurs when having learned one task makes it (*easier/harder*) to

harder   learn a later task. Positive transfer occurs when having learned one task makes it

easier   (*easier/harder*) to learn a subsequent task.

32. We do not approach each new task in life as if it were completely new. We can carry over skills learned in the past to the new situation. We can do this because

transfer of learning   of _____ of _____.

33. A special example of positive transfer studied by psychologists is called *learning to learn.* If you memorize a different list of words each day for several days, you will probably find that your learning speed improves over time; it will take you

less   (*more/less*) time to memorize the last day's list than it did the first day's. This is

to learn   an example of *learning* _____ _____.

34. A number of factors contribute to your improved performance. You may have learned to concentrate better, to ignore extraneous stimuli. You may have discovered some *principles of efficient memorization.* Both of these contribute

learning   to _____ *to learn.*

positive   **35.** Learning to learn is one form of _____ transfer.

efficient   **36.** Teaching people certain principles of _____ memorization also improves their ability to *retain* the material they have memorized.

37. One method that has proved to be a very effective aid to memory is the use of

image   *mental imagery.* This method involves forming a mental _____ge that incorporates in some way the items you wish to *associate.*

38. For example, if you want to remember that the Spanish word "pato" (pronounced "pot-oh") means duck, you could imagine a little duck hiding beneath an overturned flower pot. Then when you heard the word "pato" you would associate pot with duck and remember the meaning. This is one way that mental

memory   imagery can be used to improve _____.

mental   **39.** Studies have shown that students who use _____ images to associate vocabulary words with their meanings remember more than those who learn simply by rote.

40. It is obvious that another important factor influencing the efficiency with which people learn is motivation. Students who work through a program in algebra for the pleasure of acquiring knowledge have *intrinsic motivation,* since they desire to learn something without expecting any reward other than a feeling of inner satisfaction. Similarly, a boy or girl who wants very much to learn to drive a car needs no reward as an incentive; he or she eagerly learns to drive, spurred on by

intrinsic   _____ motivation.

41. *Extrinsic motivation* refers to performing a task for the sake of a reward that is artificially established and not inherent in the task itself. Teachers use grades as an incentive to make students study and learn. Because the students may study simply to achieve a grade of A or B instead of to acquire new knowledge, we say

extrinsic   that their motivation is _____ rather than intrinsic.

42. Jane enjoys music. She plays the violin in a string quartet composed of friends and spends hours practicing to improve her technique. Her motivation is

intrinsic   _____ because she requires no reward other than the enjoyment inherent in playing the instrument. Her brother, Dave, on the other hand, dislikes music and practices the piano only because his mother pays him a dollar

extrinsic   for each hour of practice. His motivation is _____ because he needs a reward to encourage him to perform.

43. The most genuine satisfaction in learning comes from tasks that have been

intrinsic   initiated through _____ motivation. But when an individual

extrinsic

has to be spurred on to some activity for an arbitrary reward, such as money or a grade, his motivation is _____.

extrinsic

44. The distinction between intrinsic and _____ motivation is not clear-cut, and most learning situations involve both types of motivation. John may learn to dance because he enjoys rhythm and movement; in this case the

intrinsic

motivation is _____. He may also fear the derision of his classmates if he is inept and awkward on the dance floor; so part of his

extrinsic

motivation may be _____.

45. In general, learning is more satisfying and more efficient if the motivation

intrinsic

involved is primarily _____.

46. If we wish an organism to learn some desired behavior, we must *reinforce* it in some way. We may choose to reinforce it either by *reward* or *punishment*. In more technical terms, we may choose between (1) positive reinforcement, or reward for the desired behavior, and (2) negative reinforcement, or

punishment

_____ for incorrect responses.

47. Since we may use either reward or punishment to bring about desired behavior, we must consider which is more effective. There is evidence that in most

reward

instances positive reinforcement, or _____, is more effective.

48. One of the reasons that reward is generally more effective than punishment in the control of behavior is that the reward emphasizes that the organism is

reinforces
(or strengthens)

responding correctly. Reward _____ the desired response.

49. On the other hand, punishment only tells the organism that it is wrong, without guiding it toward an alternative, correct response that may then be *rewarded.*

reward

Therefore, _____ tells the organism what the desired response is and punishment does not.

50. Furthermore, punished behavior may be temporarily suppressed but not weak-

punishment

ened, and will reappear when the _____ ceases.

51. In those instances in which punishment is effective in changing behavior, it usually accomplishes its purpose by forcing the individual to select an alternative

rewarded

response that may then be _____.

52. The above are some of the reasons that psychologists feel that

reward, punishment

_____ is generally more effective than _____ in the control of behavior.

53. Another factor that has an important influence on learning is the degree of *anxiety* connected with the task to be learned. If a student is very anxious to do well on an exam, will he perform better than a student who is less

anxious

_____?

54. Subjects who are rated as *high-anxious* perform better on simple tasks involving a single response than subjects who are rated as *low-anxious*. For example, in a classical-conditioning study in which an eye-blink response (elicited by a puff of air) is conditioned to a bell, high-anxious subjects condition more rapidly than

low-anxious   _____-_____ subjects.

better

55. High-anxious subjects perform (*better/worse*) than low-anxious subjects on simple conditioning tasks involving a single response.

56. On more complex tasks, however, low-anxious subjects usually perform better.

anxiety

On complex tasks a high state of _____ generally has a detrimental effect upon performance.

57. Bob is very anxious about his grade on a math test. He is apt to perform

worse   (*better/worse*) than Steve, who is not so concerned.

detrimental

58. One reason that anxiety is <u>det</u>_____ to performance is that anxiety arouses a number of responses that may *interfere* with learning. Worry

interfere

and concern about doing well may _____ with concentration on the task at hand.

59. On simple tasks involving only a single response the best performance is given by

high-anxious   _____-_____ subjects. On more complex

low-anxious   tasks _____-_____ subjects perform better.

60. When stress is introduced into a learning situation by telling the subjects that they are doing poorly or by emphasizing the importance of "doing well," the performance of high-anxious subjects becomes worse while that of low-anxious subjects usually improves. Thus, stress has a detrimental effect upon the perfor-

high-anxious   mance of _____-_____ subjects, but it usu-

low-anxious   ally improves the performance of _____-_____ subjects.

61. For low-anxious subjects, stress serves to focus attention on the task; for high-anxious subjects, stress may arouse a number of responses that

interfere   _____ with learning.

TERMS AND CONCEPTS FOR IDENTIFICATION

CAI _____

_____

_____

_____

linear program _____

_____

_____

_____

branching program _____

_____

_____

_____

transfer of learning _____

_____

_____

_____

doctrine of formal discipline _____

_____

_____

_____

learning to learn _____

_____

_____

_____

intrinsic motivation _____

_____

_____

_____

extrinsic motivation _____

_____

_____

_____

_____ 1. "Learning to learn" is a special example of
    a. learning set
    b. stimulus orientation
    c. transfer of training
    d. educational adaptation

_____ 2. When a monkey has formed a learning set for a particular class of problems, it
    a. can proceed on the basis of "insight"
    b. must proceed on the basis of trial and error
    c. must pay attention to positional cues
    d. becomes fixated and has trouble with additional problems

_____ 3. Which of the following is *not* one of the learning principles used in programmed instruction?
    a. progress at the student's own rate
    b. knowledge of results
    c. active participation
    d. delayed reinforcement

_____ 4. Programmed instruction presents each new item of information in a
    a. problem statement
    b. frame
    c. index blank
    d. form

_____ 5. The learning of Latin helps one to understand English because of
    a. the doctrine of formal discipline
    b. the transfer of language sets
    c. the frequency of English words with Latin roots
    d. all of the above

_____ 6. An advantage of a branching program is that
    a. the student progresses along a single track from one frame to the next
    b. where the student goes next depends upon the answer he gives
    c. the student moves along at a preprogrammed rate
    d. errors are not pointed out, so that the effects of punishment are avoided

_____ 7. Whenever possible, it is advantageous to use goals that are _____ related to the learning task.

    a. intrinsically
    b. tangentially
    c. extrinsically
    d. maximally

_____ 8. Severe punishment of a strongly motivated response may
    a. not have much effect
    b. still take some time to yield results
    c. cause grossly maladaptive behavior
    d. affect all behaviors based on that motivation

_____ 9. The CAI procedures discussed in the text are said by the authors to be
    a. possible with existing technology and economically feasible
    b. possible with existing technology, but too expensive
    c. unlikely ever to be more flexible than they are now
    d. a serious threat to human individuality

_____ 10. If a student on CAI gives a wrong answer, the computer
    a. branches to appropriate remedial work
    b. records the error
    c. evaluates the type of error
    d. all of the above

_____ 11. Extrinsic rewards may have the disadvantage of being
    a. too expensive
    b. likely to produce competition, with undesirable consequences
    c. too difficult to arrange, compared to the gains obtainable
    d. ineffective

_____ 12. The influence that learning one task has on the subsequent learning of another is called
    a. transfer of learning
    b. the priority effect
    c. sequential influencing
    d. stimulus transfer

_____ 13. According to one theory, the higher the drive level the poorer the performance, because the
    a. higher drive level reduces the subject's discriminative capability
    b. correct response is usually not the

strongest response initially

    c. higher drive level makes the subject careless

    d. higher drive level inhibits learning

_____ **14.** Trying out a new program, in order to revise it, is called
    a. program testing
    b. preliminary trial
    c. initial testing
    d. pilot testing

_____ **15.** Lessons on study skills in a high-school course resulted in
    a. substantial gains in that course alone
    b. slight gains for that course and for other courses
    c. substantial gains in that course and for other courses
    d. none of the above

_____ **16.** In the learning task in which "expected to finish" or "not expected to finish" instructions were used
    a. low-anxious subjects generally did better than high-anxious subjects
    b. high-anxious subjects generally did better than low-anxious subjects
    c. subjects' anxiety level had no effect on performance
    d. low-anxious subjects did better initially but fell behind as the task continued

_____ **17.** Punishment is less effective than reward in some cases because
    a. rewards are competitive, thus producing stronger behavior
    b. punishment leads to docility and deference to authority

    c. punishment establishes strong competitive responses, thus inhibiting learning

    d. punishment temporarily supresses a response but does not weaken it

_____ **18.** A study investigating the relationship between anxiety and academic performance found that a high level of anxiety
    a. lowers performance for very bright students
    b. lowers performance for dull students
    c. adversely affects students in the middle range of ability
    d. affects all students adversely regardless of their ability level

_____ **19.** Punishment is most effective when it
    a. is delayed
    b. provides information
    c. is given irregularly
    d. all of the above

_____ **20.** In the memory technique that used imagery in teaching Spanish words, the keyword for "caballo" was
    a. caballo
    b. horse
    c. cob-eye-yo
    d. eye

KEY TO SELF-QUIZ

20. d	15. c	10. d	5. c
19. b	14. d	9. a	4. b
18. c	13. b	8. c	3. d
17. d	12. a	7. a	2. a
16. a	11. b	6. b	1. c

INDIVIDUAL OR CLASS EXERCISE

IMAGERY VERSUS REHEARSAL IN LEARNING

Introduction

The purpose of this exercise is to determine the effectiveness of two different techniques for memorizing a list of word pairs (called paired-associates). One technique is simply to repeat the two words several times; this is the sort of procedure one might use in memorizing the vocabulary of a foreign language. The other technique involves associating the two words by means of some kind of mental image.

Equipment Needed

Stopwatch or watch with a second hand.

Procedure

Find a willing subject and read him or her the following instructions.

> The purpose of this experiment is to investigate two different techniques for memorizing word pairs. I will read a list of 20 paired nouns, one at a time. Your task is to learn the pairs so that later, when I give you the first word of a pair, you will be able to tell me the word that goes with it. There are two memory techniques I want you to use. For some pairs you are to repeat the two words aloud four times. For other pairs you are to remain silent while forming a mental image or picture in which the words are associated or interacting in some way—the more vivid or unusual the image the better. For example, if I give you the word pair "dog-bicycle," you might picture a dog dressed in a clown suit riding on a bicycle. Just before I give you each word pair, I will tell you which method of memorizing to use by saying either "repeat" or "image." For the pairs you are to rehearse aloud four times, try to avoid forming any mental images.
>
> After you have been given all 20 pairs, I will say "count" and you are to count backward from 99 until I tell you to stop. I will then test your memory by saying the first word in each pair, and you are to tell me the word that goes with it.
>
> Do you have any questions?

Answer any questions by repeating the appropriate part of the instructions. Start with the first paired-associate in the study list on page 136; give the appropriate instruction and then say the pair aloud. Continue in the same way until the list is completed. Time the presentation, allowing approximately ten seconds for the study of each pair. You should practice the procedure at least once before trying it out on your subject.

After all 20 paired-associates have been presented, ask your subject to count backward from 99 for approxi- mately 30 seconds. This task will prevent him from rehearsing the last few paired-associates. Now test your subject's memory by reading aloud the words in the first column of the test list (S_1) and recording his responses in the second column (S_2) (see page 136). After you have completed the list, check his responses for errors and tabulate the number of correct responses for repetition pairs and the number correct for imagery pairs. Record these numbers in the appropriate space. Bring your results to class so that your instructor can tabulate the results for the entire class.

Questions For Discussion

1. Which learning technique was most effective for your subject?

2. How did your subject's results compare with those from the entire class?

3. Were there individual differences in the total number of words recalled? In the effectiveness of the two memory techniques?

4. Why does the test list present the paired-associates in a different order from the study list?

5. Why does the study list present the repetition and imagery pairs in a random order rather than some fixed order, such as alternating repetition and imagery pairs?

6. How might the results of this study be applied to memorization tasks you encounter?

7. A properly controlled study would include one group of subjects who learn the list as given and a second group for whom the repetition and imagery paired-associates are switched; that is, word pairs the first group memorized by repetition would be learned by the second group through imagery, and vice versa. What variables that might have influenced the present exercise would be controlled by this procedure?

PAIRED-ASSOCIATE STUDY LIST

Instruction	Paired-associates
repeat	1. rabbit—house
repeat	2. boy—rope
image	3. shoe—mountain
repeat	4. table—skull
image	5. doctor—flag
image	6. book—fish
repeat	7. slave—party
image	8. lamp—bird
image	9. heart—water
repeat	10. ladder—baby
repeat	11. teacher—pudding
image	12. mule—dress
repeat	13. kettle—fox
image	14. snake—fire
image	15. tree—queen
repeat	16. flower—money
image	17. harp—elephant
repeat	18. bear—candle
repeat	19. clock—moon
image	20. horse—potato

PAIRED-ASSOCIATE TEST LIST

S_1	S_2
1. clock	_____
2. table	_____
3. snake*	_____
4. shoe*	_____
5. flower	_____
6. lamp*	_____
7. boy	_____
8. horse*	_____
9. book*	_____
10. rabbit	_____
11. harp*	_____
12. slave	_____
13. mule*	_____
14. heart*	_____
15. bear	_____
16. ladder	_____
17. doctor*	_____
18. kettle	_____
19. teacher	_____
20. tree*	_____

*imagery pair

Total correct (repetition)   _____

Total correct (imagery)   _____

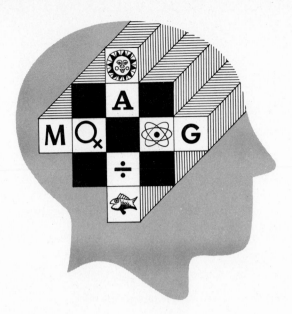

10
language and thought

LEARNING OBJECTIVES

Be familiar with the distinction between denotative and connotative meaning and the use of the semantic differential to measure the latter.

Discuss how concepts are learned and how concept formation can be studied in the laboratory.

Discuss the structure of language and the distinction between the deep structure and the surface structure of a sentence.

Describe the sequence of speech development in the child. Describe the role of operant conditioning and its limitations in accounting for grammatical learning. Give two possible explanations for the orderly sequence of language development.

Discuss the relationship between language and thought as related to concept formation and to the linguistic-relativity hypothesis.

Discuss the role of computer simulation models in understanding cognitive processes.

PROGRAMMED UNIT

1.   Thinking is a cognitive process characterized by the use of *symbolic representations* of objects and events. For instance, when you use such symbols as numbers and dollars to estimate how much it will cost you each semester to remain in

thinking   school, you are engaging in behavior called _____.

representations   **2.** In thinking, we use symbolic _____ of objects and events.

process

symbolic   **3.** Thinking is a cognitive _____ characterized by the use of _____ representations of objects and events.

    4. _Symbols_ represent, or stand for, something, and they convey _meaning_ through some reference beyond themselves. The word "book," for instance, is a

symbol   _____ that represents a collection of printed pages within a firm cover.

meaning   **5.** Symbols convey _____; that is, they provide information about some object or event to which they refer.

    6. Because they convey meaning, symbols often suggest appropriate action to the person who perceives them. For instance, the sign POISON is a

symbol   _____ that alerts a person to danger though the danger is not in the sign itself.

symbols   **7.** We think in _____. Language itself is a rich symbolic process and therefore much thinking goes on in terms of language.

    8. We sometimes use symbols to refer to other symbols. For instance, the symbol $

money   stands for, or represents, some amount of _____, another symbol.

    9. An important characteristic of symbols is that they convey

meaning   _____. When Joan says, "I get angry every time my roommates begin to chatter while I am trying to study," the word "angry" conveys a certain

meaning   _____.

    10. Likewise, if someone says, "He's an intellectual, if I ever met one," the word

meaning   "intellectual" conveys a certain _____ to us.

    11. Meanings may be _denotative._ That is, they may specify something to which one can point, and all who comprehend the meaning can agree on it. For instance, if a person says, "Please let me use that pen," the meaning is

denotative   _____, since a pen is an object to which one can point.

    12. Denotative meanings are _fixed_ and _specific._ If a sign reads DETOUR, it is specific. If a sign reads NO TRESPASSING, it, too, is specific. Such meanings

denotative   are called _____.

Denotative   **13.** _____ meanings refer to specific things or actions, such as names of objects or specific directions.

    14. _Connotative_ meanings accompany the denotative meanings of many words. Connotations are emotional, usually expressing some kind of evaluation or preference, and vary from one person to another. When someone says, "He's a

connotative   radical," the term "radical" has _____ meaning; it may mean different things to different people.

connotative   15.   In addition to denotative meanings, words may have _____ meanings, which are emotional and usually express some kind of evaluation or preference.

connotative   16.   "She's square." The word "square" in this instance has a _____ meaning, since it expresses a personal evaluation.

          17.   "If Fred were not 'chicken,' he would swim across the river." In this sentence
connotative   the word "chicken" has a _____ meaning, whereas the word
denotative   "river" has only a _____ meaning.

          18.   A method used to measure the *connotative* meanings of words is called the *semantic differential. Semantics* refers to meanings words convey, and *differential* refers to the fact that many words mean different things to different people. For instance, we could find what connotative meaning the word "politics" has
semantic   for several people by using the _____ *differential* method.

differential   19.   The semantic _____ method has people describe their feelings about a word by rating it on a number of *dimensions* such as good-bad, strong-weak, active-passive, and so on.

          20.   By determining how a person, or a group of people, rate a word on a number of
dimensions   _____, the semantic differential measures the
connotative   _____ meaning of the word.

          21.   If you wished to learn whether there are sex differences in the connotative meanings conveyed by such words as "love," "peace," and "war," you could use
semantic differential   the _____ _____ method.

          22.   When a symbol stands for a class of objects or events with *common properties,* we say that it refers to a *concept.* For example, the word "man" refers to a
concept   _____ because it stands for a class of objects that have common properties.

          23.   Words and other symbols, such as signs, stand for concepts of varying degrees of *generality.* The concept "higher education" is more general than the concept "university," which in turn is more general than the concept "department of psychology." A symbol that stands for a *class* of objects or events with *common*
concept   *properties* is a _____.

          24.   A concept is a symbol that stands for a class of objects or events with
common (or synonym)   _____ properties.

class   25.   A _____ of objects or events with common properties is represented by a concept.

          26.   The concept "mammal" is more *general* than the concept "woman," which in

turn is more *general* than the concept "mother." Words and signs may stand for

generality   concepts of varying degrees of _____.

general   **27.** The concept "art" is more _____ than the concept "painting,"

general   which in turn is more _____ than the concept "water color."

generality   Thus, concepts possess varying degrees of _____.

28. Concepts that refer to *objects* are usually more easily understood than concepts involving *higher levels of abstraction.* The concept "pencil" refers to a class of

objects   _____ and is easily understood. However, "democracy," "liberty," and "freedom" are concepts involving a higher level of

abstraction   _____ and are more difficult to understand.

objects   **29.** Usually concepts that refer to _____ are more easily under-

abstraction   stood than concepts involving higher levels of _____.

30. Language is a rich symbolic process; it provides us with verbal

symbols   _____ with which to communicate with one another, think about events, and manipulate concepts. Language can be analyzed at a number of levels. At the simplest level we can analyze a language in terms of its *elementary sounds,* or *phonemes.*

31. All languages are based on a certain number of elementary sounds, or

phonemes   _____. The English language is composed of about forty-five

elementary   phonemes, or _____ sounds, which correspond roughly to the different ways we pronounce the vowels and consonants of our alphabet. If you know a foreign language, you realize that the number of phonemes (*varies/is*

varies   *identical*) from one language to the next.

Phonemes   **32.** _____ are the elementary sounds of a language, and they may vary in number from one language to the next.

33. Each language has *rules* that specify how the elementary sounds, or

phonemes   _____, may be combined or sequenced to form a word. For example, in English we have words that start with *str* or *spl* but none beginning with *zb* or *vg* as is common in some Slavic languages.

34. Not all phonemes can be used in all combinations. Each language has

rules   _____ that specify how phonemes may be sequenced.

35. The smallest *meaningful* units in the structure of a language are called *mor-*

phoneme   *phemes.* Do not confuse the word "morpheme" with _____, which refers to the elementary sounds of a language.

meaningful   **36.** Morphemes are the smallest _____ units in the structure of a language. Morphemes may be root words, prefixes, or suffixes, and may consist of from two to six phonemes.

37. The words "banana," "god," and "sweet" are single morphemes. That is, they

meaningful   are among the smallest _____ units in the English language.

38. Some words consist of two or more morphemes. The word "sweetness" consists

morphemes   of two _____, "sweet" and "ness," since both parts have meaning (the suffix "-ness" implies "being" or "having the quality of").

39. The word "sincere" consists of a single morpheme. However, if we add the prefix "in-" (which means "without") to form "insincere," we have

two   _____ (*number*) morpheme(s).

40. The smallest meaningful units in the structure of a language are called

morphemes   _____. One word, however, may combine several morphemes and have several units of sound, or phonemes.

phonemes   **41.** In addition to analysis in terms of elementary sounds (_____)

morphemes   and meaningful units (_____), a sentence can be analyzed according to the organization of its words into *phrases.* Such an analysis is called the *phrase structure* of the sentence.

42. The diagram below shows how a sentence may be analyzed according to its

structure   phrase _____.

43. The phrase structure of a sentence shows how the words are related to one another and what role each plays in the sentence. If we want to know what role each word plays in a sentence, we can analyze the sentence according to its

phrase structure   _____ _____.

44. Language can be analyzed in terms of elementary sounds

phonemes, morphemes   (_____), meaningful units (_____), and orga-

phrase structure   nization of phrases (_____ _____). The phrase structure of a sentence, like the sequencing of phonemes and the formation of words, is governed by certain grammatical rules.

45. A psychologist studying the development of language is concerned with how a child first produces sounds, later attaches meaning to them, and eventually learns to generate and comprehend phrases and sentences. Acquiring language is a complicated psychological process that we are only now beginning to understand. At about six months of age infants begin to produce and repeat an immense variety of sounds. This repetition of elementary speech sounds, or

phonemes

_____, is called *babbling*.

46. The infant lying in his crib repeating "da-da-da" or "guh-guh-guh" to himself is

babbling

_____.

babbling

phonemes

47. During the early stage of _____ the infant produces all the sounds, or _____, that form the basis of any language. The babbling of a Chinese baby at this stage cannot be distinguished from the

babbling

_____ of a Russian or English infant.

48. Gradually, however, babies begin to restrict their babbling to the speech sounds,

phonemes

or _____, that occur in their native language.

49. Parents tend to *reinforce* those phonemes that occur in their language. If the

reinforce

infant babbles "da-da," the enthusiastic father is likely to _____ the production of this sound by giving his baby smiles and attention.

50. We could say that the infant's vocalizations are "shaped" by the reinforcement provided by the parents. When the child produces a sound that is similar to a

reinforcement

word, the parents are usually quick to provide _____.

51. In addition to learning how to produce speech sounds, the young child must also learn to *associate* speech sounds with meaning. The principle of reinforcement is important here. When a word is paired with a familiar object, as when the mother repeats "spoon" every time she hands the child a spoon, an association is established between the word and the object. The child learns to

associate

_____ the word with the object, and in this way the word acquires meaning.

babbling

52. If the child during his b_____ says "muk" and the mother, thinking that he has said "milk," hastens to provide a bottle, there is a greater probability that the child will say something similar to "muk" the next time he

reinforcement

is hungry. The appearance of the bottle serves as rein_____ for the word uttered by the child; gradually the word "milk" acquires

meaning

_____.

reinforcement

53. It is clear that the principle of _____ plays an important role in language development.

associate

54. Learning to produce speech sounds and to _____ these sounds with objects and events is only a small part of learning a language. Children must master the more difficult task of putting words together in sentences. They must learn to produce and comprehend long and complicated sentences using the proper grammatical sequences.

55. Learning to produce and understand sentences involves more than simply

associating

_____ sounds with objects or one word with the next. Children learn *rules* for generating acceptable sequences of words. The text discusses

rules

the way in which children develop grammatical _____ and how they modify these rules with experience.

56. All children appear to master the grammatical rules of their language in about the *same order,* although at *different rates.* One two-year-old girl produces quite long and complex sentences while her four-year-old playmate utters only two-word sentences. Children master the grammatical complexities of language at

rates

different _____.

57. Most children learn to use the prepositions *in* and *on* before they can use *over* and *under* properly in their speech. This illustrates the fact that children master

order

grammatical rules in about the same _____.

58. Although children master their language at different rates, they learn the various

order

grammatical constructions in roughly the same _____.

59. One explanation for the universality of the order in which children acquire

rules

grammatical _____ is that linguistic development may mirror cognitive development. In other words, a child does not use certain words correctly until he understands the concepts they represent.

60. Children understand the concept of position in space before they understand the concept of time. The fact that children use the word *in* to specify location before they use the word to express temporal relations (e.g., in a minute, in a week) suggests that the acquisition of specific word forms depends upon

cognitive

_____ development.

61. Conversely, children's ability to deal with concepts and abstract relationships is closely related to their ability to use language. For example, in a task designed to teach the concept "smaller" a child is presented with a series of pairs of boxes that vary in size; he is rewarded only when he picks the smaller of the two boxes in each pair. The child who can say to himself "the smaller one is always right" will select the correct box much more often than the child who is not able to verbalize the problem. Thus, the ability to deal with concepts is closely related

language

to the development of _____ ability.

concepts

62. Our ability to deal with _____ and abstract relationships is related to our ability to use language.

63. Thought is closely related to language. One proposal, called the *linguistic-relativity hypothesis,* assumes that *thought* is relative to the *language* in which it is conducted and that the way in which people conceive the world is *relative* to the structure of their language. If in a particular culture the word "democracy" does not exist, the concept of democracy may be very difficult for people of

think

that culture to understand because they cannot th_____ in terms of what the word "democracy" means.

relativity

relative

language

64. The linguistic-_____ hypothesis proposes that one's thinking is _____ to the language one uses. To the extent that this hypothesis has been supported by experiments, it seems clear that the way people conceive the world is relative to the structure of their _____.

65. If in a particular culture there were no verbs to indicate past tense or past action, it is conceivable that people in that culture would have difficulty thinking in historical terms. Were this true, it would lend support to the _____-_____ hypothesis.

linguistic-relativity

problem

66. We achieve our most complex use of language and concepts when we try to solve a problem. The thought processes involved in solving a _____ have many similarities to the way information is processed by a computer.

67. In the same sense that a computer processes incoming data to solve a problem, the human being can be viewed as an *information-processing* system. Some psychologists have formulated *models* of human thinking based on the methods of storing, retrieving, and operating on information used in computers. Such

models

models are called *information-processing* m_____.

processing

68. Information-_____ models of thinking are based on the methods and procedures that characterize the operation of a computer. Such models postulate sophisticated schemes for storing information in memory, and procedures for operating on the stored information to generate "new" information. The text discusses several information-processing models that have been developed to account for complex forms of human thinking and problem-solving.

TERMS AND CONCEPTS FOR IDENTIFICATION

denotative meaning _____

_____

_____

_____

connotative meaning _____

_____

_____

_____

semantic differential _____

_____

_____

_____

concept _____

_____

_____

_____

phoneme _____

_____

_____

_____

morpheme _____

_____

_____

_____

phrase structure _____

_____

_____

_____

deep structure _____

_____

_____

_____

surface structure _____

_____

_____

_____

babbling _____

_____

_____

_____

telegraphic speech _____

_____

_____

_____

linguistic-relativity hypothesis _____

_____

_____

_____

information-processing model _____

_____

_____

_____

heuristic _____

_____

_____

_____

_____ 1. We refer to the emotional, secondary meaning of a word as its _____ meaning.
   a. latent
   b. connotative
   c. hidden
   d. denotative

_____ 2. When clicks were sounded during a sentence, they were heard as occurring
   a. where they actually occurred
   b. at the nearest pause
   c. only after verbs
   d. at the pause that marked a phrase boundary

_____ 3. When a child says "What the dog can eat?" we know that the child
   a. is not yet old enough to use transformations
   b. would also say "The dog can eat?"
   c. cannot perform more than one transformation at a time
   d. is not yet using grammatical rules

_____ 4. The Logic Theorist is a
   a. simulation model
   b. heuristic
   c. means-end procedure
   d. problem-solving strategy

_____ 5. Whorf's linguistic relativity hypothesis was _____ by the study of two groups of Navajo children, because they _____.
   a. disconfirmed, did not differ in their speech patterns
   b. supported, sorted objects differently
   c. disproved, did not differ in their thinking
   d. not affected, were not tested appropriately

_____ 6. When subjects are asked to identify sentences they have previously heard, the aspect of the sentences retained the longest is
   a. stylistic detail
   b. surface structure
   c. sentence meaning
   d. sentence length

_____ 7. The results of attempts to teach language to "feral children"
   a. have been only moderately successful
   b. are confounded by possible mental retardation
   c. have become better as our knowledge of language learning improves
   d. all of the above

_____ 8. The babbling of a six-to-nine-month old Chinese baby
   a. can easily be distinguished from that of a Russian baby
   b. when expertly analyzed can be shown to include primarily the sounds in the Chinese language
   c. will soon give way to a narrower range of babbling
   d. includes primarily back consonant and front vowel pairs

_____ 9. Information-processing models suggest that human problem solving
   a. is primarily serial
   b. can process many symbols at once
   c. holds symbols being processed in LTM
   d. all of the above

_____ 10. When a symbol refers to a class of objects or events with common properties, we say that it refers to a
   a. thought
   b. category
   c. idea
   d. concept

_____ 11. The semantic differential measures word meaning in terms of three dimensions: _____, _____, and _____.
   a. evaluation, activity, analysis
   b. idealism, potency, evaluation
   c. potency, evaluation, activity
   d. formality, activity, potency

_____ 12. The easiest concepts to learn seem to be _____ concepts, while the hardest are _____ concepts.

a. object, number
b. spatial, number
c. number, object
d. object, spatial

13. The formal theory of language closest to the common-sense view is the _____ one.
a. S-R
b. cognitive
c. innate mechanism
d. rules-theory

14. Children learn to associate words with objects and events by means of
a. operant conditioning
b. classical conditioning
c. discrimination
d. all of the above

15. All languages are made up of _____ such as _____.
a. phonemes, "strange"
b. phonemes, "ess"
c. morphemes, "strangeness"
d. phonemes, "ness"

16. Studies of deaf-mute children show that language
a. and thought are identical
b. can hinder some kinds of thinking
c. is essential for the development of cognitive abilities
d. aids in solving problems of relationship

17. We always think in
a. words

b. concepts
c. symbols
d. images

18. The spontaneous speech of a two year old has been termed _____ because of such sentences as "Where Daddy coat."
a. truncated speech
b. telegraphic speech
c. abbreviated speech
d. primitive speech

19. A computer program
a. is the first step in a flow chart
b. resembles the play diagram of a football coach
c. is the same thing as a flow chart
d. is written on the basis of a flow chart

20. The deep structure of a sentence
a. refers to the thought behind the sentence
b. is the actual sound sequence used
c. is organized according to phrase-structure rules
d. is made up of the connotative meanings of the words used

KEY TO SELF-QUIZ

20. a	15. b	10. d	5. b
19. d	14. d	9. a	4. a
18. b	13. a	8. c	3. c
17. c	12. a	7. b	2. d
16. d	11. c	6. c	1. b

INDIVIDUAL EXERCISE

CONFLICT IN CODING

Introduction

We normally encode events in a manner appropriate to them. Our memory of material we have read is verbal, while our recollection of a sunset may be pictorial. This exercise, based on the Stroop Test, intentionally sets two forms of coding into conflict. It demonstrates not only how disconcerning such conflict can be, but also how difficult it is to override firmly established verbal responses.

Equipment Needed

Display cards in color, to be created from white paper and colored marker pens as described below.

Procedure

1. Make up three display sheets as follows. If you want to do the test for a group, make them as large as necessary for clear viewing by the group. (The experiment makes an interesting party game.) For individual usage, sheets of standard size typewriter paper are large enough. You should use plain white opaque paper or cardboard that will take ink well and bright felt-tip markers that will produce distinctly different colors.

2. On the first sheet, the experimental one, print the names of colors in large, thick block letters: YELLOW, GREEN, etc. But print them in *different* colors from the color names. The first word thus could be YELLOW but printed in thick block *green* letters. Make at least four or five lines, with about five words per line, a total of perhaps 25 words; each word will be repeated several times in the display, but the same word should not be used twice in succession. Use only basic color names and easily discriminable colors: perhaps red, yellow, blue, green, orange, and brown. Vary the color used to print a particular color name; that is, don't print YELLOW in green ink every time it appears.

3. Make up two control sheets, one with patches of color that are not words, the other with the color names printed all in black. Make the color patches similar in size and color density to the words on the first sheet, and make the black-ink names similar in size to the colored ones on the first sheet. (It is not necessary to have the colors and words in the same order as on the experimental sheet.)

CLASS EXERCISE

THE SEMANTIC DIFFERENTIAL

Introduction

Language makes possible the creation and transmission of man's social heritage. Without language, man could not think in terms of such abstract concepts as freedom, justice, democracy, and equality. But the use of language is not without pitfalls. Some words cause no difficulty because they refer to specific things; they have essentially denotative meanings. Other words have connotative meanings as well as denotative meanings; they generally express some kind of evaluation or preference.

4. Present the sheets to your subject (yourself, if no one else is handy) in any order. The tasks for the control sheets are to name the colors on one, and to read the color names on the other. Use a stopwatch to time each performance as precisely as possible. Subjects will of course find these tasks so easy as to be trivial. The experimental task, however, using the third sheet, is to correctly name the *ink* colors used as fast as possible; that is, to name the color that a word is printed in and not the word itself. (If the word GREEN is printed in red ink, the subject should say "red" when he comes to it.) A subject who makes a mistake must correct it before continuing. This is not nearly as easy as it sounds; a reasonably quick, errorless run through 25 names is a surprisingly difficult task.

5. Compare the time needed for the experimental task to that of the control tasks; it will undoubtedly be substantially longer.

Questions For Discussion

1. Why is this task so difficult? Would it be more or less difficult for a five-year-old child? For a nonnative speaker of English?

2. Can you figure out any way to become more proficient at the task? What do you want to do? (Hint: try turning the page upside down. Can you think of ways of achieving similar results without turning the page upside down?)

Many misunderstandings arise in communication because words have different connotations for different persons.

In order to derive more precisely the connotative meanings of words, Dr. Charles Osgood developed a method of measurement called the *semantic differential*—"semantic" because it has to do with meaning and "differential" because it provides several different dimensions of meaning. This exercise illustrates that certain words may connote various meanings to various students.

Equipment Needed

Red and blue pencils or pens.

Procedure

On page 150 rate each of the words in the left column using the rating scale in the right column. Rate each word according to your first impression or reaction and regardless of how unrelated the word and scale appear. There are no right or wrong answers. Work rapidly. Do not struggle over particular items. There are seven spaces or steps in the scale, and each word should be rated by a check in one of the spaces. An example follows:

ARITHMETIC   easy_:_:_:_:_:_:_hard

If your first impression is that arithmetic is very hard, you should check the space at the extreme right toward "hard." If your first impression is that arithmetic is fairly easy, you should check one of the spaces toward "easy." If your first impression is that arithmetic is neither hard nor easy, you should mark the middle of the scale.

Treatment of Data

Your instructor will collect your ratings so that the profiles can be plotted on the scales below. Median responses for the entire group can be shown by a heavy black line. If the group wishes to find out whether there are sex differences in connotative meanings, median responses for males and females can be plotted separately using different colors.

LOVE

good_:_:_:_:_:_:_bad
tense_:_:_:_:_:_:_relaxed
strong_:_:_:_:_:_:_weak
dirty_:_:_:_:_:_:_beautiful
deep_:_:_:_:_:_:_shallow

MOTHER

shallow_:_:_:_:_:_:_deep
bad_:_:_:_:_:_:_good
relaxed_:_:_:_:_:_:_tense
strong_:_:_:_:_:_:_weak
dirty_:_:_:_:_:_:_beautiful

SEX

relaxed_:_:_:_:_:_:_tense
beautiful_:_:_:_:_:_:_dirty
good_:_:_:_:_:_:_bad
deep_:_:_:_:_:_:_shallow
weak_:_:_:_:_:_:_strong

FATHER

dirty_:_:_:_:_:_:_beautiful
weak_:_:_:_:_:_:_strong
tense_:_:_:_:_:_:_relaxed
good_:_:_:_:_:_:_bad
deep_:_:_:_:_:_:_shallow

PEACE

strong_:_:_:_:_:_:_weak
deep_:_:_:_:_:_:_shallow
tense_:_:_:_:_:_:_relaxed
beautiful_:_:_:_:_:_:_dirty
bad_:_:_:_:_:_:_good

Questions For Discussion

1. Does your rating on certain words differ considerably from that of the group? Why?

2. Some of the evaluative words were arranged in a positive-to-negative order; others, the opposite. Can you think why?

3. Did your group find sex differences in the connotative meanings of some of the words?

4. What other connotative words might have been used?

LOVE   good_:_:_:_:_:_:_bad

MOTHER   shallow_:_:_:_:_:_:_deep

SEX   relaxed_:_:_:_:_:_:_tense

FATHER   dirty_:_:_:_:_:_:_beautiful

PEACE   strong_:_:_:_:_:_:_weak

LOVE   tense_:_:_:_:_:_:_relaxed

MOTHER   bad_:_:_:_:_:_:_good

SEX   beautiful_:_:_:_:_:_:_dirty

FATHER   weak_:_:_:_:_:_:_strong

PEACE   deep_:_:_:_:_:_:_shallow

LOVE   strong_:_:_:_:_:_:_weak

MOTHER   rélaxed_:_:_:_:_:_:_tense

SEX   good_:_:_:_:_:_:_bad

FATHER   tense_:_:_:_:_:_:_relaxed

PEACE   tense_:_:_:_:_:_:_relaxed

LOVE   dirty_:_:_:_:_:_:_beautiful

MOTHER   strong_:_:_:_:_:_:_weak

SEX   deep_:_:_:_:_:_:_shallow

FATHER   good_:_:_:_:_:_:_bad

PEACE   beautiful_:_:_:_:_:_:_dirty

LOVE   deep_:_:_:_:_:_:_shallow

MOTHER   dirty_:_:_:_:_:_:_beautiful

SEX   weak_:_:_:_:_:_:_strong

FATHER   deep_:_:_:_:_:_:_shallow

PEACE   bad_:_:_:_:_:_:_good

11
physiological basis of motivation

LEARNING OBJECTIVES

Be able to discuss the development of motivational concepts from instincts through drive-reduction theory to incentive theory.

Be familiar with the mechanisms that control hunger and thirst. Give the current theories of obesity.

Describe how internal variables interact with environmental ones in determining sexual behavior. Discuss the influences of experience and culture on patterns of mating behavior.

Give some examples of motives that have no apparent physiological basis. Explain them according to the concept of arousal level.

PROGRAMMED UNIT

1. By a *motive* we mean something that incites the organism to *action.* Hunger can incite an organism to action; therefore hunger can act as a _____.

motive

2. When an organism is quiescent, we say that it is *not* motivated; when it is incited to action, we say that it is _____.

motivated

3. Motivated behavior is also characterized by *direction.* When an organism is incited to action by hunger, it does not simply act at random; its action (or behavior) is in the _____ of food.

direction

action

4. Motivation has to do with two variables: _____ and direction.

direction

5. An animal motivated by thirst will go in the _____ of water.

6. Any behavior, then, that is characterized by action and direction is called

motivated

_____ behavior.

7. Most of the motives discussed in this chapter are based on bodily needs; these are called *physiological* motives. Hunger is a function of certain bodily needs that

physiological

result from lack of food. Hunger is thus classed as a _____ motive.

8. Thirst results from dryness of the throat and mouth plus other specific bodily

needs that occur from lack of water. Thirst is thus a _____

physiological

motive.

9. In discussing physiological motives a distinction is made between the terms *need* and *drive*. A *need* is defined as a *bodily deficit*. If we lack food, we have a *need*

need

for food. If we lack water, we have a _____ for water.

deficit

10. A lack of food creates a bodily _____; we call this lack a need.

11. Any bodily deficit, or state of deprivation (such as lack of oxygen, food, or

need

water), can be defined as a _____.

12. The need for food is physiological, not psychological, but a state of physiological need has *psychological consequences*. The psychological consequences of a

drive

need are called a *drive*. The need for food leads to the hunger dr_____. While need and drive are related, they are not the same. For example, drive does not necessarily get stronger as need gets stronger. People who have fasted for a long time report that their feelings of hunger come and go, although their need for food persists. The need persists but the psychological consequences of the

hunger

need, the _____ drive, fluctuate.

psychological

13. Drive, then, refers to the _____ consequences of a need.

14. The body attempts to maintain a state of *homeostasis,* that is, to maintain a *constant internal environment.* Body temperature, for example, is maintained within a few degrees in a healthy individual. When you get hot you perspire, and perspiration evaporating from the body surface has a cooling effect. Perspiring is

homeostasis

thus one of the automatic mechanisms that helps maintain homeo_____ by keeping body temperature within normal range.

constant

15. Homeostasis refers to the body's attempt to maintain a _____ internal environment.

16. When the concentration of sugar in the blood drops below a certain level, the liver releases stored sugar (in the form of glycogen) to restore the proper blood

homeostasis

sugar level. This is another example of _____.

17. Homeostasis refers to the body's attempt to maintain a constant

internal

_____ environment. There are many internal states that must be maintained within narrow limits; presumably, there are sensors in the body that detect changes from the optimal level and activate certain mechanisms that

homeostasis

correct the imbalance and restore homeo_____.

18. When the amount of water in the body cells becomes low, you feel thirsty and are motivated to drink water to restore the balance of fluid in the cells. This is

homeostasis

another example of _____.

need

19. Any bodily deficit, or n_____, alters the state of homeostasis and initiates

drive

a _____, the psychological consequences of a need. When homeostasis is restored, the drive is reduced, and motivated activity ceases.

20. But not all motivated activity is initiated by internal drives. *Incentives* in the environment can motivate behavior even in the absence of an internal

drive
(or need)

_____.

21. An hour after lunch, feeling not a bit hungry, you pass a bakery window full of delicious-looking cakes and go in to buy one. Your behavior in this instance is

incentive

not motivated by an internal drive but by an _____ in the environment.

22. An object or condition in the environment that motivates behavior is called an

incentive

_____. There are *positive incentives* that an individual will *approach* and *negative incentives* that he will *avoid.*

23. If you are hungry and thirsty, food and water would be

positive

_____ incentives. A live electric wire or a clump of poison ivy

negative

is a _____ incentive because you are motivated to avoid it.

24. A positive incentive is any object or condition in the environment that the

approach

organism is motivated to _____. A negative incentive is any

avoid

object that the organism is motivated to _____.

25. Motivation is best understood as an interaction between certain objects in the

incentives

environment, called _____, and the physiological state of the organism. Drives alone do not provide a complete explanation of motivated behavior.

26. Hunger as a source of motivated behavior is aroused by bodily needs as well as

incentives

by external _____. Psychologists have tried to pinpoint some of the internal and external stimuli that *regulate food intake.*

intake

27. Because regulation of food _____ is crucial to the survival of the organism, nature has provided several homeostatic controls. These control systems are integrated in a region of the brain called the *hypothalamus.*

28. One area of the hypothalamus, the *lateral hypothalamus,* initiates eating; it is a

hypothalamus

"feeding center." Another area of the hypo_____, the *ventromedial hypothalamus,* inhibits eating; it is a *"satiety center."*

29. If the lateral hypothalamus is stimulated with a mild electric current, an animal that has just completed a large meal will begin to eat again. This is evidence that

hypothalamus
feeding

the lateral _____ is a _____ center because its stimulation initiates eating.

30. If the ventromedial hypothalamus is stimulated electrically, a hungry animal will stop eating in the midst of a meal. This is evidence that the

ventromedial

_____ hypothalamus is a satiety center, be-

inhibits (or stops)

cause its stimulation _____ eating.

lateral

31. The feeding center is the _____ hypothalamus; the satiety

ventromedial

center is the _____ hypothalamus.

32. Knowing this much you would guess that if a large part of the ventromedial

hypothalamus
much

_____ is removed or destroyed, the animal will eat too (*much / little*).

33. And this is exactly what happens. When tissue in the ventromedial hypothalamus is destroyed the animal overeats until it becomes obese. This is so because the

satiety

ventromedial hypothalamus is a _____ center, and if it is destroyed the animal doesn't know when to stop eating.

34. You might guess that in the opposite case, when tissue in the lateral hypothala-

little

mus is destroyed, an animal will eat too (*much / little*).

35. What actually happens when the lateral hypothalamus is destroyed is that the animal refuses to eat at all and will die unless fed artificially. This provides

lateral

further evidence that the _____ hypothalamus functions as a feeding center.

opposite

36. These two regions of the hypothalamus thus appear to act in (*the same / opposite*) way(s) to regulate food intake.

37. Moreover, there appear to be two kinds of control systems in the hypothalamus: a *short-term control system* that responds to the organism's immediate nutritive needs and tells it when to start and stop a meal, and a *long-term control system* that attempts to maintain a stable body weight over a long period of time regardless of how much the organism eats in any one meal. The fact that most people maintain the same body weight from year to year (give or take a few

long

control

short

blood

fullness

ventromedial

feeding

blood-sugar,
fullness

less

blood-sugar, fullness,
temperature

weight

lateral, ventromedial
(either order)

lateral hypothalamus

ventromedial

pounds) suggests that the body must have some kind of _____-*term* control system for regulation of food intake.

38. The hypothalamus appears to have both short-term and long-term _____ systems for regulating eating.

39. Experiments have pinpointed three physiological variables that are related to our immediate feeling of hunger: *blood-sugar level, stomach fullness,* and *body temperature.* These are variables to which the hypothalamus responds in controlling when we start and stop eating a given meal; they are thus important to the _____-*term* control system.

40. When our blood-sugar level is low we feel weak and hungry; studies indicate that certain cells in the hypothalamus are sensitive to the level of sugar in the bl_____.

41. But we usually stop eating before the food we have consumed can raise the blood-sugar level significantly. A more immediate result of eating, stomach _____, apparently signals the brain that food is on the way.

42. Certain cells in the hypothalamus appear to respond to a full stomach to inhibit further eating. As you would expect, these cells are in the (*lateral*/*ventromedial*) region of the hypothalamus.

43. When the stomach is empty we have periodic contractions of the stomach walls called hunger pangs. This increased activity of the stomach walls signals cells in the lateral hypothalamus or (*feeding*/*satiety*) center to start the organism eating.

44. Two variables that affect the short-term control of eating are _____-_____ level and stomach _____. A third short-term control variable is temperature: decreased brain temperature initiates eating; increased brain temperature inhibits eating. This is probably one reason why you have (*more*/*less*) of an appetite in hot weather.

45. Three variables that are important to the short-term hunger control system are _____-_____ level, stomach _____, and _____.

46. The physiological variables that affect the long-term control system so as to keep our body w_____ about the same from year to year are not fully known. But experimental evidence suggests that the two hypothalamic regulatory centers, the _____ and the _____ hypothalamus, interact reciprocally to maintain an individual's weight at a set point. These studies have implications for problems of obesity.

47. Let's review. The two important brain areas for the regulation of food intake are the _____ _____, a feeding center, and the _____.

hypothalamus, satiety _____, a _____ center.

body These two centers act reciprocally to maintain a stable _____ weight. They also provide for short-term control of food intake by responding differ-

blood-sugar, entially to three bodily variables: _____-_____ level,

fullness, temperature stomach _____, and _____.
(The text discusses how learning and environmental factors influence hunger and their importance in obesity. The programmed unit has concentrated on the physiological variables because they are less familiar and more difficult to understand.)

48. Human beings can go without food for weeks, but they cannot survive without water for more than a few days. *Thirst,* then, is another important

physiological _____ motive.

49. The hypothalamus is important to the regulation of water intake, just as it is for

food _____ intake.

50. If water is placed directly into a thirsty dog's stomach via a tube that bypasses the mouth and throat, it will still drink its usual amount of water if allowed immediate access to its water bowl. However, if there is a delay of several minutes before the dog is given access to water, the amount consumed decreases as the delay increases; and after 20 minutes the dog does not drink at all. In this

time experiment the important variable is (*time/degree of thirst*).

51. The results suggest that a certain amount of water must be absorbed through the stomach wall into the blood stream before the mechanism that responds to

water _____ intake is activated.

52. Although all the details of water regulation are not yet known, current theories postulate two kinds of internal "receptors" that control thirst: *osmoreceptors* are sensitive to the concentration of certain chemicals in the blood and body fluids; *volumetric receptors* are sensitive to the total volume of blood and

body _____ fluids.

53. If you go for a while without water the chemicals in your blood and in the fluids

more surrounding your cells become (*more/less*) concentrated. This increased concentration causes water to pass out of the cells, through osmosis, leaving them *dehydrated.*

increased 54. One result of water deficit is (*increased/decreased*) concentration of body fluids

dehydrated which causes the cells to become _____.

55. All body cells become dehydrated when there is a water deficit, but certain

dehydration nerve cells in the hypothalamus respond specifically to de_____.

hypothalamus 56. These specialized cells in the _____ are assumed to be the osmoreceptors; when they become dehydrated, they stimulate the organism to drink.

57. Osmoreceptors are cells in the hypothalamus that respond to the dehydration that occurs when a water deficit causes the blood and body fluid to become too

concentrated
    _____.

dehydration
58. But cellular de_____ is not the only signal for thirst. During a fast game of tennis in hot weather your body loses salt through

fluids
decreased
    perspiration. The salt concentration of your blood and body _____ is thus (*decreased/increased*), yet you feel thirsty. There must be receptors that are sensitive to the *total volume* of blood and body fluids regardless of their

concentration
    con_____.

59. Thus, in addition to osmoreceptors that are sensitive to the

concentration
    _____ of blood and body fluids, there are

volume
    volumetric receptors that respond to the total _____ of blood and body fluids. Both of these receptors act together to control thirst. (The text describes in more detail how the volumetric receptors operate.)

60. Another important physiological motive is sex. Sex is not vital to the survival of

water
    the organism, as are food and _____, but it is essential to the survival of the species.

61. Sexual behavior depends on internal factors, primarily *hormones,* and *stimuli in the environment.* If a female rat is injected with a male hormone, it will try to mount other females when placed in a cage with them. This illustrates the

hormones
    influence of h_____ on sexual behavior.

62. If the same rat is placed in a cage with male rats, it will revert to the female sexual pattern when confronted with a sexually aggressive male. This illustrates

environmental
(or external)
    the influence of _____ stimuli on sexual behavior.

63. As we go from lower to higher mammals experience and learning play an increasingly important role in sexual behavior. If a rat is raised in isolation with no contact with other rats, it will usually show the proper sexual response when first confronted with a receptive mate. Thus, sexual behavior in the rat appears

innate
    to be largely (*learned/innate*).

64. A monkey raised in isolation, on the other hand, seems to have no clear idea of the appropriate sexual behavior when confronted with a receptive member of the opposite sex. In monkeys, sexual behavior is primarily influenced by

learning
(or experience)
    _____.

65. Harry Harlow, a psychologist who has done extensive research on the importance of early experience in monkeys, has suggested that normal heterosexual behavior in primates depends on three factors: (a) the influence of *hormones;* (b) the development of the *appropriate sexual responses* in early play with other monkeys; and (c) an *affectional bond* between members of the opposite sex which is formed as an outgrowth of early interactions with the mother and other monkeys.

66. Monkeys reared in isolation do not lack the appropriate sex hormones; but because they have never had the chance to play with other young monkeys they

sexual

have not learned the appropriate _____ responses. And because they have never interacted with either a mother or other monkeys, they have not

bond

learned the trust necessary to form an affectional _____.

67. Although we cannot automatically extend these findings with monkeys to sexual development in humans, observations indicate that the same three factors may be important to the development of normal heterosexual behavior: hormones,

sexual responses

the development of appropriate _____ _____,

affectional

and an _____ bond between members of the opposite sex.

68. Among humans an additional influence on sexual behavior is provided by the *culture* in which a person is raised. All cultures place some restrictions on sexual behavior, and what the culture says is right or wrong will have a significant

behavior

influence on the sexual _____ of its members.

69. Some cultures are very *permissive,* encouraging sex play among the children and placing few restrictions on adult sexual relationships. Some cultures are very *restrictive,* frowning on any indication of sexuality in childhood and restricting adult sexual behavior to narrowly prescribed forms. Most societies would fall

restrictive

somewhere between the very permissive and the very _____.

70. Until recently how would you have classified American society in terms of its

restrictive

attitudes toward sexual behavior? Fairly (*restrictive/permissive*)? If you said "restrictive," you are closer to the opinions of most authorities in evaluating the attitude of the average American up until the 1960s.

71. There are indications, however, that the United States, along with most other western nations, has become more permissive in its attitudes toward sexual

behavior

_____. (The text discusses the reasons and evidence for this change.)

72. The three physiological motives we have discussed so far are

hunger, thirst, sex
(any order)

_____, _____, and _____. Two other physiological motives covered in the text are *maternal behavior* and *avoidance of pain.*

pain

The motivations to care for one's young and to avoid _____ are important determiners of behavior.

73. All of these motives have some basis in the physiological condition of the organism. But there is another determiner of action, important to both animals and humans, whose physiological correlates are unknown—the need for *sensory stimulation.* Both animals and people enjoy exploring new places and manipulat-

stimulation

ing objects. They appear to need a certain amount of sensory _____.

74. When people participate in experiments where the normal amount of stimulation is greatly reduced, their functioning is impaired and they cannot tolerate the

sensory

situation for very long. A certain amount of _____ stimulation is necessary for the well-being of the organism.

TERMS AND CONCEPTS FOR IDENTIFICATION

rationalism _____
_____
_____
_____

instinct _____
_____
_____
_____

need _____
_____
_____
_____

drive _____
_____
_____
_____

homeostasis _____
_____
_____
_____

drive-reduction theory _____
_____
_____
_____

incentive theory _____
_____
_____
_____

positive incentive _____
_____
_____
_____

negative incentive _____
_____
_____
_____

lateral hypothalamus_____
_____
_____
_____

ventromedial hypothalamus_____
_____
_____
_____

osmoreceptors _____
_____
_____
_____

volumetric receptors _____
_____
_____
_____

_____ 1. The best current overall statement about motivational theories is that
a. each theory has a grain of truth but is incomplete in itself
b. biological needs are less important for humans than social needs
c. drive-reduction theory comes closest to a complete explanation of behavior
d. the concepts of homeostasis and incentive together describe most motivated behavior

_____ 2. Humans have more trouble than animals do in maintaining a regular weight throughout their lifetime, primarily because
a. human diets are less natural and thus confuse the control mechanisms
b. with evolution the LH and VMH centers have become less well developed
c. human eating is more strongly influenced by social and emotional factors
d. by wearing clothes humans distort the temperature mechanism for controlling diet

_____ 3. Psychologists usually narrow the broad concept of motivation to those particular factors that _____ and _____ behavior.
a. organize, control
b. energize, direct
c. activate, modify
d. determine, control

_____ 4. The hormone prolactin has been found to be remarkably influential in maternal behavior. For example,
a. an injection of it will bring out proper maternal behavior in a monkey raised with a terry-cloth "mother"
b. it has been found to be at very low levels in human mothers who batter their children
c. an injection of it will cause a male rat to build a nest and care for young
d. all of the above

_____ 5. Incentive theory adds to our understanding of motivation and helps explain some problems of drive-reduction theory by
a. focusing attention on the motivational effects of external stimuli
b. providing an explanation for seeking the thrills of horror movies or roller-coaster rides
c. looking at the interaction between bodily states and environmental stimuli
d. all of the above

_____ 6. When obese subjects were tricked into thinking that the time was 6:05 instead of 5:30, they
a. were affected by it, while normal subjects were not
b. ate more crackers
c. reported more frequent hunger pangs
d. all of the above

_____ 7. Study of neural mechanisms for the control of sexual behavior have shown us the complexity of such control. For example, it has been found that
a. men with severed spinal cords can have erections and ejaculate
b. male rats stimulated electrically in the hypothalamus will indiscriminately mount any available partner
c. male monkeys can be switched from eating to sexual behavior by switching electrodes in the posterior hypothalamus
d. all of the above

_____ 8. The drive-reduction theory and homeostatic models of motivation are
a. useful for understanding hunger, thirst, and pain
b. contradicted by the evidence on sensory deprivation
c. not very appropriate to a maternal drive
d. all of the above

_____ 9. Hunger and thirst are good examples of drives which fit the homeostatic mechanism approach, because they
a. initiate behavior to restore the balance of substances in the blood
b. are both necessary to sustain life
c. operate through both internal and external cues
d. are common to all species

_____ 10. When water is placed directly into a thirsty dog's stomach, it

a. drinks less than it would have otherwise
b. drinks the same amount as it would have otherwise
c. does not drink at all
d. any of the above, depending on how soon afterwards it is allowed to drink

____ 11. Subjects who experienced experimental sensory deprivation
a. became bored, restless, irritable, and upset
b. found it created a soothingly altered state of consciousness akin to meditation
c. were often better able to concentrate on problems in the absence of distractions
d. experienced subjective time distortions, but gave no evidence of this in the pattern of their response to the experimenters

____ 12. Studies of hunger and eating in animals show us that taste and smell are
a. necessary for an animal to regulate its food intake
b. not essential to regulation of food intake
c. less useful in food regulation for rats with VHM lesions
d. not sensed at all by rats with VMH lesions

____ 13. Freud can be said to be an instinct theorist because he believed that behavior was determined by two basic instincts: _____ and _____.
a. sex instincts, competitive instincts
b. social instincts, competitive instincts
c. life instincts, death instincts
d. sex instincts, destructive instincts

____ 14. Hormones control sexual behavior
a. by producing a state of readiness to respond
b. according to both the type and amount of hormone present in the bloodstream
c. less as we go from lower to higher vertebrates
d. all of the above

____ 15. In examining centers in the hypothalamus that regulate food intake, researchers have found that
a. the LH inhibits eating
b. the VMH initiates eating

c. both long-term and short-term systems are involved
d. all of the above

____ 16. Drug dependency helps us to understand the complexity of motivation, since it shows that
a. incentives can be simultaneously pleasurable and aversive
b. the physiological basis of a drive can be acquired
c. incentives can be classically conditioned
d. some motives can never be fully satisfied

____ 17. Injured persons who have lost a lot of blood help us to understand the mechanisms of _____ by the fact that they _____.
a. thirst, are intensely thirsty
b. hunger and thirst, are neither hungry nor thirsty
c. obesity, will overeat if allowed to
d. pain, are less sensitive to it

____ 18. Cultures differ with regard to their sexual taboos; _____ is prohibited by most cultures while _____ are viewed with varying degrees of tolerance.
a. homosexuality, masturbation and incest
b. sexual activity among children, incest and premarital sex
c. incest, masturbation and homosexuality
d. masturbation, premarital sex and homosexuality

____ 19. The concepts of need and drive are parallel but not identical, even though they are sometimes used interchangeably. One crucial difference, for example, is that
a. as need gets stronger drive gets weaker
b. need is a hypothetical construct
c. as drive gets stronger it arouses greater need
d. as need gets stronger drive may get stronger or weaker

____ 20. When rats have been fed on a fat-free diet, they
a. eat much more than normal rats
b. show a marked preference for fat
c. prefer it to a normal diet
d. eat enough of it to maintain their calorie intake above normal levels

1. a	6. b	11. a	16. b
2. c	7. a	12. b	17. a
3. b	8. d	13. c	18. c
4. c	9. a	14. d	19. d
5. d	10. d	15. c	20. b

INDIVIDUAL EXERCISE

MEASURING MOTIVATION

Introduction

Psychologists study motivation in many ways. In laboratory studies precise instruments that measure physiological responses in motivated behavior can be used. However, for classroom purposes it is difficult to make the necessary arrangements to measure physiological changes. For that reason the sentence-completion test that follows has been chosen. Many psychologists feel that it has clinical value in the study of personal adjustment.

Equipment Needed

None

Procedure

Below are 50 incomplete sentences. You will have about 30 minutes to complete all the sentences. Try not to omit any item. Be sure to express your real feeling toward each item. The results will be more valuable if you write down thoughts that occur to you spontaneously, as soon as you see the first word or words of each item. You will be the only person to score the test and to see the results. Therefore, try to be frank and honest by writing the first thought that comes to mind.

After completing the test, score your sentences according to the directions given on page 295 of the Appendix.

1. College _____

_____

_____

2. I need _____

_____

3. My nerves _____

_____

_____

4. Girls _____

_____

5. Secretly, I _____

_____

6. My father _____

_____

7. I wish _____

_____

_____

8. I'm afraid _____

_____

9. People _____

_____

10. The future _____

_____

_____

11. I worry about _____

_____

12. Boys _____

_____

_____

13. I know _____

_____

_____

14. At night _____

_____

_____

15. Marriage _____

_____

_____

16. My mother _____

_____

_____

17. If I could _____

_____

_____

18. My studies _____

_____

_____

19. My friends _____

_____

_____

20. I get annoyed _____

_____

_____

21. I daydream about _____

_____

_____

22. There are times when _____

_____

_____

23. My feelings _____

_____

24. My goal _____

_____

_____

25. I find it difficult _____

_____

_____

26. Most of my friends _____

_____

_____

27. I know it is silly but _____

_____

_____

28. When I was a youngster _____

_____

_____

29. When I marry _____

_____

_____

30. My father thinks my mother _____

_____

_____

31. My family _____

_____

_____

32. I would do anything to forget _____

_____

_____

33. A real friend _____

_____

_____

34. Most of my friends don't know _____

_____

_____

35. I think a mother _____

_____

_____

36. I could be happy if _____

_____

_____

37. Ten years from now _____

_____

_____

38. Most of all, I _____

_____

_____

39. Sex _____

_____

_____

40. Compared with others, I _____

_____

_____

41. I can't understand _____

_____

_____

42. My father and I _____

_____

_____

43. Dating _____

_____

_____

44. My mother thinks my father _____

_____

_____

45. What I want most _____

_____

_____

46. My mother and I _____

_____

_____

47. My biggest fault _____

_____

_____

48. Sometimes I _____

_____

_____

49. My dreams _____

_____

_____

50. My appearance _____

_____

_____

Questions For Discussion

1. Does your score place you above or below the median? What does this mean?

2. Which items were most difficult for you to complete? Why?

3. Does your score correspond to your own evaluation of your adjustment?

4. Does the test reveal some of your current difficulties? Why or why not?

5. How might a clinical psychologist find your responses helpful in diagnosing your difficulties?

6. What are some of the cautions that should be observed in interpreting the results?

12
human motivation and emotion

LEARNING OBJECTIVES

Discuss the psychoanalytic and social learning theory approaches to motivation and show how they differ in their interpretation of aggression.

Is the expression of aggression cathartic? Be able to cite evidence in support of your conclusion.

Be familiar with the physiological changes that occur during emotion.

Be able to compare the three theories of emotion.

Understand the contributions of maturation and learning in the development of emotional expression.

Discuss the useful and harmful effects of emotion.

PROGRAMMED UNIT

1. Human beings engage in a vast variety of complex activities. Physiological motives, as we saw in the preceding chapter, can account for some of these activities. But many of our motives are *psychological;* they are learned in interaction with other people and are little influenced by biological needs. Security, self-esteem, and acceptance by others are important psychological

motives _____.

physiological

psychological

biological
(or physiological)

psychological

psychoanalytic

unconscious

unconscious

unconscious

unconscious

slips

motives

unconscious

sex, aggression
(either order)

2. Hunger is a _____ motive, while the need to feel competent is a _____ motive.

3. Psychological motives are influenced primarily by learning and the kind of society in which the individual is raised rather than by _____ needs.

4. Not all societies consider it important for a person to acquire wealth or material goods. Consequently, we assume that avarice is a _____ rather than a physiological motive.

5. Of the numerous motivational theories the text discusses two: *psychoanalytic theory* and *social learning theory.* Psychoanalytic theory, which originated with Freud, views human actions as determined by internal impulses which are often unconscious. The idea of unconscious motivation is important to _____ theory.

6. When a person engages in behavior but is *not* aware of the real reason for his behavior, he is directed by *unconscious* motivation. If you meet a stranger and dislike him at first sight, there are probably _____ motives operating, especially if you are unaware of why you do not like him.

7. If a person is not aware of the real reason for his behavior, we say that his motivation is _____.

8. Freud believed that unconscious motives reveal themselves in several ways. In dreams the dreamer often expresses desires of which he or she is unaware. *Dreams,* then, are one way in which _____ motives may be expressed.

9. *Slips of speech* may also reveal unconscious motives. While expressing sympathy, John says to his ailing sister, "I regret that you will soon be well." His speech slip may express _____ hostile feelings toward her.

10. Dreams and _____ of speech are two ways in which hidden or unconscious _____ may be expressed.

11. Freud believed that the two basic drives or instincts that motivate human behavior are sex and aggression. Because parents and society place certain taboos on the child's expression of sexual or aggressive impulses, these impulses are often repressed from conscious awareness. They remain active only as _____ motives.

12. According to psychoanalytic theory, the two most important sources of motivation are _____ and _____.

13. Because of taboos on the expression of sex and aggression, such impulses may be

repressed

banished from awareness, or re_____.

14. Repressed impulses remain active as unconscious motives and may find expression indirectly in _____ or slips of _____.

dreams, speech

15. A father resents the time and attention his wife devotes to their young son. His resentment leads to aggressive feelings toward the child. But since it is not considered acceptable to feel or express aggression towards one's offspring, these feelings remain largely un_____.

unconscious

16. A second theory of motivation, *social learning theory*, proposes that much of human motivation is *learned* through coping with the social environment as the individual grows. Psychoanalytic theory maintains that behavior is motivated by instinctual drives. Social learning theory, in contrast, claims that many motives are not innate but are _____.

learned

17. Behavior patterns that are rewarded will tend to be repeated, while those that produce unfavorable results will be discarded. This is the basic premise of social _____ theory.

learning

18. Every time Margaret, who is four, strikes out in anger her mother hastens to placate her with a cookie or toy. When she enters kindergarten Margaret is the most aggressive child in the class. Aggressive behavior patterns have been re_____.

rewarded
(or reinforced)

learned

19. In this case it is clear that Margaret's aggressiveness is (*learned*/*innate*).

20. Not all behavior is learned directly. Many behavior patterns are learned by watching the behavior of others and observing its consequences for them. This is called *vicarious learning.* Mary observes that every time her older brother takes out the garbage mother praises him. Mary begins to take out the garbage. Her learning in this case is _____ because she was not rewarded herself but observed someone else being rewarded.

vicarious

21. Vicarious learning saves a lot of time. We don't have to experiment with different behaviors and determine whether they produce reward or punishment. Instead, we can observe their consequences for other people and *model* our behavior after theirs. Vicarious learning is an important principle of (*social learning*/*psychoanalytic*) theory.

social learning

22. The motivation of aggression is of great concern to psychologists. Some distinguish between *hostile aggression* and *instrumental aggression.* Hostile _____ is designed solely to inflict injury. Instrumental aggression is aimed at obtaining rewards other than the victim's suffering.

aggression

23. A young man shot a store clerk during a robbery. This would probably be called _____ aggression.

instrumental

24. However, the distinction between instrumental aggression and _____ aggression is not always clear-cut. Several motives may be

hostile

involved in any aggressive act.

25. Quite different explanations of aggression are proposed by psychoanalytic theo-

learning

ry and social _____ theory. As we have seen, Freud con-

instincts (or drives)

sidered aggression to be one of the two basic _____.

sex

The other was _____.

26. Freud believed that aggression was an innate drive. Later psychoanalytic theorists proposed that aggression was a drive produced by frustration. The *frustration-aggression hypothesis* states that when a person is thwarted in efforts to

aggression

reach a goal, that person will display _____ toward
the source of this frustration.

is not

27. According to the frustration-aggression hypothesis agression (*is/is not*) innate.
But since all of us encounter frustration in our daily existence, an aggressive
drive is fairly universal.

28. In contrast, social learning theory views aggression as a learned response rather

produced

than either an innate or a *frustration-*_____ drive.

learned

29. According to social learning theory, aggression is (*innate/learned*). Frustration
produces an unpleasant emotion; how the individual responds to this emotion
depends on the kinds of responses he or she has found successful in coping with
stress in the past.

30. Whenever Judy is thwarted she runs to mother who always solves the problem.

dependent

In the future Judy will probably respond with (*aggressive/dependent*) behavior
when frustrated.

drive

31. Psychoanalytic theory sees aggression as a (*drive/learned response*), while social

learned response

learning theory views aggression as a (*drive/learned response*).

32. Studies have shown that children will imitate aggressive behavior they see
modeled by adults. These findings lend support to the (*psychoanalytic/social*

social learning

learning) theory of aggression.

33. Motivation and emotion are closely related. Emotions can activate and direct

motives

behavior in the same way as biological or psychological _____.
When we talk about motivation we usually focus on the goal-directed activity; in
discussing emotion our attention is drawn to the subjective, affective experiences
that accompany the behavior.

34. Most emotions can be classified according to whether they are *pleasant* or
unpleasant. Joy and love would be considered pleasant emotions, while anger

unpleasant

and fear would be classed as _____.

35. Emotions can also be scaled according to the *intensity* of the experience. Rage

unpleasant

and panic would be classified as intensely un_____

intensely

affective states, ecstasy and joy as _____ pleasant emotions.

36. Intense emotions are accompanied by widespread *bodily changes.* Most of these changes are controlled by the *sympathetic division* of the *autonomic nervous system* which prepares the body for emergency action. The increased heart and respiration rate and the elevated blood sugar level that occur when one is

sympathetic

nervous

frightened result from activity of the _____ division of the autonomic _____ system.

37. In fear, also, blood is diverted from the stomach and intestines and sent to the brain and skeletal muscles. These changes prepare the body for

emergency

sympathetic

autonomic

_____ action. They result from activity of the (*sympathetic/parasympathetic*) division of the _____ nervous system.

bodily

38. Because emotions are accompanied by widespread _____ changes, it might be possible to classify emotions according to the bodily responses involved. If a person always became red-faced and breathed rapidly when angry and became pale and breathed slowly when afraid, these differences in bodily

changes (or responses)

fear

_____ might prove a useful means of distinguishing between anger and _____.

39. Unfortunately, attempts to differentiate emotions on the basis of

bodily

_____ changes have not proved very successful. The physiological symptoms of the different emotions vary from one individual to the next, and there is considerable overlap between the symptoms. The face may flush during

would not

fear as readily as during anger. Hence redness of the face (*would/would not*) be a useful measure for distinguishing between the two emotions.

40. The problem of distinguishing among emotional states is further complicated

changes

because the *situation* in which the bodily _____ of emotion occur will often influence how the person *labels* the emotion.

41. For example, if a subject is given a drug that produces profound bodily changes, he will tend to label his emotional state in accordance with the behavior of those around him. If his fellow subjects are acting in a gay and euphoric manner, the person will tend to label his emotional state as euphoria; if his fellow subjects are

label

expressing angry feelings, he will tend to _____ his emotion as anger.

42. The label that a person attaches to the bodily changes of emotion depends to

situation

label

some extent upon the s_____ in which these changes occur. Situational factors influence how a person will _____ his emotional state.

43. One of the earliest theories of emotion was the *James-Lange theory,* which proposed that what we feel as emotion is the *feedback* from the bodily changes.

James

According to the _____-Lange theory, we see a wildcat, start to run, and then experience the emotion we call fear.

44. The notion that the feeling of sorrow results from the tears that flow when a

James-Lange

person hears tragic news is a statement of the _____-_____ theory of emotion.

bodily

feedback

45. The James-Lange theory maintains that emotion is defined by _____ responses that are perceived and labeled after they occur. The experience of emotion is fe_____ from the bodily changes.

emotion

46. An alternative explanation of emotion, proposed by Walter Cannon, is that the bodily changes and the experience of emotion occur at the same time. According to Cannon's theory of _____, butterflies-in-the-stomach and the felt emotion of fear occur together; the brain and the sympathetic nervous system are aroused simultaneously by an emotion-producing situation.

James-Lange

47. Because an emotional experience is not a momentary event but takes place over time, it is difficult to determine whether the physiological responses precede or accompany the emotion. When you are suddenly confronted with possible danger (e.g., a loud sound that might be an explosion, a narrowly avoided accident), your pounding heart and feeling of weakness in the knees may precede full awareness of the danger. In this instance the (*James-Lange/Cannon*) theory of emotion is correct.

Cannon

48. More often, however, physiological arousal follows the appraisal of a situation as dangerous. You realize that the gray shape behind the door is not a shadow but a man with a gun; the emotional experience of fear precedes or occurs at the same time as the autonomic activity. In this case the (*James-Lange/Cannon*) theory is correct.

bodily

49. Regardless of what point in the emotional sequence bodily changes have their effect, they influence the *intensity* with which we experience emotion. Even though fear cannot be differentiated from anger on the basis of the kind of bodily changes that occur, the intensity with which we feel either emotion is dependent upon the degree of _____ changes or arousal.

intensity

50. People whose spinal cords have been injured so that they receive no sensations from the internal organs report that their experience of emotion is less intense than it was before their injury. Feedback from internal bodily changes is important to the _____ of the emotional experience.

cognitive

51. *Cognitive factors* also influence our conscious experience of emotion. We noted earlier that the label a person attaches to an emotion depends upon the situation in which the physiological arousal occurs. The *cognitive-physiological theory* of emotion proposes that emotional states depend upon the interaction of physiological arousal with cog_____ processes.

intensity

cognitive

52. Physiological arousal is important to the _____ with which we experience an emotion. But _____ factors determine how we interpret the emotional experience.

physiological

53. The cognitive-_____ theory of emotion assumes that how we interpret the situation that causes physiological arousal will determine the label we attach to the emotion.

cognitive	**54.** According to the _____-physiological theory emotional
	states depend upon the interaction of physiological arousal with
cognitive	_____ processes.
	55. Studies have shown that a person's emotional response to a stressful situation (as
	measured by bodily changes) can be increased or decreased depending on the
	interpretation of the situation. This shows that emotional reactions are influ-
cognitive	enced by _____ factors.
James	**56.** The two theories of emotion discussed earlier, the _____-Lange and
Cannon	_____ theories, are concerned with how the emotion-producing
	stimuli and internal bodily changes interact to produce an emotional experience.
	A third theory, which focuses on the way the individual interprets the emotion-
cognitive-physiological	producing situation, is the _____-_____
	theory of emotion.
	57. Some of the ways in which we express emotions are *innate,* appearing at birth or
	developing through *maturation.* As soon as he is born the infant can cry. Crying
	is thus an innate expression of emotion. When he is about six months old the
	infant will laugh when his mother smiles or makes funny faces. Laughing is thus
innate	an inborn, or _____, expression of emotion. But it requires a
maturation	period of mat_____ before it appears.
	58. Although the infant is born with the capacity to cry and develops the capacity
maturation	to laugh through _____, most aspects of emotional
	behavior are acquired through *learning.*
	59. As they grow older children learn the *occasions* when it is appropriate to cry and
	when it is appropriate to laugh. They also learn the *form* of emotional expres-
learn	sion that is proper in their culture; for example, they _____ to express
	anger verbally rather than by hitting.
	60. In our society women express sorrow by crying; men usually inhibit their tears.
learning	This is an example of the influence of l_____ on emotional
	expression.
	61. To recapitulate: Some expressions of emotion are innate; they appear at birth or
maturation	develop through _____. Crying and laughing are
innate	examples of _____ emotional expressions. However, learning is
occasions	important in determining the o_____ when certain emo-
form	tions are appropriate and in shaping the f_____ of expression acceptable
	within the culture.
	62. How do emotions affect our performance? When they are mild they keep us
	alert and interested in what we are doing. But intense emotions, whether
	pleasant or unpleasant, generally disrupt performance, making it less effective. If

impaired

you are experiencing an intense emotion, your performance on a complex task will probably be (*impaired/improved*).

63. Emotional states that are prolonged may lead to actual illness. *Psychophysiological disorders* are a group of illnesses in which the symptoms are physical but the causes may lie in the person's *emotional* life. If continued worry over your job causes you to have high blood pressure, then the disorder is considered

psychophysiological

psycho_____.

64. Psychophysiological disorders are a group of illnesses in which the symptoms are

emotional

physical but the causes may lie in the person's em_____

life.

65. Asthma, ulcers, and migraine headaches are considered

psychophysiological

_____ disorders when they are caused

primarily by emotional stress.

TERMS AND CONCEPTS FOR IDENTIFICATION

psychological motive_____

_____

_____

_____

unconscious motive _____

_____

_____

_____

vicarious learning_____

_____

_____

_____

hostile aggression_____

_____

_____

_____

instrumental aggression _____

_____

_____

_____

frustration-aggression hypothesis_____

_____

_____

_____

GSR _____

_____

_____

_____

James-Lange theory _____

_____

_____

_____

Cannon's theory _____

_____

_____

_____

cognitive-physiological theory _____

_____

_____

_____

psychophysiological disorder _____

_____

_____

_____

_____ 1. In a psychophysiological disorder
a. continued emotional tension is the cause
b. the cause is primarily psychological
c. the symptoms are physical
d. all of the above

_____ 2. Pain, a loud noise, and certain other stimuli arouse fear in young organisms of many species. The common fear-arousing element in these situations seems to be
a. strangeness
b. the threat of bodily harm
c. pain
d. danger to the species

_____ 3. From a psychologist's viewpoint, much of the controversy over whether aggressive behavior should be displayed on TV centers around the question of whether it is
a. frightening to children
b. cathartic as opposed to stimulating aggressive acts
c. excessively violent
d. justified by the circumstances

_____ 4. According to Freud, motives that cannot be expressed openly are repressed and remain active as unconscious motives. Such unconscious motives are believed to be shown by
a. slips of speech
b. symptoms of mental illness
c. dreams
d. all of the above

_____ 5. The frustration-aggression hypothesis
a. assumes that aggression is a basic instinct
b. claims that frustration and aggression are both instinctive patterns
c. assumes that frustration produces aggression
d. was developed by social learning theorists

_____ 6. The James-Lange theory of emotion says that
a. the thalamus has the central role in arousal
b. we are afraid because we run
c. perception of the emotion leads to physiological changes
d. all of the above

_____ 7. Maslow aided our understanding of the relationships among motives by
a. pointing out that psychological motives are based on physiological needs
b. describing them in terms of vicarious learning and self-control techniques
c. arranging them in a hierarchy, from biological ones to more complex psychological ones
d. showing the importance of instinctive aggressive patterns in more complex motives

_____ 8. According to social learning theorists, reinforcement has two basic sources, _____ and _____, which sometimes coincide and sometimes conflict.
a. external, self-evaluative
b. family, peers
c. motives, incentives
d. sexuality, aggression

_____ 9. Researchers studying the influence of TV aggression on children found that watching violent TV programs increased aggressive behavior in boys but not in girls. This difference may be related to the fact that
a. girls in our society are seldom reinforced for aggression
b. most of the aggressive TV models are male
c. in general, girls in our society imitate aggression less than boys
d. all of the above

_____ 10. The concept of an aggressive drive is supported in the popular media by accounts of explosive outbursts in meek individuals such as Charles Whitman. Investigation of such episodes _____ this concept, noting that _____.
a. confirms, the stories are well founded
b. contradicts, these people have previously been aggressive
c. is unable to confirm or deny, the evidence is mixed

d. supports, more often than not it is an accurate summary

_____ 11. Freud believed in two forms of instinct (Eros and Thanatos) which he felt were represented by the behaviors normally said to reflect the motives of
a. dependency and aggression
b. sex and death
c. sex and aggression
d. affiliation and dominance

_____ 12. The facial expressions, postures, and gestures used by children blind from birth to express emotion
a. often develop appropriately through maturation
b. are unlike those of normal children
c. resemble the simple movements of an infant
d. must be carefully taught to them by others

_____ 13. Using the polygraph to detect guilt is not foolproof because
a. an innocent subject may also respond emotionally
b. a knowledgeable subject can "beat" the machine
c. a practiced liar may be able to control his emotions
d. all of the above

_____ 14. When children were shown a film of adults expressing aggression against a Bobo doll, many of them imitated the aggression. When tested eight months later, the children
a. still remembered many of the aggressive responses
b. had forgotten about half of the aggressive responses
c. remembered seeing the movie, but no longer remembered specific aggressive responses
d. did not remember seeing the movie

_____ 15. In addition to taking a more generally cognitive position than strict S-R theorists, social learning advocates stress the importance of _____ learning, i.e., learning by _____.
a. operant, reinforcement
b. vicarious, observation

c. latent, non-reinforced trials
d. self-discovery, doing

_____ 16. Which of the following is *not* a true statement regarding emotional arousal level and performance?
a. the optimum level of arousal differs for different tasks
b. individuals are very similar in the extent to which their behavior is disrupted by arousal
c. intense arousal can seriously impair the performance of organized behavior
d. performance is optimal at moderate levels of arousal

_____ 17. When veterans with spinal-cord injuries were interviewed about their emotions, it was found that the _____ the lesion, the more emotionality _____ following injury.
a. lower, increased
b. lower, decreased
c. higher, decreased
d. higher, increased

_____ 18. Some psychologists distinguish between two forms of aggression. They would call assault committed during a robbery _____ aggression.
a. instrumental
b. secondary
c. hostile
d. conditioned

_____ 19. Psychologists have in the past devoted much effort to trying to classify emotions. A classification that has proved useful is to divide emotions into _____ and _____.
a. arousing, soothing
b. innate, learned
c. pleasant, unpleasant
d. all of the above

_____ 20. Schachter's cognitive-physiological theory of emotion states that
a. cognitions give rise to the physiology of emotion
b. physiological responses create the cognitions in emotions
c. cognitions are involved in some emotions, physiological responses in others
d. cognitions and physiological responses interact to form emotions

1. d	6. b	11. b	16. b
2. a	7. c	12. a	17. c
3. b	8. a	13. d	18. a
4. d	9. d	14. a	19. c
5. c	10. b	15. b	20. d

INDIVIDUAL EXERCISES

LISTENING WITH A THIRD EAR

Introduction

While psychologists differ in their conception of a "subconscious" or "unconscious" portion of the mind, most would agree that some of our thoughts, motives, and emotional responses are more available for self-inspection than others. A variety of techniques have been developed to aid us in better understanding such "unconscious" mental activity. These range from Freud's free association to Zen and other forms of meditation. The two techniques presented below fall into this spectrum. However, they are not accepted research techniques as are most of the other procedures in this workbook. (One of them, the Chevreul Pendulum,[1] has been widely used in the manner to be described below, but rarely as part of a carefully controlled scientific study.) They are presented as possible ways for getting more in touch with ourselves or listening to ourselves "with a third ear."

[1] Named after the Frenchman, Michael Chevreul, who investigated the phenomenon in 1883, relating it to the use of a divining rod to discover water or precious metals beneath the earth.

A. THE COIN-FLIP DECISION MAKER

Equipment Needed

A coin

Procedure

1. This procedure allows you to "focus" on your emotional responses when you are conflicted or confused about a decision. You have weighed the pros and cons but cannot decide on the evidence alone; you wonder just how you would really *feel* after deciding one way or the other. Next time you have this problem, try the coin technique, as follows.

2. Take out your coin and tell yourself that you will let a flip of the coin determine the decision. Put one choice on heads, the other on tails and flip the coin.

3. The instant the coin lands and you realize what the outcome is, pay special attention to your own reaction, i.e., listen with that third ear. Do you hear a sigh of relief? Or a still small voice asking, "Two out of three?"

4. Frivolous as it may seem, such a technique may be useful. It appears to provide an instant role-playing situation, in which you sense how you would really feel if the decision had been made for you, rather than trying to predict your feelings through logic alone.

B. THE CHEVREUL PENDULUM

Equipment Needed

A pendulum, made up of a small weight on six to ten inches of string or fine chain. A locket on a chain will do. Or make a pendulum from a fishing weight, an eraser, etc., tied to a length of string.

Procedure

1. The Chevreul Pendulum is a device for what hypnotists term "ideomotor answering." The "answering" refers to the subject's answering questions, while "ideomotor" means doing so by a special kind of motor performance, one which reflects a thought yet is different from normal, deliberate body movements. Those hypnotists who use the "unconscious" as an explanatory system say this device allows the unconscious to answer. Others, less convinced of an unconscious "mind" lurking in our heads somewhere, still agree that such answering may yield responses different from simple verbal replies.

2. The pendulum works by allowing very fine muscular movements to provide answers to questions, movements so fine as to seem to happen by themselves. To help this happen, sit down, hold the string of the pendulum between your index finger and your thumb, and rest your elbow on a table. Pick a comfortable angle of the arm and let the pendulum hang to within an inch or two of the table. You will find that you can cause the pendulum to oscillate along a line, forward and back or left and right, and to rotate in either direction by very small, almost imperceptible movements.

3. In order to answer questions you should have pendulum movements for "yes," "no," "maybe," "I don't know," and perhaps "I don't want to answer." A typical set-up could be right-left for "yes," forward-back for "no," an indeterminate movement for "maybe," a circle one way for "I don't know," and the other way for "I don't want to answer." But don't just use these movements; let the pendulum tell you. Rest your elbow comfortably with the pendulum motionless and tell yourself, out loud or silently, that the pendulum will soon move appropriately for "yes." The movement may be uncertain at first, but don't force it. Just keep thinking "yes" and expecting some movement. If all goes well the pendulum will slowly begin to move. Use the same procedure for the other answers.

4. If you can get the answering to work, then ask yourself questions—ones, for example, about which you are confused. You may get a "maybe" or "I don't know" answer, but you may be surprised to find a definite answer forthcoming.

5. You might also let someone else try the pendulum while you ask the questions.

6. Note that there is no suggestion of magic, spirits, or other psychic causation in this procedure. The answers come from you. But normal verbal consciousness is not the totality of all our thoughts and desires. The pendulum may simply allow you to listen to parts of yourself usually overridden or overlooked.

Questions For Discussion

1. Do you think these techniques might be related to the differences between the two hemispheres of your brain, as discussed in Chapter 2 of the text? If so, why?

2. Do you think that the pendulum might react differently when you use your left hand than when you use your right or vice versa? (Try it.)

13
personality and its assessment

LEARNING OBJECTIVES

Give examples of the way in which inborn potential, common experiences, and unique experiences help to shape personality.

Understand the methods used to identify and measure basic traits.

Discuss the contribution of psychoanalysis, both as a dynamic and a developmental theory, to the understanding of personality.

Be familiar with the two projective tests discussed in the text.

Discuss social learning theory as an alternative to theories that stress the consistency of personality.

Discuss the concept of the self as an approach to the study of personality.

PROGRAMMED UNIT

1. *Personality* is a difficult concept to define, but we will begin by referring to personality as the *characteristic patterns of behavior and modes of thinking* that determine an individual's adjustment to the environment. According to this definition, every person (*has/does not have*) personality.

has

2. The characteristic patterns of behavior and modes of thinking that determine an individual's adjustment to the environment may be said to make up his

personality _____.

3. When we speak of Margaret's personality, we are referring to the characteristic

behavior, thinking

patterns of _____ and modes of _____ that determine her adjustment to her environment.

4. Some of the characteristics that influence personality are *inborn,* that is, present at birth. Robert, a large, sturdy baby, lies placidly in his crib and is not easily

inborn
(or innate)

upset. These in_____ characteristics, physical size and emotional reactivity, may well influence his personality in later life.

5. Susan at three weeks of age is a small, frail infant who is fussy and continually

inborn
(or innate)

active. These _____ characteristics may well contribute to her

personality

_____ as an adult.

6. The characteristics that are present at birth constitute the individual's *potential—* a potential that develops through maturation and learning as the person grows up. The experiences encountered in growing up shape or modify the inborn ·

potential

po_____. Some of these experiences are *common experiences,* shared by most individuals growing up in a certain *culture.*

7. If a particular culture emphasizes the value of cleanliness and early toilet training, then most individuals growing up in this culture will share

common

_____ experiences in these areas.

8. If a culture expects females to be docile and submissive, then most of the girls growing up in this culture will share some common

experiences

_____ that tend to develop these qualities. These

inborn
(or innate)

experiences will *modify* the girls' _____ potential. A girl who is active and vigorous as an infant may become more placid as her personality is

culture

shaped or modified by the _____.

modify

9. Some of the experiences that shape or _____ the person's inborn

culture

potential are common to most individuals in a certain _____. Other experiences are *unique* or *individual;* they cannot be predicted from knowledge of the culture in which the person was raised.

10. John grew up with a drunken father who beat John unmercifully. This would be

unique

an example of an individual or _____ experience for John—one

common

that is not _____ to most children in his culture.

inborn
(or innate)
common
unique

11. Thus the _____ potential of the individual is shaped or modified by _____ experiences (those shared by most members of the culture) as well as by _____ or individual experiences to form the

personality

_____ we see in the adult.

12. Many theories attempt to explain and describe personality, but most can be grouped into one of *four* types or classes: *trait, psychoanalytic, social learning,*

four

and *humanistic*. We will look at each of these _____ (*number*) types of theories in turn.

13. Trait theories assume that people can be distinguished from one another on the basis of certain *measurable* and *persisting* characteristics called *traits*. A trait is a

measured

persisting characteristic that can be m_____.

persisting (or synonym)

14. Thus, one may think of intelligence as a trait since it is a measurable and relatively _____ characteristic.

trait

15. Aggressiveness may also be considered a _____ to the extent that it is a measurable and persisting personality characteristic.

16. When we attempt to describe a personality in terms of certain persisting

trait

characteristics that can be measured, we are using a _____ theory.

17. One method for measuring personality traits is a *personality inventory*. A

inventory

personality in_____ asks questions about an individual's attitudes, feelings, and experiences. The questions are designed to measure *certain traits*.

18. A personality inventory asks the same questions of each person and the answers are given in a form that can be easily scored. An individual's scores can be compared with the scores of other people to see how he compares on certain

traits

_____.

19. A test used in personality assessment in which the person responds to a number of

personality inventory

questions about himself is a _____ _____.

20. One of the most widely used personality inventories, the Minnesota Multiphasic Personality Inventory (abbreviated MMPI), was designed at the University of Minnesota to measure various phases of personality—thus the word "*multiphasic*." The Minnesota Multiphasic Personality Inventory (abbreviated

MMPI

_____) measures a number of different personality characteristics or

traits

_____.

21. One way to assess personality traits is by using a personality inventory such as

Multiphasic

the Minnesota _____ Personality Inventory. Another method uses a *rating scale* to record *judgments* about a trait.

scale

22. A rating _____ is a device by which a rater can record his judgments of another person according to the traits defined by the scale. A sample item from a rating scale is given below.

Place a check at the point that describes the individual's poise.

| Nervous and ill at ease | Somewhat tense; easily upset | Average poise and security | Sure of himself | Very composed; adapts well to crises |

judgment

23. In this example the rater would record his ju_____ of the individual's poise by placing a check at the appropriate point on the

scale

s_____.

24. In rating personality traits it is important to avoid the *"halo effect."* The halo

effect

_____ refers to the tendency to rate someone high on all traits because of a good impression on one or two traits, or to rate the person low

traits

throughout because of a poor impression on one or two _____.

25. Gladys M has a very friendly and pleasant manner. Her employer rates her high on her ability to get along well with others; he also rates Gladys M high on honesty and efficiency although he has little information on which to base his

halo

judgment of the latter two traits. This example shows how the _____

effect

_____ interferes with objectivity in rating others.

rating

26. The halo effect is a possible source of error in the use of _____

scales

_____. Another possible source of error is the tendency of raters to be influenced by *social stereotypes.*

27. Unless the raters know the persons being rated fairly well, they may base their

stereotypes

judgments as much on social _____, how they *believe* a "housewife" or a "high school athlete" or a "long-haired college student" acts and thinks, as on observations of actual behaviors.

halo

28. Two possible sources of error in the use of rating scales are the _____

effect, social

_____ and _____ stereotypes.

scales

29. Rating _____ are most often used when one person assesses the traits of another, but they can also be used for self-ratings. If you were asked "How well do you control your emotions?" and were requested to rate yourself by placing a check mark at the appropriate place on a line that runs from "tend to be unresponsive" to "tend to be overemotional," you would be using a

rating scale

_____ _____ to evaluate your own personality traits.

personality

30. Two methods used to assess personality traits are _____

inventories, rating
scales (either order)

_____ and _____ _____.

31. Theories of personality that describe people by measuring their persisting charac-

trait

teristics are called _____ theories. A quite different approach to personality is provided by *psychoanalytic theory* as formulated by Sigmund Freud.

32. Freud conceived of personality as composed of three major systems: the *id,* the *ego,* and the *superego.* The id represents the innate instinctual drives (including sex and aggression). The id seeks immediate gratification of impulses without regard for the consequences. A person who acts impulsively, without concern for

id

more remote consequences, is likely to be expressing the _____ portion of his personality.

33. In psychoanalytic theory the pleasure-seeking, impulsive portion of personality

id   is called the _____. It is manifested in early childhood but is never completely outgrown, so that behavior stemming from this part of the personality can be found in the most sober of adults.

34. It is obvious that if the id were given full rein we could never have a civilization. We need a part of the personality that will exert control in such a way as to make our behavior conform to reality and social constraint. This is called the *ego.* The aspect of personality that takes into account the real consequences of

ego   our search for pleasure is, then, the _____.

35. The id is the pleasure-seeking aspect of personality that ignores reality; the

ego   _____ is the more rational portion and tries to take reality into account.

36. Because it seeks immediate pleasure, the _____ is said to be controlled by the

id

ego   *pleasure principle;* because it conforms to environmental realities, the _____ is said to be controlled by the *reality principle.*

37. The third part of the personality, according to psychoanalytic theory, is the *superego,* an aspect that develops out of the ego's experiences with social reality and parental prohibitions. Parental commands are made part of the individual, who then feels guilt if he violates this internalized code. The common word for the *superego* is *conscience.* If the ego proposes a course of action that is

ego   opportunistic but somewhat in violation of conscience, the _____ will be

superego   opposed by the s_____.

38. Let us set up a hypothetical situation involving a young boy, in which his thoughts may be attributed to these three aspects of personality. The boy is angry at one of his classmates and thinks, "I'd sure like to beat him to a pulp!"

id   This statement would be an expression of the _____. Next the boy thinks, "But

ego   he's bigger than I and might beat *me* up." This is the _____ at work. Finally the boy thinks, "Well, fighting is wrong anyhow." This would be the judgment

superego   of the _____. A person's approach to such problem situations reflects the way in which he has learned to cope with the conflicting demands of the three parts of his personality. (The text also discusses the developmental aspects of the psychoanalytic theory of personality which are concerned with the form the id impulses take during the various stages of psychosexual development and some of the personality characteristics that develop if a person becomes fixated at any of these stages.)

39. Psychoanalytic theory assumes that many aspects of an individual's personality are *unconscious.* Since unconscious conflicts and impulses are unknown to the

would not   person, we (*would/would not*) expect him to report them in answering questions on a personality inventory. A different kind of test, called a *projective test,* is used to tap motives and feelings that a person may be unaware of or may be unwilling to reveal.

scales   **40.** Unlike personality inventories and rating _____, projective tests are *unstructured* and require the person to reveal (project) himself by responding imaginatively to ambiguous stimuli. For example, in the *Rorschach Test* a person is shown a series of irregularly shaped inkblots and asked to tell what they suggest. Since the inkblots are relatively unstructured and ambiguous stimuli, the

projective   Rorschach Test is a _____ test.

unstructured   **41.** Projective tests are <u>un</u>_____ and ambiguous stimuli to which a person responds with an imaginative production rather than a specific answer.

42. Tests composed of relatively unstructured and ambiguous stimuli that elicit

projective   projections of the personality are called _____ tests.

Rorschach   **43.** One example of a projective test is the <u>R</u>_____ Inkblot Test. Another projective test, the Thematic Apperception Test, consists of a series of pictures about which the person tells stories. In so doing the subject may say things about the characters in the stories that apply to himself. The

inkblots   Rorschach Test utilizes _____ as stimuli, whereas the Thematic Apperception Test utilizes a series of pictures.

Thematic   **44.** The _____ Apperception Test utilizes a series of pictures to which the subject responds with stories. Certain themes that recur in the person's imaginative productions are analyzed by the psychologist to arrive at basic motives and conflicts.

45. The Thematic Apperception Test is so called because certain "themes" recur in the imaginative productions of a person. "Apperception" means a readiness to perceive in certain ways, based on prior experience. Hence, the person interprets

picture   an ambiguous stimulus, in this case a _____, according to his apperceptions and elaborates his stories in terms of preferred themes that reflect his personality.

Rorschach   **46.** Both the _____ Test, which utilizes inkblots, and the

Thematic Apperception   _____ _____ Test,

projective   which utilizes pictures, are _____ tests of personality.

trait   **47.** We have discussed two theoretical approaches to personality: _____ theory which uses structured methods such as personality

inventories, rating   _____ and _____ scales to measure

psychoanalytic   personality traits, and _____ theory which stresses unconscious motives in personality and measures them by means

projective, Rorschach   of _____ tests, such as the _____

Apperception   Inkblot Test and the Thematic _____ Test. A third theoretical approach to the study of personality is *social learning theory*.

learning   **48.** Social _____ theory assumes that personality is shaped by the *conditions of learning* a person encounters in the course of growing up.

49. Thus, differences in personality from one person to the next can be explained in

learning

terms of differences in their l_____ experiences.

50. Trait theories assume that personality traits are consistent and

measurable

m_____ characteristics of an individual. Social learning theorists maintain that many personality traits are not consistent but depend instead on the *specific situation* in which the behavior occurs.

51. Harriet considers herself to be an "honest" person. She is careful to give the correct change when she works part-time as a store clerk, she is scrupulous about filling out her income-tax return, and she has never cheated on an examination. However, when she finds a wallet full of money on the sidewalk, she fails to return it, even though the owner's address is clearly indicated. This example

honesty

points to the fact that there is no unitary trait called h_____.
Whether a person behaves in an "honest manner" depends upon the

specific

_____ situation.

52. Social learning theorists assume that many personality traits are not consistent

situation

but depend on the specific _____ in which behavior occurs.

social

53. According to _____ learning theory, people behave in ways that are likely to produce *reinforcement.*

54. Ted's parents praise him whenever he acts aggressively toward his classmates and wins a fist fight, but they punish him whenever he shows any aggression toward them. Social learning theory would predict that Ted will display aggression only

reinforcement

in those situations where he has received r_____.
He will not show aggression in all situations.

is not

55. Thus, according to social learning theory, aggression (*is/is not*) a trait; it is a learned response to a specific situation. Social learning theorists assess personality by determining the environmental conditions that maintain certain behaviors and discovering how these conditions can be changed to modify behavior. (The text discusses these procedures in more detail.)

56. So far we have examined three approaches to the study of personality:

trait, psychoanalytic
(either order)
social learning

_____, _____, and
_____ _____ theories. A fourth group of personality theories are called *humanistic* because they emphasize those characteristics of people that are uniquely *human,* not shared by the lower animals.

57. Humanistic personality theories stress those aspects of personality that are

human

uniquely _____. They consider the basic force motivating behavior to be *self-actualization*—an innate human tendency toward growth and fulfillment (actualization) of all of one's potentials.

58. According to humanistic theorists the basic force motivating behavior is

actualization

self-_____.

growth   **59.** Self-actualization refers to an innate human tendency towards g_____

potentials   and the fulfillment of one's p_____.

60. One of the most influential of the humanistic psychologists is Carl Rogers, whose theory of personality centers around the *concept of the self.* The self,

Rogers   according to Carl _____, consists of all the *ideas, perceptions,* and *values* that characterize "I" or "me."

values   **61.** Your self-concept includes all of the ideas, perceptions, and _____

concept   that characterize you. Your self-_____ influences both your perception of the world and your behavior. If you do something that

self-concept   is not consistent with your s_____-_____, you feel uncomfortable and may even distort or deny your actions to preserve your self-concept.

62. Rogers proposes that we all have an *ideal self* in addition to our self-concept. An ideal self is the kind of person we would like to be. The closer our self-concept is

ideal   to our i_____ self, the more fulfilled and happy we will be.

ideal self   **63.** The person we would like to be is the _____ _____. If we are close to our ideal self and have fulfilled most of our potential, then we have come close to self-actualization.

64. Self-actualization is the basic force motivating behavior according to

humanistic   _____ psychologists.

65. Each of the theoretical approaches we have discussed looks at personality from a slightly different viewpoint. Can you identify each of these approaches from their main emphasis?

psychoanalytic   a. Unconscious motivation: _____ theories

social learning   b. Reward and punishment: _____ _____ theories

humanistic   c. Self-actualization: _____ theories

trait   d. Consistent and enduring personality characteristics: _____ theories

TERMS AND CONCEPTS FOR IDENTIFICATION

trait _____

_____

_____

_____

introvert _____

_____

_____

_____

extravert _____

_____

_____

_____

factor analysis _____

_____

_____

_____

personality inventory _____

_____

_____

_____

rating scale _____

_____

_____

_____

halo effect _____

_____

_____

_____

moderator variable _____

_____

_____

_____

free association _____

_____

_____

_____

id _____

_____

_____

_____

ego _____

_____

_____

_____

superego _____

_____

_____

_____

projective test _____

_____

_____

_____

self-concept _____

_____

_____

_____

self-actualization _____

_____

_____

_____

_____ 1. In seeking to help a woman who suffered from severe asthma attacks, social learning theorists did *not*
a. ask her to keep a several-month diary
b. find a correlation between her attacks and visits with her mother
c. subject her to a series of fear-inducing stimuli
d. ask for a detailed report of her symptoms

_____ 2. The complex statistical technique for reducing a large number of measures to a smaller number of independent dimensions is
a. limited to certain kinds of measures
b. called trait analysis
c. useful only for the analysis of personality measures
d. called factor analysis

_____ 3. According to Freud
a. defense mechanisms defend against repression
b. repression reduces anxiety
c. individuals are similar in their balance of id, ego, and superego systems
d. all of the above

_____ 4. Studies with the Self-Disclosure Questionnaire show that
a. college students applying for counseling typically had low self-disclosure scores
b. greater mutual disclosure takes place between mother and daughter than in any other relationship
c. contrary to popular belief, men show more self-disclosure than women
d. the emotionally disturbed individual most typically shows excessive self-disclosure

_____ 5. Personality is defined in the text as the characteristic _____ and _____ that determine a person's adjustment to the environment.
a. thoughts, emotions
b. patterns of behavior, modes of thinking
c. desires, behaviors
d. systems of beliefs, ways of perceiving

_____ 6. Carl Rogers' view of the self may be compared to Freud's in some ways. For example, Rogers' _____ is similar to Freud's _____.
a. unsymbolized feelings, repressed feelings
b. ideal self, ego ideal
c. neither a nor b
d. both a and b

_____ 7. In Freud's theory of personality
a. the ego obeys the reality principle
b. the id operates by secondary process thinking
c. the superego obeys the pleasure principle
d. the ego operates by primary processs thinking

_____ 8. Social learning theorists focus on several "person variables" that determine what an individual will do in a particular situation. These do *not* include
a. competencies
b. subjective value of outcome
c. traits
d. cognitive strategies

_____ 9. Although cultural and subcultural measures impose some personality similarities, an individual personality is never completely predictable from a knowledge of the group in which the person was raised because
a. individuals differ in their inherited characteristics
b. a given culture is not applied uniformly to all members of it
c. individuals have different life experiences
d. all of the above

_____ 10. Initial enthusiasm for the Rorschach test has begun to dim because
a. it has not been subjected to enough research to establish its usefulness
b. formal scoring systems have not been devised for it
c. it has not proved to have much predictive value
d. all of the above

11. In the development of his personality theory, Abraham Maslow did *not* make major use of
   a. peak experiences
   b. antisocial needs
   c. self-actualization
   d. the experience of being

12. Trait theories have been criticized on the grounds that
   a. traits may be highly dependent on the situation
   b. moderator variables are often very influential
   c. they often do not specify how traits are organized within the personality
   d. all of the above

13. Freud's major contribution to our understanding of personality is probably
   a. the recognition that unconscious needs and conflicts motivate much of our behavior
   b. the recognition that sexual conflicts cause most personality disturbances
   c. his definition of psychosexual stages
   d. his definition of defense mechanisms

14. Analyses of the controversy between trait and social learning theorists, as to whether differences in behavior arise from people or situations, have found that the largest proportion of the variability in behavior is accounted for by
   a. different situations
   b. persisting individual differences
   c. the interaction between persons and situations
   d. none of the above

15. The personality inventory called the MMPI
   a. is based on the method of empirical construction
   b. only works if those who take it answer truthfully
   c. is based on factor analysis
   d. was originally designed as a college admission test

16. Social learning theorists believe that
   a. reinforcement is not necessary for learning
   b. much human learning is vicarious

   c. reinforcement is crucial for performance of learned behavior
   d. all of the above

17. While type theories have a certain appeal, they are misleading because
   a. they do not give enough weight to genetic factors
   b. most people fall on a continuum between types
   c. they place too much emphasis on early development
   d. most people fit one of the types, leaving only a few to be sorted into the other types

18. Freud compared the human mind to an iceberg. In this analogy the portion below the water was the _____.
   a. unconscious
   b. conscience
   c. id
   d. superego

19. Which of the following is *not* a true statement about Freud's psychosexual stages?
   a. the phallic stage is marked by pleasure obtained from fondling the genitals
   b. deprivation at a stage may produce fixation at that stage
   c. the genital stage is marked by pleasure obtained from fondling the genitals
   d. overindulgence at a stage may produce fixation at that stage

20. Future personality theories will probably concentrate on two areas:
   a. self-actualization and situational factors
   b. cognitive processes and social role factors
   c. intellectual abilities and traits
   d. aggressive instincts and social needs

KEY TO SELF-QUIZ

1. c	6. d	11. b	16. d
2. d	7. a	12. d	17. b
3. b	8. c	13. a	18. a
4. a	9. d	14. c	19. c
5. b	10. c	15. a	20. b

INDIVIDUAL EXERCISE

PERSONALITY DESCRIPTION

The text discusses four approaches to the study of personality. This exercise will give you some feeling for the way these approaches differ. Select an historical figure, a character from literature or drama, or a contemporary public personality about whom you know a great deal. Write a brief synopsis of his or her life from each of the viewpoints listed below. You may want to focus on only one or two events in your subject's life, explaining the motivation for the person's action in these situations from each of the following viewpoints.

1. trait theory

2. psychoanalytic theory

3. social learning theory

4. humanistic or self theory

Questions For Discussion

1. Which account was the easiest to write? Why?

2. Which account was most helpful in understanding the person? Why?

3. How useful do you think these accounts are from a scientific viewpoint? How interesting are they from a literary viewpoint?

CLASS EXERCISE

A PROJECTIVE TEST

Introduction

The Rorschach test, introduced by Dr. Hermann Rorschach in 1921, consists of a series of complex inkblots. Subjects are asked to tell what they see in each inkblot, and their responses are then scored and interpreted by experienced testers.

In this demonstration we will use the Rorschach inkblot reproduced on the next page. The exercise is designed to demonstrate that people looking at the same blot will see different things. No attempt at interpretation will be made by your instructor.

Equipment Needed

The inkblot presented here.

Procedure

Your instructor will ask six volunteers, preferably three men and three women, to leave the room. While they are out of the room, write below what the blot looks like to you. They will be called in one at a time and will be asked to relate what the blot looks like to them or what it makes them think of. You are to write each student's response in the space provided below.

Your own impression:

Student 1:

Student 2:

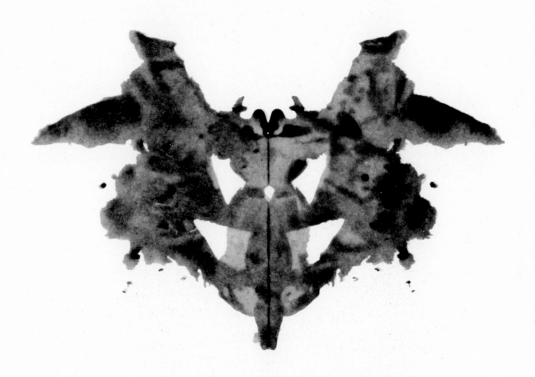

Student 3:

Student 4:

Student 5:

Student 6:

Questions For Discussion

1. Were there differences in the responses of the six subjects? If so, can you think why?

2. Although the sample used was small, did there seem to be sex differences in perception?

3. Do you think people "project" aspects of their personality in responding to such a blot?

4. What are the advantages of using stimuli as unstructured as this to assess personality? The disadvantages?

5. How does this test differ from the Thematic Apperception Test?

6. Would it be easy to derive objective scoring methods for a test of this type?

14
ability testing and intelligence

LEARNING OBJECTIVES

Understand the distinction between aptitude and achievement tests. Describe how reliability and validity are measured and how critical scores are used in prediction.

Be familiar with the assumption underlying a mental-age scale. Describe two methods of selecting and two of testing items in an intelligence test.

Be familiar with the general structure of the Stanford-Binet and the Wechsler Scales. Be able to write the formula for the IQ and discuss how it is interpreted.

Describe how factor analysis is used to determine the components of intelligence. Discuss the results obtained by Thurstone and Guilford using this method.

Discuss the stability of the IQ and the changes in intelligence that occur with age.

Be familiar with the evidence supporting the importance of genetic and environmental factors in intelligence.

Discuss the classification and causes of mental subnormality.

PROGRAMMED UNIT

1. Individuals differ in *aptitudes, knowledge,* and *skills.* In order to match the talents of each person to the appropriate job, we need some way of assessing or measuring his or her abilities. *Ability testing* is one way of assessing individual

skills   *differences* in aptitudes, knowledge, and _____.

2. The study of individual differences in aptitudes, knowledge, and skills is often
ability testing   carried on by means of _____ _____.

3. In attempting to appraise an individual's abilities, psychologists distinguish between what the person can do now and what the person might do if trained. Ability tests that identify what you can do now, or skills already accomplished, are *achievement tests.* Sally has had two years of typing instruction in high school. If a psychologist were interested in how fast and how accurately she can
achievement   type *now,* he would administer an _____ test.

4. When you take your final examination in this course, your instructor will
achievement   administer an _____ test to find our how well you have learned the various concepts and generalizations covered in the lectures and the textbook.

5. Ability tests designed to measure *capacity to learn*—that is, to predict what you can accomplish with *training*—are known as *aptitude tests.* Tests designed to measure skills already attained, or what a person can do now, are called
achievement   _____ tests.

6. Suppose a company has fifty unskilled applicants for a job as machinist and intends to train only ten of the fifty applicants to become machinists. An industrial psychologist employed by this company would probably administer an
aptitude   _____ test to determine which of the fifty applicants have the greatest capacity to learn to become machinists.

7. Tests designed to measure capacity to learn—that is, to predict what one can
aptitude   accomplish with training—are known as _____ tests.

capacity   **8.** Aptitude tests are designed to measure _____ to learn, that
training   is, to predict what one can accomplish with _____.

9. Before lawyers are admitted to the bar, they must pass a test of knowledge and
achievement   understanding of legal precepts. The test they take is an (*achievement/aptitude*) test.

10. If a law school can admit only forty out of several hundred applicants, an
aptitude   _____ test might be administered to determine which applicants have the greatest capacity to learn to become skilled lawyers.

11. Tests designed to measure skills already attained are called
achievement   _____ tests. Tests designed to predict what one can accomplish with training or to measure capacity to learn are called
aptitude   _____ tests.

ability   **12.** Both achievement and aptitude tests are tests of _____.

13. If test scores are to be used for scientific purposes, they must be *trustworthy.* In scientific terms this means that they must meet two requirements: *reliability* and

trustworthy

validity. Test scores that are not _____ are not likely to be regarded as useful by scientists.

14. If they are to be regarded as trustworthy, all test scores used for scientific purposes must meet two requirements. These two requirements are *reliability*

validity

and <u>val</u>_____.

15. By *reliability* we mean that the scores are dependable and reproducible, that they measure *consistently* whatever it is they measure. To be regarded as

reliability

trustworthy, test scores must have both _____

validity (either order)

and _____.

16. Test scores that measure consistently are said to have the characteristic of

reliability

_____, since the scores are dependable and reproducible.

17. Few of us would want to use a ruler made of rubber, because the measurements could vary considerably from one measurement to the next and would not give

reliability

consistent and reproducible results. Such measurements would lack _____.

18. A steel ruler, however, should give us consistent, dependable, and reproducible results from one measurement to the next and would therefore have the charac-

reliability

teristic of _____.

19. Psychologist X has developed a new intelligence test, which she has administered to a large group of students. She administered the same test twice to the same group of students and found that the pattern of scores on the second test compared quite closely to the pattern on the first test. Because her test gave consistent results, which are dependable and reproducible, her test presumably

reliability

has _____.

20. By reliability we mean that the scores are dependable and reproducible, that

consistently

they measure _____ whatever it is they measure.

21. By *validity* we mean that the test scores measure what the tester *intended* to measure. For instance, if your instructor desires to measure what you have learned in this course and the test does measure your actual achievement, the

validity

test has the characteristic of _____.

22. If your instructor desires to measure knowledge achieved in the course, but the test measures your intelligence rather than your achievement, he is not measuring what he intended to measure and the test therefore would lack

validity

_____.

23. By validity we mean that the test scores measure what the tester

intended

_____ to measure.

reliability	**24.** By _____ we mean that the scores measure consistently whatever it is they measure; by _____ we mean that the scores measure what the tester intended to measure.
validity	
	25. A test may be reliable but invalid. That is, a test may measure consistently yet
intended	not measure what the tester _____ to measure.
	26. Suppose that a psychologist designed a new test intended to measure intelligence. He administered the same test to the same subjects on two occasions and found that the scores for all subjects on both occasions were quite consistent, but that his test results correlated poorly with those of well-established intelli-
validity	gence tests. His test has reliability but probably lacks _____.
	27. The psychologist, in attempting to learn how reliable his new test is, administered it twice to the same group of students. To compare the first and second sets of scores, he needs to know the *degree of relationship* between the two sets of scores. This relationship is provided by the *correlation coefficient* (commonly abbreviated as *r*), a term already familiar to you as a measure of the degree of correspondence between two sets of scores. In this case the correlation
coefficient	_____ between the two sets of scores is a *reliability coefficient*.
	28. To estimate the degree of relationship between two sets of scores in order to
reliability	find out how reliable a test is, we need a re_____ coefficient.
	29. Well-constructed psychological tests of ability commonly have reliability coefficients above *r* = .90. The psychologist who designed a new intelligence test
.90	should find an *r* of _____ or above for his test if it is to be considered as reliable as other well-constructed ability tests.
	30. To measure *validity* we must also have two scores for each person taking the test, one being the test score and the other a score on a *criterion* of some sort. For instance, if we designed a test of ability to sell life insurance and obtained
criterion	scores for a number of persons, we would also need a _____ of some sort, which in this case might be the total value of insurance policies sold by those taking the test.
	31. A criterion might be a standard selected as the goal to be achieved in a task, or a set of scores or other records against which the success of a predictive test is verified. For instance, if effective life insurance salesmen sell at least $100,000
criterion	of insurance in a year, this figure might serve as a standard, or _____.
	32. If we want to measure a test's validity, we need not only each person's score on
criterion	the test, but also his score on a _____ of some sort.
	33. To measure validity we need to derive the *degree of relationship* between test scores and a criterion measure. This correlation coefficient is known as a *validity coefficient*. The correlation coefficient that tells us how well the test measures
validity	what it is supposed to measure is a (*validity/reliability*) coefficient.

34. When we derive the degree of relationship between test scores and a criterion

validity

measure, we obtain a _____ coefficient.

35. In using test performance as a basis for selecting candidates, psychologists often use *critical scores.* These are scores selected after experience with tests used for a given purpose; persons scoring below the critical level are rejected as unlikely to

critical

succeed. A _____ score on a scholastic aptitude test for college students is one below which no candidate is accepted for admission to college.

36. Students applying for admission to college X must have achieved a total scholastic score that places them at or above the fortieth centile. This figure is a

critical

_____ score, since no students obtaining scores that place them below the fortieth centile gain admission to this particular college.

37. Alfred Binet invented the intelligence test as we know it and devised a scale of *mental age.* In Binet's system, *average* mental-age (MA) scores *correspond* to chronological age (CA), that is, to the age determined from the date of birth. Thus, a child of normal intelligence with a chronological age of ten should have a

mental

_____ age of ten.

38. A child with a chronological age of thirteen who has normal intelligence would

thirteen

also have a mental age of _____.

correspond

39. If a child has normal intelligence, his mental age will _____ to his chronological age.

Chronological

40. _____ age refers to the age determined from the date of birth.

41. A bright child's mental age is above his chronological age; one would expect,

below

then, that a dull child's mental age would be _____ his chronological age.

mental

42. A retarded child has a _____ age below his chronological age.

43. The *intelligence quotient* (IQ) is a convenient index of brightness. It expresses intelligence as a ratio of the mental age to chronological age:

$$IQ = 100 \ \frac{\text{Mental Age (MA)}}{\text{Chronological age (CA)}}$$

The 100 is used as a multiplier to remove the decimal point and to make the average IQ have a value of 100. If a child with a chronological age of nine has a

100

mental age of nine, his IQ or intelligence quotient, is _____.

44. What is Tim's IQ if his mental age is eight and his chronological age is ten?

80

_____

140

45. A child with an IQ *below 70* is considered *mentally subnormal.* A child with an IQ of *140 or above* is considered *gifted.* If Jill has a mental age of fourteen and a chronological age of ten, her IQ would be _____.

70

140

46. Persons with IQs below _____ are considered mentally subnormal; those with IQs of _____ or above are considered gifted.

47. As the text points out, however, these cut-off points are quite arbitrary. Whether a person with an IQ below 70 is considered mentally _____

subnormal

depends upon his or her social skills and the complexity of the environment in which he or she lives. Whether a person with an IQ above 140, supposedly a

gifted

_____ individual, succeeds in using his or her ability depends largely upon social adjustment and motivation.

48. Two of the most widely used intelligence tests are the *Stanford-Binet* and the

Binet

Wechsler Intelligence Scale. The Stanford-_____ is a revision of the

Binet

earlier test devised by Alfred _____.

Stanford

49. The _____-Binet Intelligence Test, like the earlier Binet

mental

tests, is a _____-*age scale.* It consists of a number of different

age

items at each *age level.* The number of test items passed at each _____ level determines the child's *mental-age score.*

Intelligence Scale

50. The Wechsler _____ _____ is *not* a mental-age scale. The test items are grouped according to *type* of item rather

level

than age _____. The child obtains *separate* scores on twelve subtests. Six of these subtests are *verbal,* testing such abilities as mathematical reasoning,

subtests

vocabulary, and recall of series of digits; the other six sub_____ are nonverbal, or *performance,* tests that involve assembling picture puzzles, manipulating blocks to form specific designs, or recognizing the missing detail in a

Wechsler

picture. The final IQ score on the _____

Intelligence

_____ Scale is obtained by averaging all the

subtest

sub_____ scores. Separate IQ scores can also be obtained for the sum of the verbal tests and for the sum of the performance tests.

51. Since the test provides more information about a child's abilities than just

age

a single mental-_____score, or IQ score, the Weschler

Intelligence Scale

_____ _____ is frequently used for diagnostic pur-

verbal

poses. By analyzing the scores on both the _____

performance (either order)

subtests and the _____ subtests, it is possible to determine a child's special abilities and weaknesses.

mental-age

52. To recapitulate: the Stanford-Binet is a _____-_____ scale; it

does not

(*does/does not*) group test items according to type so as to permit a diagnostic analysis of different abilities. A test that does provide separate scores for various

Wechsler Intelligence
Scale

subtests is the _____ _____ _____.

53. Christina is having trouble coping with the work in second grade. Her teacher suspects that she is quite bright but that difficulty in recognizing visual patterns hinders her reading. Of the two intelligence tests we have discussed, the

Wechsler Intelligence

_____ _____

Scale

_____ might provide more helpful information than the

Stanford-Binet

_____-_____.

54. What are the abilities that underlie intelligence? One method used to identify clusters of abilities that combine to make up the IQ scores obtained on tests

Stanford-Binet

such as the _____-_____ and the Wechsler Intelligence Scale is called *factor analysis.*

analysis

55. Factor _____ is a statistical procedure used to determine the *common factors* that contribute to a body of data. (Also discussed in Chapter 13 of the text.) The same people are given a large number of tests, each individual test composed of similar items. The scores on all the tests are then intercorrelated. If two tests correlate highly with each other, they have a lot in *common* with each other. Tests that show high intercorrelations have much in

common

_____ with each other.

little

56. Tests that have low intercorrelations would have (*little/much*) in common with each other.

factor

57. This is the basic method of _____ analysis. It is a statistical procedure that provides a systematic way of finding a small number of *common factors* that can account for a large array of intercorrelations.

analysis

58. Factor _____ attempts to discover underlying traits or abilities that produce intelligence test results. In one study by Thurstone an analysis of more than sixty different tests yielded seven *primary abilities.* These

common

primary abilities were the _____ factors that emerged from the

factor

application of _____ analysis.

primary

59. Thurstone concluded that these _____ abilities were the basic abilities that comprise intelligence.

60. A later investigator, Guilford, also used factor analysis and found many more abilities underlying intelligence. Guilford found more abilities than did

Thurstone

Th_____ because he broadened the concept of intelligence beyond that measured by the usual IQ test.

61. The usual IQ test measures *convergent thinking,* that is, thinking that leads to a specific "correct" answer. A test item such as "How many eggs in a dozen?"

convergent   measures con_____ thinking, since it requires a specific correct answer.

62. The question "What is the capital of Italy?" measures _____ thinking, since it requires a specific _____ answer.

convergent

correct

63. Guilford proposed that *divergent thinking,* which is concerned with many "possible" answers rather than a specific correct answer, is an important aspect of intelligence. Divergent thinking is more creative than convergent thinking because it is concerned with many _____ answers.

possible

64. The question "How many uses can you think of for a paper clip?" asks for a number of possible answers and is thus a measure of _____ thinking.

divergent

65. The item "Imagine all of the things that might happen if the force of gravity suddenly disappeared" is a measure of _____ thinking.

divergent

66. Convergent thinking is concerned with a specific _____ answer, while divergent thinking is concerned with many _____ answers.

correct

possible

67. Intelligence tests consist primarily of questions that require _____ thinking.

convergent

68. A question frequently debated is "How much of our intelligence is *innate* and how much is *acquired* through experience?" One way to find evidence on this question is to compare the IQs of people who are *related genetically.* If people who are related _____ are no more alike in IQ than total strangers, then we would assume that intelligence is entirely (*innate/acquired*).

genetically

acquired

69. Studies of this type generally have found that the closer the genetic relationship, the more similar the IQ. Thus, the average correlation between the IQs of identical twins is about .90, while the average correlation between the IQs of siblings who are not twins is about .55. Since identical twins are closer genetically than ordinary siblings (having developed from the same ovum), these results indicate that there (*is/is not*) a genetic component to intelligence.

is

70. But if identical twins are reared from birth in different homes, the correlation between their IQs is not as high as if they were raised together. This finding points to the importance of (*heredity/environment*) in the development of intelligence.

environment

71. Experts differ in the importance they attribute to genetic and to environmental factors in the determination of intelligence. But it is clear that an individual's tested IQ depends upon both h_____ and en_____.

heredity

environment

TERMS AND CONCEPTS FOR IDENTIFICATION

aptitude test _____

_____

_____

_____

achievement test _____

_____

_____

_____

test battery _____

_____

_____

reliability _____

_____

_____

_____

validity _____

_____

_____

_____

reliability coefficient_____

_____

_____

_____

validity coefficient _____

_____

_____

_____

critical score _____

_____

_____

_____

basal mental age _____

_____

_____

_____

intelligence quotient (IQ) _____

_____

_____

_____

factor analysis _____

_____

_____

_____

convergent thinking _____

_____

_____

_____

divergent thinking _____

_____

_____

_____

heritability _____

_____

_____

_____

mentally retarded _____

_____

_____

_____

mentally defective _____

_____

_____

_____

_____ 1. When IQ changes over a lifetime are examined for large numbers of adults, it is found that
   a. mental ability peaks at age 21, then steadily declines
   b. the decline after age 60 is very steep because most people show physical deterioration after that age
   c. some people show an increase in IQ after age 26
   d. mental abilities requiring speed tend to peak between ages 20 and 25

_____ 2. The intellectually gifted children studied by Terman were _____
   a. comparatively pale and sickly
   b. mostly ahead of their age group in school
   c. socially introverted
   d. all of the above

_____ 3. According to the intelligence quotient index suggested by Stern and adopted by Terman, IQ is computed as
   a. $100 \dfrac{\text{Mental Age}}{\text{Chronological Age}}$
   b. $100 \dfrac{\text{Chronological Age}}{\text{Basal Mental Age}}$
   c. $100 \dfrac{\text{Basal Mental Age}}{\text{Chronological Age}}$
   d. $100 \dfrac{\text{Mental Age}}{\text{Basal Mental Age}}$

_____ 4. In measuring abilities we need ways of considering both present and potential ones. Which of the following is *not* a true statement?
   a. aptitude tests and achievement tests are both ability tests
   b. achievement tests measure accomplished skills
   c. aptitude tests measure capacity to learn
   d. intelligence tests are intended to be achievement tests

_____ 5. In considering public attacks on psychological testing, it is worth noting that
   a. among the lower class, blacks favor the use of ability tests in job selection more than do whites

   b. intelligence tests are excellent predictors of success in life
   c. test scores are the only indications children have of their own intelligence
   d. all of the above

_____ 6. _____ developed the first tests designed to measure intelligence.
   a. Alfred Binet
   b. Lewis Terman
   c. Sir Francis Galton
   d. Louis Thurstone

_____ 7. Guilford's structure-of-intellect model of intelligence is notable because
   a. it separates operations from content and product
   b. it rejects the idea of a general factor
   c. it yields 120 unique intellectual factors
   d. all of the above

_____ 8. It is important to note that heritability estimates for intelligence
   a. are always above .65
   b. apply to populations but not to individuals
   c. imply that environmental conditions are not important
   d. all of the above

_____ 9. A good test must be trustworthy, i.e., it must be both reliable and valid. In considering these qualities we note that
   a. scores are reliable if scores on half the test correlate highly with the other half
   b. valid scores are those that are reproducible
   c. the reliability of scores is tested by use of criterion scores
   d. a test cannot be reliable without being valid

_____ 10. The concepts of convergent and divergent thinking help our understanding of the complexities of intelligence testing. It has been found, for example, that
   a. convergent thinking tests are a good measure of creativity
   b. highly intelligent people are certain to show up as highly creative
   c. divergent thinking is closely related to creativity

d. creativity is not related to intelligence

11. The National Merit Scholarship Qualifying Test
     a. is an achievement test, since it measures the effectiveness of prior schooling
     b. is an aptitude test, since it predicts success in college quite well
     c. illustrates the blurring of the distinction between aptitude and achievement tests
     d. all of the above

12. In the contemporary versions of the Stanford-Binet tests, basal mental age is
     a. set at 21 years for the adult tests
     b. the level at which a child passes all items
     c. computed by adding two months for every correct answer in the level above the child's own age
     d. the mean level of performance for all children of a particular age

13. In studying the stability of IQ over time (i.e., as one gets older), it has been found that IQ tests at age
     a. 7 predict one's IQ at age 18 well
     b. 2 do not predict one's IQ at age 7 well
     c. 18 predict one's adult IQ well
     d. all of the above

14. The most important criterion of whether an individual should be considered retarded is that individual's
     a. social competence
     b. mental age
     c. IQ
     d. ability to learn to speak

15. A critical score might be used in
     a. determining the validity coefficient of a test
     b. selecting applicants for admission to graduate training
     c. determining the reliability coefficient of a test
     d. all of the above

16. Psychologists who use the technique of factor analysis see intelligence as
     a. a general capacity for comprehension and reasoning
     b. a generally invalid concept

c. an array of correlated special abilities
d. all of the above

17. In seeking to understand the influence of genetics in IQ, we examine family members and environment in various combinations. When we do, we find that the correlation between the IQs of identical twins reared apart in separate homes is _____ the correlation between the IQs of fraternal twins raised together.
     a. higher than
     b. about the same as
     c. less than
     d. only half as great as

18. The proposed classification of mentally defective, as compared to mentally retarded,
     a. means the same but sounds more medical
     b. implies defective genetics are the cause of the problem
     c. implies some identifiable defect in the nervous system
     d. applies to those with IQs below 30

19. Thurstone objected to Spearman's conclusions but used his methodology, factor analysis. With it he identified
     a. the general intelligence factor (g) involved in intelligence
     b. seven primary mental abilities
     c. 120 unique intellectual factors
     d. over 30 special factors important in intelligence

20. The assumptions of an intelligence test
     a. include the expectation that it predicts other important performances
     b. can never be strictly met
     c. include the subject's familiarity with the standard language of the test
     d. all of the above

KEY TO SELF-QUIZ

20. d	15. b	10. c	5. a
19. b	14. a	9. a	4. d
18. c	13. d	8. b	3. a
17. a	12. b	7. d	2. b
16. c	11. d	6. c	1. c

CLASS EXERCISE

INDIVIDUAL DIFFERENCES

Introduction

Despite the fact that humans resemble one another in some fundamental ways, they also differ from one another in many important characteristics, such as skills, attitudes, intelligence, aptitudes, interests, and personality. In many practical situations, as in the selection of employees, the measurement of these individual differences is important, especially if one wishes to select the best performers and eliminate the poor performers at a given task. This exercise is intended to show that individual differences exist even on relatively simple tasks.

Equipment Needed

None

Procedure

When your instructor gives you instructions to begin, immediately rearrange the following scrambled sentences to make meaningful sentences. Write your meaningful sentence in the space provided below each scrambled sentence. You will be permitted ten minutes for this task. You may not be able to finish in the time allowed, but do the best you can.

1. MEN THEM LIVES GOOD DO AFTER THE THAT

   _____

2. EYES YOU THEIR UNTIL SHOOT OF WHITES DON'T SEE THE

   _____

3. THE HUMAN WORLD IS THING MOST FREE VALUABLE THE MIND THE IN

   _____

4. TELL YOUR DEVIL GO THE TO STYLE YARN YOUR AND LET

   _____

5. IT MOMENTS WE THAT RARE LIVE ONLY IS AT

   _____

6. DO MUCH TOO KNOWING ANSWERS NOT BLAME ME FOR THE ALL NOT

   _____

7. THE FAULTS CONSCIOUS IS OF TO NONE OF GREATEST BE

   _____

8. MISUNDERSTAND BETTER IS UNDERSTAND LOT A THAN TO LITTLE A IT TO

   _____

9. THE BOASTING IT OF THAT MADE OF CAN SUCCESS BE USE WORST IS

   _____

10. BETTER FOOLISH FOOL THAN WIT A WITTY A

_____

11. FIRST CURIOSITY OF LOT ONLY LOVE IS FOOLISHNESS AND A LITTLE A

_____

12. THE LAUGHTER OF ASTONISHING IS POWER

_____

13. MONEY UNHAPPINESS CURE CANNOT

_____

14. FAILURE GROWS WITH REPUTATION YOUR EVERY

_____

15. HOURS FOR MAN HIMSELF AND WILL HE ABOUT A LISTEN TO TALK

_____

16. THE NOBODY BELIEVE WILL ONE IS THE THING TRUTH

_____

17. MY TRUTH THE TO TELL OF JOKING IS WAY

_____

18. LIVING IS MAKES WORTH THAT LIFE PLEASURE NOT IT

_____

19. RIGHT BE RATHER PRESIDENT I HAD THAN

_____

20. VERY MINDS COMPLEX OF IDEAS SIMPLE WITHIN LIE REACH THE ONLY

_____

Total number unscrambled _____

Treatment of Data

1. The unscrambled sentences are given on page 296 of the Appendix; if your sentence is meaningful it need not have precisely the same word order as that given in the Appendix. Count the number of meaningful sentences you wrote from the scrambled sentences.

Enter your score where it reads "Total number unscrambled _____."

2. Your instructor will ask you to submit your score on a small slip of paper so that the data for the class as a whole can be plotted on the graph that appears on page 206.

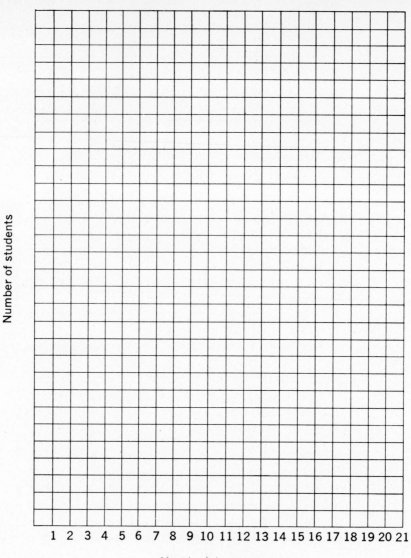

Number of students

1 2 3 4 5 6 7 8 9 10 11 12 13 14 15 16 17 18 19 20 21

Meaningful sentences

Questions For Discussion

1. Is the curve bell-shaped or skewed?

2. Is there a clustering around the central tendency?

3. Which of the scrambled sentences took the longest time to unscramble? Why?

4. What conclusions can you draw regarding individual differences in performing a simple task such as this?

5. What would you conjecture about the particular abilities of those students who unscrambled the most sentences in the time allotted?

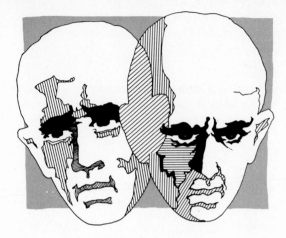

15
conflict, anxiety, and defense

LEARNING OBJECTIVES

Discuss sources of frustration and types of conflict.

Understand how the principles of approach and avoidance gradients explain ambivalent behavior.

Describe the immediate consequences of frustration.

Understand how the concept of anxiety helps explain reactions to frustration.

Describe and give examples of each of the defense mechanisms. Understand the ways in which defense mechanisms may hinder or help satisfactory adjustment.

PROGRAMMED UNIT

1. No matter how resourceful we may be in coping with problems, we are bound to encounter *frustration* and *conflict.* Frustrating situations vary all the way from petty annoyances to major defeats and disappointments. Frustration occurs when progress toward a *desired goal* is blocked or delayed. You have only a few minutes to catch a plane and you find yourself snarled in a traffic jam at the entrance to the airport. Since your progress toward a desired goal is blocked,

frustration   you are experiencing _____.

goal   2. Frustration occurs when progress toward a desired _____ is blocked or delayed. Frustration, as used in the text, refers to the *thwarting circumstances* rather than the emotional state that results from blocked goal-seeking.

3. There are many barriers to the attainment of goals. The physical environment presents such obstacles as floods and snowstorms; the social environment presents obstacles through the restrictions imposed by other people. All of these are

frustration   possible sources of _____.

4. Sometimes we are kept from reaching a desired goal because of our own *deficiencies* or *limitations.* You may want to become a professional musician, yet you don't have the ability. In this case, the source of frustration is your own

limitations   l_____.

frustration   5. If you set goals beyond your ability, then _____ will result. Another source of frustration is a *conflict* between two *opposing*

conflict   *goals* or *motives.* When two motives _____, frustration will result.

goal   6. Frustration refers to the blocking of progress toward a _____. It may

environment   result from obstacles in the physical or social en_____,

limitations   from personal deficiencies or l_____, or from

conflict   c_____ between two goals.

7. Sometimes the conflict is between a motive and a person's *internal standards* of

goals   behavior rather than between two external _____. Frank needs to pass chemistry in order to graduate and since he feels unsure of his ability, he is tempted to cheat on the exam. But he is deterred by the knowledge that he would feel ashamed if he did so. His conflict is between his desire to succeed and

standards   his internal _____ of what constitute acceptable behavior.

8. Most conflicts involve goals that are simultaneously desirable and undesirable, goals about which we feel *ambivalent.* You want to go to the movies but are worried about the consequences of lost study time. Your attitude toward a

ambivalent   possible evening at the movies is am_____.

9. Conflicts involving goals that are simultaneously desirable and

undesirable   un_____ are called *approach-avoidance* conflicts.

avoidance   10. One's attitude toward the goal in an approach-_____

ambivalent   conflict is _____. To be ambivalent is to both like and

dislike   _____ something at the same time.

11. In an approach-avoidance conflict the goal is both liked and

disliked   dis_____ at the same time. Approach-avoidance conflicts tend to result in *vacillation.* At some distance from the goal the positive aspects predominate and the person approaches; nearer to the goal the negative aspects become influential and the tendency is to withdraw. These conflicting tenden-

vacillation

cies may result in a period of _____ before a final decision is reached.

12. Frustration—whether it is the result of obstacles, personal limitations, or

conflicts

c_____—may have a number of immediate consequences. One common consequence is a state of *restlessness* and *tension.* Joan has neglected her studies throughout the semester and is now staying up late to cram for the final exam. If she chain smokes and frequently paces around her room,

tension

she is displaying restlessness and _____ as an immediate consequence of her frustration.

13. Restlessness and tension are common immediate consequences of

frustration

_____. Another immediate consequence may be destructiveness, or *aggression.* If Tommy kicks his older sister in the shins when

aggression

she takes his ball away from him, he is displaying _____ toward his sister as a consequence of frustration.

14. When a frustrated person directly attacks the frustrating object or person, we say he is displaying *direct* aggression. If after Tommy's sister takes the ball away

direct
is not

from him, he kicks her, he is displaying _____ aggression. If he kicks the door instead, he (*is/is not*) displaying direct aggression.

15. If we cannot satisfactorily express our aggression against the source of frustration, we may shift, or *displace,* the aggression toward an innocent person or object. Sandra, who is angry with her father, pulls the cat's tail. She is probably

displaced

exhibiting _____ aggression.

16. The football player who has caught and then dropped a pass stamps the ground.

displaced

This is an example of _____ aggression.

17. Sometimes when frustrated we may simply act indifferent or attempt to withdraw from the situation—that is, we may react with *apathy.* Ann, who has been told that she cannot attend a movie with her friends, does not display active aggression but goes to her room and sulks. Her behavior could be described as

apathy

_____, which is the opposite of aggression.

18. The immediate consequences of frustration we have discussed so far include

tension, displaced
apathy

restlessness and _____, direct or dis_____ aggression, and _____.

19. When problems become too much for us, we sometimes seek the "solution" of escape into a dream world, a solution through *fantasy* rather than through

more

realistic means. Fantasy is (*more/less*) difficult to observe directly than aggression.

20. Mr. L has just learned that another employee has been promoted to the job he was hoping to get. If Mr. L constructs a daydream in which he pictures his rival as being a complete failure in the new assignment, he is engaging in

fantasy

_____ as a consequence of frustration.

21. Joan, who postponed her studying until the night before the final exam, has learned that she has failed the exam and may have to leave school. She returns to her room, shuts the door, and sits quietly staring out the window. Based on her *observed* behavior, we can say that, of the four immediate consequences of frustration we have studied so far, Joan is *not* displaying

restlessness (or tension), aggression (either order)

apathy

fantasy

_____ or _____. However, she *might* be demonstrating _____ or engaging in _____.

22. Another possible consequence of frustration is *stereotypy* in behavior, that is, a tendency to *blind, repetitive, fixated* behavior. The same faulty behavior that produced the frustration is repeated again and again; the organism has lost its flexibility in problem-solving. Stereotypy is more easily identified in laboratory

aggression

animals than in human beings; in contrast, direct or displaced _____ can easily be observed in humans.

23. The tendency to blind, repetitive, fixated behavior, called

stereotypy

_____, is another consequence of frustration.

24. Behavior in response to frustration sometimes shows a childish quality. Such behavior, in which the individual returns to behavior patterns characteristic of an earlier stage of development, is called *regression*. A return to thumb-sucking or a lapse in toilet training in a young child may be an example of

regression

_____ as a consequence of frustration.

25. We have examined six behavior patterns that may occur as immediate conse-

restlessness

quences of frustration. These are _____ and

tension, direct

_____, aggression (either _____ or

displaced, apathy, fantasy
stereotypy, regression
(any order)

_____), _____, _____, _____, and _____.

26. In explaining these reactions to frustration psychologists use the concept of *anxiety.* Any situation that threatens a person's well-being is assumed to produce a state of anxiety. Conflicts and other types of frustration threaten a person's

anxiety

feeling of well-being and thus create a state of _____.

27. Threats of physical harm or threats to one's self-esteem are also sources of

well-being

anxiety since they threaten a person's well-_____.

28. Any situation that threatens a person's well-being can produce

anxiety

_____. By anxiety we mean that unpleasant emotion characterized by the terms "worry," "apprehension," and "fear" that we all experience at times.

29. Because anxiety is an unpleasant _____ that threatens our

emotion

well-being

well-_____, we are motivated to do something to alleviate it.

30. One way of coping with anxiety is to take direct action to deal with the anxiety-producing situation. If you are anxious because you are about to fail a course, you can cope with your anxiety directly by finding out what you need to do to improve your grade and devising a plan for doing it. This is a (*direct/indirect*) method of coping with anxiety.

direct

31. Another way of coping with anxiety in this situation would be to refuse to acknowledge the possibility of failure or to convince yourself that the course is worthless so it doesn't matter whether you fail or not. Both of these alternatives

anxiety

are attempts to *defend* yourself against an_____ without dealing directly with the anxiety-producing situation. These indirect methods of coping with anxiety are called *defense mechanisms.*

mechanisms

32. Defense _____ are methods of coping with anxiety that *distort reality* in some way. They do not alter the objective situation; they simply change the way the person thinks about it.

33. Defense mechanisms are methods of coping with anxiety that

distort

dis_____ reality in some way. They do not change the anxiety-producing situation.

34. They are called defense mechanisms because they are ways of defending the

anxiety

individual against _____.

mechanisms

35. Two basic defense _____ are *denial* and *repression.* Denial of reality is a defense against external threat; the person tries to block out disturbing realities by refusing to acknowledge them.

36. A woman whose husband is unfaithful may refuse to admit to herself that anything is wrong even though she has ample evidence to the contrary. By

anxiety

denying reality she tries to defend herself against an_____.

37. The mother of a child who is fatally ill may refuse to admit that there is anything seriously wrong with her child even though she has been fully informed of the diagnosis and the expected outcome of the illness. In this case, the

denial

defense mechanism of _____ protects her against intolerable anxiety.

38. Repression is similar to denial but it refers to an *internal* threat. Impulses or

anxiety

memories that might cause unbearable _____ are excluded from conscious awareness.

repression

39. Denial is a defense against external threat, while _____ is a defense against internal threat.

40. A young woman feels intensely hostile toward her mother. But because such feelings are totally inconsistent with her concept of herself as a loving daughter, they would cause anxiety if she were aware of them. Consequently, her feelings

repressed

of hostility are re_____ and banished from memory.

41. A young boy was partially responsible for his brother's death. As an adult he has no memory for the events surrounding the tragedy. This is another example of

repression

_____.

distorting

42. Both denial and repression defend against anxiety by _____

external

reality. Denial usually refers to an individual's defense against an _____ threat by refusing to acknowledge some disturbing aspect of reality; repression

internal

usually refers to an individual's defense against an _____ threat by banishing anxiety-producing impulses or memories from conscious awareness.

43. George is frequently criticized by his employers for poor workmanship, but he fails to perceive their dissatisfaction or to admit to himself that there is anything wrong with his work. This would most likely be considered an example of

denial

(*denial*/*repression*).

44. Lucy felt very jealous and resentful of her younger sister and often wished something fatal would happen to her. If, as an adult, Lucy has no memory of

repression

these feelings, one would assume that _____ has occurred.

mechanisms

45. Repression and denial are the two basic defense _____. The text discusses six additional defense mechanisms that may be used to aid denial or repression. They help keep anxiety-producing thoughts from awarness

reality

by distorting re_____ in some way. They include (1) *rationalization*, (2) *projection*, (3) *reaction formation*, (4) intellectualization, (5) *undoing*, and (6) *displacement*.

46. Assigning logical reasons or plausible excuses for what we do impulsively is known as *rationalization*. The statement, "I'd have been here on time but my

rationalization

alarm clock didn't go off," might very well be a _____.

47. A young boy refuses to share his candy with his younger sister and gives as the reason, "If I give her some candy, it will only make her teeth decay." If the boy is giving a "good" reason but not the "true" reason for not sharing, he is using

rationalization

the defense mechanism of _____.

rationalization

48. In _____ we give "good" reasons but not "true" reasons for our behavior.

49. In *projection* we protect ourselves from recognizing our own *undesirable* qualities by assigning them in an exaggerated amount to other people, thereby justifying our own tendencies. If a man says, "You can't trust people any farther than you can throw them," it is possible that he himself has been untrustworthy in the past and is attempting to protect himself from acknowledging his own

projection

failings by using the mechanism of _____.

projection

50. In the defense mechanism known as _____, we attribute to others traits we find undesirable in ourselves.

51. Sally is overly critical but does not readily acknowledge this as one of her traits. She is overheard saying that her roommate is a very critical person. Sally is attributing to another individual an undesirable trait that she herself possesses.

projection

This illustrates the mechanism of _____.

52. In projection we protect ourselves from recognizing our own

undesirable

_____ qualities by assigning them in an exaggerated amount to other people.

53. "Most people cheat on examinations," says Mark. In order to justify his own unacknowledged tendencies, he is assuring himself that everyone else cheats on

projection

examinations. This example also illustrates _____.

54. In *reaction formation* we *conceal a motive* from ourselves by giving strong expression to its *opposite.* The mother who unconsciously resents the demands and restrictions upon her time that result from having a child may be excessively fussy and particular in her care of the child, devoting more time than is necessary. She conceals her real feelings through the mechanism of

formation

reaction _____.

55. Concealing a motive by giving strong expression to its opposite describes the

reaction formation

defense mechanism known as _____ _____.

56. When we conceal a motive by giving strong expression to its

opposite

_____, we are using the defense mechanism known as reaction formation.

57. Mrs. Z, once an alcoholic but now a teetotaler, is an ardent prohibitionist and engages in a personal crusade to convert everyone from drinking any kind of alcoholic beverage. She may be displaying the defense mechanism called

reaction formation

_____ _____.

58. *Intellectualization* is an attempt to gain *detachment* from an emotionally threatening situation by dealing with it in abstract, intellectual terms. A young man watches his mother slowly die from cancer. In talking about her death to a friend he focuses on the medical details of her condition and treatment. He is

intellectualization

using intell_____ to defend against very stressful emotions.

detachment

59. In intellectualization the person tries to gain de_____ from an emotionally threatening situation by dealing with it in abstract,

intellectual

_____ terms.

60. The defense mechanism whereby we assign logical reasons or plausible excuses

rationalization

for what we do impulsively is known as _____.

61. An individual who attributes to others qualities that he finds undesirable in

projection

himself is engaging in _____.

62. When we try to detach ourselves from an emotionally threatening situation by dealing with it in abstract, intellectual terms, we are using

intellectualization

_____ as a defense mechanism.

63. Concealing a motive by giving strong expression to its opposite is known as

reaction formation

_____ _____.

anxiety

reality

repression

64. All of these mechanisms are ways of protecting oneself against _____ by distorting _____ to some extent. They may be used as aids to the basic defense mechanisms of denial and re_____ which block the anxiety-producing feelings completely from awareness.

65. In repression an impulse or memory that might provoke feelings of *anxiety* or *guilt* is completely banished from awareness. A ten-year-old boy has strong feelings of hostility and resentment toward his father. Yet he has been brought up to feel that one should love one's parents. To protect himself from anxiety

guilt

repression

and g_____ he has succeeded in burying these feelings of hostility and is not aware they exist. The defense mechanism known as _____ is operating in this case.

66. Refusal to acknowledge an unpleasant or anxiety-producing situation is similar to repression, in that it keeps the unpleasant thoughts out of awareness. In this

denial

case, the mechanism is called _____ because it defends against external rather than internal threat.

67. Two additional defense mechanisms discussed in the text are *undoing* and *displacement.* Undoing refers to *ritualistic* and *repetitive* actions designed to prevent or atone for some unacceptable thought or impulse. Washing one's hands every time thoughts of unacceptable sexual impulses occur would be an example

undoing

of un_____.

68. In displacement a motive whose gratification is blocked in one form is *displaced* or directed into a different, more *socially acceptable* channel. If one's hostile impulses are expressed in boxing or wrestling, this is an example of

displacement

dis_____. Sexual impulses that cannot be expressed directly may be expressed indirectly in such creative activities as art and

displacement

music. This is another example of _____.

69. Freud felt that displacement was the most satisfactory way of handling blocked aggressive and sexual impulses, because it allowed these impulses to be expressed

acceptable

indirectly in more socially _____ forms.

70. To the extent that defense mechanisms help a person through difficult times until he can learn more *mature* and *realistic* ways of coping with

anxiety

_____-producing situations, they contribute toward satisfactory adjustment.

71.   If, however, the individual continues to rely upon defense mechanisms so that he

mature   is never forced to learn more m_____ and realistic ways of behaving,
then such mechanisms would constitute a barrier to satisfactory adjustment.

TERMS AND CONCEPTS FOR IDENTIFICATION

frustration_____

_____

_____

_____

conflict _____

_____

_____

_____

ambivalence_____

_____

_____

_____

approach-avoidance conflict _____

_____

_____

_____

displaced aggression _____

_____

_____

_____

learned helplessness _____

_____

_____

_____

stereotypy_____

_____

_____

_____

regression _____

_____

_____

_____

objective anxiety _____

_____

_____

_____

neurotic anxiety _____

_____

_____

_____

defense mechanism_____

_____

_____

_____

denial _____

_____

_____

_____

repression_____

_____

_____

_____

rationalization _____

_____

_____

_____

projection_____

_____

_____

_____

reaction formation _____

_____

_____

_____

intellectualization _____

_____

_____

_____

undoing _____

_____

_____

_____

displacement _____

_____

_____

_____

_____ 1. Amnesia is a striking form of behavior which illustrates some aspects of the defense mechanism called
   a. displacement
   b. undoing
   c. reaction formation
   d. repression

_____ 2. If you find these questions too difficult, and respond by telling yourself psychology is all nonsense anyway, you are relieving your anxiety by
   a. direct coping
   b. defensive coping
   c. hostile aggression
   d. projection

_____ 3. Studies have been made of inmates of concentration or prisoner-of-war camps, who are subjected to frustrating conditions of long duration from which there is no hope of escape. Such studies show that the most common reaction to these conditions is
   a. scapegoating
   b. fantasy
   c. apathy
   d. stereotyping

_____ 4. The text points out that defense mechanisms are not simply sources of problems; they also contribute to satisfactory adjustment in several ways. Which of the following is *not* one of these ways?
   a. intellectualization may lead to future intelligent conduct
   b. they permit experimentation with new roles
   c. they give us time to solve problems that might otherwise overwhelm us
   d. rationalization may lead to future rational conduct

_____ 5. The text defines frustration as
   a. an unpleasant emotional state that results from blocked goal-seeking
   b. thwarting circumstances
   c. obstacles presented by the social environment
   d. obstacles presented by the physical environment

_____ 6. The text points out three important precautions to be kept in mind when considering defense mechanisms. Which of the following is *not* one of them?
   a. all of them are found in everyday behavior of normal people
   b. a label for behavior is not an explanation of it
   c. there is no experimental evidence for any of them
   d. defense mechanisms are psychological constructs

_____ 7. Regression may be interpreted as
   a. retrogressive behavior
   b. primitivation
   c. a return to earlier behavior patterns
   d. all of the above

_____ 8. The defense mechanism that best serves its function of reducing anxiety while still allowing some gratification of the unacceptable motive is
   a. displacement
   b. rationalization
   c. intellectualization
   d. reaction formation

_____ 9. The common element in defense mechanisms is
   a. primitivation
   b. self-deception
   c. covert aggression
   d. undoing

_____ 10. Studies on approach and avoidance gradients help us to understand how we can be repeatedly drawn into an old conflict situation. This happens, in part at least, because in such circumstances the
   a. tendency to approach a positive goal is stronger further away from it
   b. tendency to avoid a negative goal is stronger further away from it
   c. avoidance gradient tends to be steeper than the approach gradient
   d. all of the above

_____ 11. When subjects respond to a posthypnotic suggestion, they sometimes feel so embar-

rassed that they _____
the behavior.
a. repress
b. rationalize
c. project
d. displace

_____ 12. In Freud's view, defense mechanisms "defend" by
a. keeping certain impulses out of awareness
b. gratifying the id's impulses
c. strengthing the superego
d. all of the above

_____ 13. In our society the most pervasive and difficult approach-avoidance conflicts occur in three areas. Which of the following is *not* one of them?
a. impulse expression vs. moral standards
b. independence vs. dependence
c. cooperation vs. competition
d. privacy vs. social gregariousness

_____ 14. If you suspect the local, self-appointed censors of enjoying all the pornography they must read in order to protect you, you don't just call them dirty old men (women); you exercise your new knowledge and say they are displaying the defense mechanism of
a. undoing
b. reaction formation
c. suppression
d. regression

_____ 15. "Scapegoating" as an outcome of frustration illustrates a typical response, called _____ aggression.
a. direct
b. frustrated
c. instrumental
d. displaced

_____ 16. According to the learning-theory approach, a lifelong fear of dogs that stems from a frightening experience with a dog in childhood persists because
a. it occurred during a critical period in development
b. it was reinforced by later experiences with snarling dogs

c. by avoiding dogs the person never learns that most dogs are friendly
d. people can fool themselves into thinking they are afraid

_____ 17. One of the first and most general responses to frustration by children in the half-toy experiment was
a. an excess of restless behavior
b. crying
c. passive refusal to play with the half toys
d. a demand to end the play and go home

_____ 18. It is possible to solve personal problems rationally. We often do not, however, because
a. sometimes our motives distort our view of the problem
b. the problem may not have a rational solution
c. our emotions may keep us from seeing some of the evidence necessary to solve the problem
d. all of the above

_____ 19. Freud was one of the first theorists to focus on the importance of anxiety. He
a. differentiated between objective anxiety and neurotic anxiety
b. viewed neurotic anxiety as synonymous with fear
c. felt objective anxiety stemmed from an unconscious conflict
d. all of the above

_____ 20. One example of a defense mechanism as a helpful coping device is the use by doctors and nurses of the mechanism of
a. repression
b. displacement
c. intellectualization
d. rationalization

KEY TO SELF-QUIZ

20. c	15. d	10. c	5. b
19. a	14. b	9. b	4. a
18. d	13. d	8. a	3. c
17. a	12. a	7. d	2. b
16. c	11. b	6. c	1. d

INDIVIDUAL EXERCISES

A. REACTIONS TO FRUSTRATION

Introduction

People react differently to stress and frustration. The text discusses some of the immediate reactions to, and ways of coping with, frustrating situations. This exercise should help you analyze your own responses to frustration.

Equipment Needed

None

Procedure

1. Think back over the past two months and list any occasions on which you were frustrated either by other people or by circumstances. Some of these events may be trivial (e.g., you were late to class because you failed to awake in time or your car wouldn't start); others may be major disappointments (e.g., you failed a test in an important course or were rejected by someone you love). If you can't recall any frustrations during the past two months, you lead a blessed life or are good at repressing unpleasant experiences. Whatever the reason, keep going back in time until you have listed five to ten frustrating experiences. Write down a few phrases to identify each episode. Don't read further until you have recalled at least five or more events.

2. Now think about each event and try to recall your immediate reactions (e.g., anger, tension, feelings of helplessness) and your method of coping with your feelings (e.g., tried to forget about the situation, went out for a milk shake and pizza, went to a movie, sought the comfort of friends, took some action to remedy the situation). You may have had more than one reaction to each situation; if so, list all your reactions.

3. Examine your list of reactions. Do you discern a characteristic way of handling frustration?

4. As a final step keep a record for the coming week, listing any frustrating situations and your reactions as they occur.

Questions For Discussion

1. Was it difficult to recall past reactions to frustration? If so, why do you think this is the case?

2. Did you notice any difference in reactions recorded for earlier events and those recorded for the past week? If so, what factors might contribute to this difference?

3. Does your increased awareness of your reactions to frustration make it easier to change the way you respond?

B. RATIONALIZATION

Complete each of the following sentences with the first answer that comes to mind. Work quickly without pondering your responses. No one else need see them.

1. My grades would be higher if _____

_____

_____ .

2. I would feel more comfortable in social situations if

_____

_____

_____ .

3. I would be more popular with the opposite sex if __

_____

_____ .

4. I would have done better in my last exam in this course if _____

_____

_____ .

5. I would have achieved more honors and recognition for extracurricular activities if _____

_____

_____ .

6. Sometimes my grades are lower than they should be because _____

_____

_____ .

7. I could work better if _____

_____

_____

8. I do not engage in many extracurricular activities because _____

_____

_____ .

9. I would have more friends if _____

_____

_____ .

10. I could manage my finances better if _____

_____

_____ .

Someone else looking at your answers might discern some evidence of rationalization—the tendency we all have to give "rational" and "good" explanations rather than "true" reasons. (See page 444 in the text for some examples of rationalization.) Examine each of your answers above carefully and objectively, as if you were an outside observer. Do you find any evidence of rationalization—instances where the reasons you give are not exactly the real ones? In which, if any, areas of your life are you more likely to use this defense?

16 psychopathology

LEARNING OBJECTIVES

Know the four criteria that enter into the definition of abnormality as well as the characteristics that are considered indicative of good mental health.

Be able to define and distinguish among the various forms of psychopathology described in the text.

Describe how anxiety is handled in each of the neurotic reactions.

Understand the distinction between organic and functional disorders, between process and reactive schizophrenia, and between conversion reactions and psychophysiological disorders.

Be familiar with research on the causes of schizophrenia.

PROGRAMMED UNIT

1. The term *psychopathology* covers a wide variety of disorders in which a person's behavior is considered *abnormal*. But defining what we mean by abnormal is

abnormal

difficult. The word itself, ab_____, means *"away from the norm."* So one definition of abnormality is any behavior that is *statistically*

norm

infrequent or deviant from the n_____.

2. But this definition is not completely satisfactory. People who are very gifted intellectually or unusually well adjusted deviate from the norm in the sense of

infrequent

being statistically (*frequent/infrequent*), yet we would not consider them abnormal.

3. A second method of classifying behavior as normal or abnormal is by determining whether the behavior is in accord with *society's standards.* Anthropological studies have revealed, however, that what is considered normal in one society may be considered abnormal in another. Therefore, this definition of abnormality, which really constitutes a *social* definition, also has its limitations. For example, homosexuality is considered normal behavior in some cultures, but

abnormal   in other cultures it is considered _____.

statistical   **4.** A definition of abnormality in terms of st_____
frequency is not satisfactory because some very desirable traits may fall outside

social   the normal range. Likewise, we cannot be content with a _____
definition of abnormality, since the standards of normality and abnormality vary
from one culture to the next.

5. A third definition of abnormality is based on *adaptiveness of behavior.* Behavior
is abnormal if it is *maladaptive;* that is, if it has adverse effects either for the
individual or for society. According to this definition a person who is so fearful
of enclosed places that he cannot enter an elevator or a windowless room would

maladaptive   be considered abnormal because his behavior is mal_____;
it has adverse effects for him.

6. A person whose anger explodes in assaultive attacks on others would also be
considered abnormal by this definition, because his behavior has adverse effects

society   for s_____.

7. A fourth criterion looks at abnormality from the viewpoint of the individual's
subjective feelings—his *personal distress*—rather than his behavior. According to
this criterion a person who functions very effectively at his job and whose
behavior appears quite normal to observers, may still be considered

abnormal   _____ if he feels acutely miserable most of the time.

8. A fourth definition looks at abnormality in terms of the individual's personal

distress   _____ rather than his behavior.

9. Our four definitions of abnormality take into account statistical

frequency, society   f_____, the standards of _____, adap-

behavior, distress   tiveness of _____, and personal _____.
In most instances all four criteria are used in diagnosing psychopathology.

abnormality   **10.** Normality is even more difficult to define than _____.
Some of the characteristics discussed in the text as possessed *to a greater
degree* by normal individuals than by those diagnosed as abnormal include an
efficient perception of reality, self-knowledge and *self-acceptance,* ability to
control one's behavior and to *form affectionate relationships,* and *productivity.*
These characteristics do not distinguish sharply between the mentally healthy
and the mentally ill; they are simply traits that the normal person possesses to a

greater   _____ degree than one diagnosed as abnormal.

11. The major *diagnostic categories* of psychopathology, based on *behavioral symp-*

toms, include *neuroses, psychoses, psychophysiological disorders,* and *personality disorders.* Each of these is further divided into a number of subcategories,

symptoms

also based primarily on behavioral sym_____.

12. A major distinction is made between the *neuroses* (singular, *neurosis*) and the psychoses (singular, *psychosis*). The *neurotic* disorders are less severe than the *psychotic* disoders; they do *not* involve *personality disintegration* or *loss of contact with reality.* A person who is so disturbed that he cannot distinguish his own fantasies from reality would be classed as (*neurotic/psychotic*).

psychotic

13. The neurotic disorders may be viewed as exaggerated forms of the normal *defense mechanisms* used in an attempt to resolve a persistent conflict. When a person cannot achieve a realistic solution to a persistent conflict but instead habitually resorts to exaggerated forms of defense mechanisms to relieve his

neurotic

problems, he may be considered _____tic.

14. The neuroses are characterized by the habitual use of exaggerated forms of the

defense

normal _____ mechanisms in response to a persistent conflict.

15. Unresolved conflicts create *anxiety.* Consequently, it is not surprising that the

anxiety

chief symptom of neurosis is an_____.

16. We noted in the preceding chapter that defense mechanisms serve to protect our

anxiety

self-esteem and to defend against _____. A person who cannot resolve a persistent conflict either remains in a state of anxiety or resorts to

defense mechanisms

habitual use of one of the _____ _____, often in exaggerated form, to defend against anxiety.

17. Everyone resorts to defense mechanisms at one time or another. It is only when these defenses become the dominant method of handling problems that the

neurotic

person is called _____.

neuroses (or neurotics)

18. Anxiety is the chief symptom of the _____. Sometimes the anxiety is very obvious—the individual appears tense, restless, and may be unable to eat or sleep. *Anxiety reactions* are a type of neurosis in which the chief

anxiety

symptom, _____, is obvious.

anxiety

19. In the type of neurosis called _____ reactions the person habitually appears tense and restless, and reacts to even the slightest difficulty with strong feelings of anxiety.

20. Since the unresolved conflicts that underlie a neurosis are frequently *unconscious,* persons suffering from anxiety reactions usually have no clear idea of why they feel so tense and apprehensive. The reasons behind their anxieties are

unconscious

often un_____.

21. When a person feels tense and anxious much of the time without being able to

anxiety reaction

specify exactly what he is afraid of, he is suffering from an _____

_____.

22. In anxiety reactions the person's anxiety is quite apparent. In another **type** of neurosis, called *conversion reaction,* the anxiety is *converted* into *physical*

symptoms

symptoms. These physical _____ have no organic cause; they serve unconscious purposes of the patient.

23. A pilot becomes afraid to fly following an emergency landing in which he nearly lost his life. He develops a paralysis of the right arm for which the doctors can

conversion

find no organic basis. This is an example of a _____ reaction.

24. A woman is afraid that her husband may leave her. She suddenly loses her sight so that she is totally dependent upon his care. Since no physical cause can be found for her blindness, this appears to be another case of a

conversion reaction

_____ _____.

physical

25. In conversion reactions anxiety is converted into _____ symptoms that serve unconscious purposes for the individual. It should be emphasized, however, that the person is not faking. In conversion

reactions

_____ the physical disability seems quite real to the

unconscious

person, and the purposes served are un_____.

26. In anxiety reactions the anxiety is quite obvious. In conversion reactions, however, the person usually seems calm and relaxed. His anxiety is

converted

_____ into physical symptoms. He may be somewhat concerned about his physical condition, but he is not overwhelmed by anxiety.

27. The chief symptom in all types of neurosis is anxiety. The anxiety may be

anxiety reaction

readily apparent, as in a(n) _____ _____,

conversion reaction

or it may be converted into physical symptoms, as in a(n) _____

_____.

reactions

28. A third type of neurosis is the *phobic* reaction. Phobic _____ are *excessive fears* of certain situations in the *absence of real danger.* Jane is so fearful of closed places that she will never take the elevator to her ninth-floor office but insists upon climbing the stairs instead. She has a

phobic reaction

_____ _____.

29. Tom is so fearful of fire that he cannot stay in a room in which there is a fire burning in the fireplace. Since Tom's fear is excessive in a situation in which

phobic reaction

there is no real danger, it is another example of a _____

_____.

absence

30. Phobic reactions are excessive fears in the _____ of real danger. The assumption is that the anxiety that stems from some other conflict in the individual's life is channeled into a highly specific fear.

anxiety

31. So far we have discussed three kinds of neurotic disorders: (1) _____

reactions, in which feelings of tension and anxiety are predominant;

conversion

(2) _____ reactions, in which the anxiety is con-

phobic

verted into a physical symptom; and (3) _____ reactions, in which the person experiences excessive, irrational fear in the absence of real danger. The fourth major type of neurosis is the *obsessive-compulsive* reaction.

32. *Obsessive-compulsive* reactions take three forms: (1) *obsessive thoughts,* (2) *compulsive acts,* and (3) a *combination* of obsessive thoughts and compulsive

obsessive

acts. You might guess that a person with _____ thoughts has persistently unwelcome, disturbing thoughts and that a person with a compulsion has an irresistible urge to repeat a certain stereotyped or *ritualistic*

act

_____.

33. *Obsessive thoughts* frequently involve aggressive or sexual impulses that are quite unacceptable to the conscious feelings of the person who has them. Because these unacceptable impulses would cause great anxiety if the person acknowledged them as his real feelings, they are repressed and appear as

obsessive

_____ thoughts that the individual experiences as not being really his own.

impulses

34. Obsessive thoughts thus involve unacceptable _____ that the person cannot acknowledge as his own.

35. A young mother had frequent thoughts of murdering her two small children. She professed nothing but love for them and maintained that "these awful thoughts that pop into my head" had nothing to do with her real feelings. In this case

obsessive

_____ thoughts protected the mother from the anxiety she would feel were she to acknowledge these impulses as her own.

36. *Compulsive acts* are stereotyped or ritualistic acts that are designed to protect the individual from feelings of anxiety or guilt. A young boy who suffered guilt feelings whenever he masturbated felt compelled to scrub his hands many times

compulsive

a day. In this case the _____ act served to relieve his feelings of guilt.

37. Obsessive thoughts and compulsive acts thus serve to protect the individual

anxiety

against _____ or guilt. They are characteristic of an

obsessive-compulsive

_____-_____ reaction.

38. We have discussed four types of neuroses, all of which are characterized by

anxiety, conversion

anxiety: (1) _____ reactions; (2) _____

phobic

reactions, in which anxiety is converted into physical symptoms; (3) _____ reactions, in which there is excessive fear in the absence of real danger; and

obsessive-compulsive

(4) _____-_____ reactions, in which a person has persistent, unpleasant thoughts or feels the need to perform a ritualistic act of some sort to ward off aggressive or sexual impulses he does not wish to acknowledge to himself.

39. A fifth type of neurotic reaction is *neurotic depression.* In neurotic

depression

de_____ the person reacts to a distressing event with more than the usual amount of sadness and fails to recover within a reasonable amount of time.

40. After losing her job Barbara spends all her time lying in bed and crying. She has no interest in anything, feels worthless, and contemplates suicide. Since her depression seems out of proportion to the precipitating event and shows no signs

neurotic

of improving, it would be classed as _____.

41. If, in addition to the above symptoms, Barbara becomes so immersed in her own thoughts and fantasies that she can no longer distinguish her fantasies from what is going on in the real world, she would be diagnosed as *psychotic* rather than

neurotic

n_____.

42. *Psychotic* disorders are much more serious than neuroses. The personality is disorganized and normal social functioning is greatly impaired. The psychotic individual often requires hospitalization. While the neurotic tries to cope with

psychotic

his anxiety in order to continue functioning, the p_____ is no longer able to function adequately and has lost contact with reality so that he can no longer distinguish between his fantasies and what is actually happening.

43. Some psychoses are due to *physical* damage or malfunctioning. These are called the *organic* psychoses. Others are called *functional* psychoses because no

physical

ph_____ basis for them has been demonstrated. Functional

psychoses

_____ are presumed to be primarily psychological in origin, although genetic and other biological factors may play a significant role.

44. *Manic-depressive* psychoses are a form of functional psychosis characterized by recurrent and exaggerated mood swings from the normal to either the depressive phase (deep depression) or the manic phase (wild excitement). If a person feels complete worthlessness and despondency, we might suspect that he is in the

manic-depressive

depressive phase of a _____-_____ psychosis.

45. Most people suffering from manic-depressive psychoses do not exhibit both phases of the mood cycle. They tend to swing from normal to one of the extreme phases. Thus, a person who at times felt normal and at other times felt

manic

deep depression, never showing the m_____ phase of the disorder, could still be classified as manic-depressive.

46. Schizophrenic psychoses are the most common of the functional psychoses and are characterized by a split between the thought processes and the emotions. For example, a schizophrenic may smile as he describes a sad event, showing an emotion that is inappropriate to the thought being expressed. *Withdrawal from*

schizophrenic

reality is also a common characteristic of a sch_____ psychosis.

schizophrenic

47. In a sch_____ psychosis a person may have

hallucinations. That is, he may hear voices or see visions that are not real. A person suffering from this disorder often seems to withdraw from r_____ity in order to build a more satisfying fantasy world of his own.

reality

48. Likewise, a schizophrenic may have *delusions,* which are simply *false beliefs* that are clung to in spite of contrary evidence and common sense. Do not confuse delusions with _____, such as "hearing voices," which refer to false *sensory perceptions* without an appropriate external stimulus.

hallucinations

49. Patient X thinks he is God and has come back to earth to save us. He is evidently experiencing a _____, since he is clinging to a false belief. Patient Y hears voices talking to her and threatening her that no one else hears. She is probably experiencing a _____.

delusion

hallucination

50. Delusions are false _____, whereas hallucinations are false sensory _____.

beliefs

perceptions

51. We have mentioned several *symptoms* of schizophrenia. The schizophrenic may experience *disturbances of affect,* which means that his affect, or emotion, may be inappropriate to the thoughts he is expressing or the situation in which he finds himself. He may experience *delusions* and *hallucinations.* He may exhibit *autism,* which means that he is absorbed in an inner fantasy life that he finds more satisfying than the real world. He often manifests *"bizarre" behavior,* such as peculiar gestures, movements, and repetitive acts. His speech and writing are often incoherent and disconnected, indicating *disturbances of thought.* These are all symptoms of the psychosis we call _____ although any one schizophrenic will usually not exhibit all of these _____.

schizophrenia

symptoms

52. A person who becomes so absorbed in his inner fantasy life that he loses contact with the world of reality is showing the symptom of schizophrenia that we call _____.

autism

53. One of the symptoms of schizophrenia, in which withdrawal from reality is accompanied by almost complete absorption in an inner fantasy life, is called _____. Some of the other symptoms include withdrawal, or a loss of interest in the realistic environment; _____, which are false sensory perceptions, and _____, which are false beliefs; "_____" behavior, such as peculiar gestures and movements; disturbances of _____ as well as disturbances of thought.

autism

hallucinations

delusions

bizarre

affect

54. A two-category scheme for classifying schizophrenia has been proposed. The scheme is not based upon a patient's current symptoms, but rather upon his pre-illness adjustment and the prognosis for recovery. *Process schizophrenia* is one category; it involves a history of *long-term, progressive deterioration* in adjustment. Because the illness has been long term, you might guess that the prognosis for recovery is relatively (*good/poor*).

poor

55. The second category is *reactive schizophrenia,* in which the person has had a fairly adequate adjustment in the past but has been precipitated into illness by some sudden severe *stress,* such as death of a loved one or loss of a job. You might surmise that for reactive schizophrenia the prognosis for recovery is relatively (*good/poor*).

good

Process

poor

Reactive

stress

good

56. _____ schizophrenia involves a history of long-term, progressive deterioration in adjustment, and the prognosis is relatively _____. _____ schizophrenia, however, involves a history of fairly adequate adjustment but is precipitated by sudden _____, and the prognosis is relatively _____. (The text discusses some of the research aimed at determining the causes of schizophrenia.)

57. We have discussed two major types of psychosis, the most common type being _____, which is characterized by disturbances of affect and by withdrawal from reality. The _____-_____ psychosis involves violent mood swings.

schizophrenia

manic-depressive

58. A third form of psychopathology that differs from either the n_____ or the p_____ are the *psychophysiological disorders.* As you might guess from the label, a psychophysiological disorder is a physical illness that has psychological causes. The older term is *psychosomatic illness.*

neuroses

psychoses

59. In psychophysiological or psychosomatic disorders the physical symptoms are real, but the causes are assumed to be _____.

psychological

60. Don't confuse psychophysiological disorders with conversion reactions. In conversion reactions, which you will recall are classed as (*neuroses/psychoses*), no physical cause can be found. In psychophysiological disorders the illness (*is/is not*) real.

neuroses

is

61. Although asthma is related to certain allergies, asthmatic attacks are frequently triggered by emotional factors. Thus, we can say that asthma may be in some cases a _____ disorder.

psychophysiological

62. Ulcers brought about by emotional stress would be another example of a _____ disorder.

psychophysiological

63. Psychophysiological disorders come about through the effect of psychological or em_____ factors on the body.

emotional

64. So far we have discussed three major forms of psychopathology: _____, _____, and

neuroses, psychoses
(either order)

psychophysiological _____ disorders. A
fourth category includes the *personality disorders.*

65. Personality disorders are a group of *behavior patterns* that are pathological more from *society's viewpoint* than in terms of the individual's own discomfort or unhappiness. *Psychopathic personality,* for example, is a form of personality disorder in which the individual has a lifelong history of socially deviant behavior but experiences little, if any, anxiety concerning himself or his actions.

society's   The psychopath's behavior is deviant more from _____'s viewpoint than from his own.

psychopathic   **66.** One form of personality disorder is the <u>psych</u>_____ personality. The chief characteristic of the *psychopath* is his lack of moral development or *conscience.* He is highly impulsive, manipulative, seeks immediate gratification of his needs, and cannot tolerate frustration. "I want what I

psychopath   want when I want it" sums up the behavior of the _____.

conscience   **67.** The psychopath's chief characteristic is his lack of _____. He acts impulsively, like a young child, has little tolerance of

frustration   _____, and seeks immediate

gratification   _____ of his needs.

prison   **68.** These characteristics frequently bring the psychopath in conflict with the law. He is more likely to be found in a (*hospital / prison*). (The text discusses some of the biological and environmental factors that may be responsible for the psychopathic personality.)

anxiety   **69.** Let's review. The chief symptom of the neuroses is _____. The
anxiety   five major types of neuroses include _____ reactions, in which
conversion   anxiety is predominant; _____ reactions, in which anxiety is converted into a physical symptom such as paralysis, blindness, or
phobic   deafness; _____ reactions, in which the person suffers excessive
obsessive-compulsive   fear in the absence of real danger; _____-
_____ reactions, in which persistently disturbing thoughts keep recurring or the person feels an irresistible urge to carry out some ritualistic act as a means of warding off dangerous impulses; and, finally, neurotic
depression   _____, in which the individual's sadness and dejection are exaggerated out of proportion to the precipitating event.

70. The psychoses are more severe disorders, of which the most common is
schizophrenia   _____, often characterized by withdrawal from reality into one's own private world. Another type of psychosis, characterized by violent mood swings, is the _____-
manic-depressive   _____ psychosis.

71. When psychological factors produce physical illness, as in some cases of ulcers or asthma, we have a third category of psychopathology known as the

psychophysiological

_____ disorders.

72. Finally, reactions characterized by socially deviant behavior, such as the psychopathic personality, are classified as _____

personality disorders

_____.

TERMS AND CONCEPTS FOR IDENTIFICATION

neuroses _____

_____

_____

_____

psychoses _____

_____

_____

_____

psychophysiological disorders _____

_____

_____

_____

personality disorders _____

_____

_____

_____

anxiety reaction _____

_____

_____

_____

obsessive-compulsive reaction_____

_____

_____

_____

phobic reaction_____

_____

_____

_____

conversion reaction _____

_____

_____

_____

neurotic depression _____

_____

_____

_____

organic psychosis_____

_____

_____

_____

functional psychosis _____

_____

_____

_____

manic-depressive psychoses _____

_____

_____

_____

schizophrenia_____

_____

_____

_____

autism _____

_____

_____

_____

delusion _____

_____

_____

_____

hallucination _____

_____

_____

_____

process schizophrenia _____

_____

_____

_____

reactive schizophrenia _____

_____

_____

_____

schizoid _____

_____

_____

_____

psychopathic personality _____

_____

_____

_____

_____ 1. A major defining characteristic of personality disorders is that they
a. are pathological more from society's
view than from that of the persons who
have them
b. reflect a lack of contact with reality
c. are comparatively easy to treat
d. are frequently reactive, i.e., short-term
responses to stress

_____ 2. A person who has to some extent given up
the struggle to function in the world, and
who has thereby lost contact with reality,
is termed
a. schizophrenic
b. neurotic
c. paranoid
d. psychotic

_____ 3. Each of the several criteria for the classification of abnormal behavior has both advantages and drawbacks. The only useful
criterion for some neuroses, for example, is
a. adaptiveness of behavior
b. social standards
c. personal distress
d. statistical frequency

_____ 4. Schizophrenia usually occurs during
a. youth (ages 10-20)
b. young adulthood (ages 25-35)
c. middle age (ages 45-55)
d. old age (ages 65-75)

_____ 5. If in preparing for an exam in this course,
you find yourself having recurring thoughts
about shouting something wildly obscene
at your professor, you can take comfort in
the fact that you now know how to label
this behavior. You are exhibiting (a mild
form of)
a. anxiety attack
b. phobic reaction
c. obsessive-compulsive reaction
d. conversion reaction

_____ 6. Studies of the populations of mental hospitals show that
a. 30 percent of first admissions are diagnosed schizophrenic
b. 50 percent of first admissions are for
depressive disorders

c. 3 of 10 babies will be so hospitalized at
some time in their lives
d. all of the above

_____ 7. Conversion reactions
a. of the most dramatic type are becoming
more frequent
b. may be diagnosed by _belle indifférence_
c. convert a normal situation into one
which causes anxiety
d. are a form of malingering

_____ 8. A study of children born to schizophrenic
mothers but raised in foster homes found
that
a. all of them became schizophrenic eventually
b. the incidence of schizophrenia was no
higher than for controls
c. 66 percent became schizophrenic
d. many more became schizophrenic than
controls

_____ 9. Our popular concept of the "raving mani-
ac" is grossly oversimplified and misleading
as an image of psychopathology in general.
It is not completely useless, however; such
an individual, with his pacing, screaming,
and general disorientation, is
a. in an extreme anxiety reaction
b. diagnosed as hypermanic
c. a psychopath
d. the typical manic-depressive

_____ 10. The most widely accepted classification
system for abnormal behavior groups people into four major categories, which are
then further subdivided. The four major
categories are
a. psychophysiological disorders, neuroses,
personality disorders, psychoses
b. neuroses, psychoses, personality disorders, conversion reactions
c. schizophrenias, personality disorders,
neuroses, psychoses
d. psychoses, psychophysiological disorders, anxiety reactions, personality
disorders

_____ 11. The "executive" monkeys who developed
ulcers attracted a lot of attention. Further
research with rats showed that an impor-

tant factor in *preventing* ulcers is
a. immediate feedback
b. ability to make an effective response
c. both a and b
d. neither a nor b

_____ 12. Normal people are characterized in the text as possessing a series of traits to a greater degree than individuals diagnosed as abnormal. Which of the following is *not* one of these characteristics of the psychological healthy individual?
a. self-esteem and acceptance
b. social conformity
c. productivity
d. self-knowledge

_____ 13. The behavioral interpretation of depression relates it to "learned helplessness." The most obvious symptom of this condition is
a. passivity
b. increased appetite
c. excessive counteraggressiveness when threatened
d. an increase in random maladaptive behavior

_____ 14. A process schizophrenic
a. has a history of long-term deterioration in adjustment
b. has an adequate premorbid social development, with the illness being precipitated by a sudden stress
c. has a good prognosis for recovery
d. has a history of brain damage or deficit

_____ 15. The college student described in the text as worried about his sexual identity, fearful of many things, and panicky when heading for class, represents a
a. typical college student
b. schizophrenic reaction
c. conversion reaction
d. phobic reaction

_____ 16. Which of the following statements is not true of individuals diagnosed as schizophrenics? They
a. occupy an estimated 50 percent of neuropsychiatric hospital beds
b. often display bizarre behavior

c. exhibit multiple personalities
d. are characterized by thought disorders

_____ 17. One notable aspect of the behavior of neurotics has been called the "neurotic paradox." This refers to the fact that they
a. can behave normally and simultaneously experience anxiety
b. are often successful yet belittle themselves
c. show chronic lack of energy yet drive themselves too hard
d. cling rigidly to self-defeating behavior patterns and don't recognize this

_____ 18. While the complete answer is not fully known, the choice of *which* neurotic reaction a person develops in response to stress has been shown to be influenced by
a. the person's age
b. how stressful the situation is
c. behavior patterns learned as a child
d. all of the above

_____ 19. The person characterized as a psychopathic personality
a. typically comes from a home marked by intense conflict or skewed relationships
b. is best characterized by "lovelessness" and "guiltlessness"
c. has been said to have an overreactive autonomic system
d. suffers from anxiety attacks

_____ 20. Studies of the family background of schizophrenics have found that
a. schizophrenics are more likely than normals to have lost a parent early in life
b. disturbed home life is much more common for schizophrenics than normals
c. no single pattern of family interaction leads to schizophrenia
d. all of the above

KEY TO SELF-QUIZ

20. d	15. d	10. d	5. c
19. b	14. a	9. b	4. b
18. c	13. a	8. d	3. c
17. d	12. b	7. b	2. d
16. c	11. c	6. a	1. a

INDIVIDUAL EXERCISE

CLASSIFYING ABNORMAL BEHAVIOR

Descriptions of individuals displaying various kinds of psychopathology are given below. In each instance, attempt to classify the disorder on the basis of the behavioral symptoms. Consult the textbook for a discussion of the different types of psychopathology. The *neuroses* include anxiety reactions, obsessive-compulsive reactions, phobic reactions, conversion reactions, and neurotic depression. The *psychoses* include two functional psychoses, manic-depressive psychosis and schizophrenia, as well as psychoses resulting from organic conditions. *Psychopathic personality* and *psychophysiological disorders* are not included under the neuroses or psychoses.

It is important to remember that clinical cases in real life show a wide variety of symptoms and seldom fit as neatly into categories as do our hypothetical cases. The correct diagnoses are given on page 297 of the Appendix.

CASE 1

John, a patient at the state mental hospital, appears to be happy and elated. He frequently makes humorous remarks, laughs at them himself, and is successful in making others laugh too. In expressing his thoughts he jumps from one topic to another without following any particular course. If, while he is talking about his family, the psychologist suddenly interjects a comment about the weather, John immediately switches his conversation to the weather or any other topic the psychologist introduces. Furthermore, he is hyperactive. He is either drumming with his fingers, playing with a pencil, or engaging others with his rapid talk. There is no deterioration of intellectual and emotional faculties, however. His present illness will probably be followed by several years of "normal" behavior.

CASE 2

Jack has been hearing for several months the same voice, which makes derogatory accusations about his being a sexually immoral pervert. This same voice often commands him to do such things as throw furniture out of the window. His speech is monotonous except when he is talking about his troubles, at which time it becomes quite animated and vehement. His sentence structure is often shattered and his statements are usually incoherent, since they consist of a sequence of apparently unconnected words. An example of his "word-salad" is "The pipe tail on the bed, the TV said, a brown came out of the lawn, the flowers are board walk." He also coins new words such as "lapicator," which he said was an important chemical that will be used to purify the world.

CASE 3

Jim, a soldier, is in an Army medical hospital. He complains of a loss of sensation in his fingers. He also complains that he cannot see, although a competent oculist examined his eyes and found nothing wrong. It seems strange that Jim is calm about his disorder even to the point of feeling indifferent about it. Except for this, his personality seems intact.

CASE 4

Jane has been referred to a psychiatrist by her local physician, who can find nothing physically wrong with her. She complains, however, of feeling that something terrible is going to happen to her or to her family. She realizes that her fear is irrational, but she can't seem to help it. She has also become fearful of doing things she formerly did without any apprehension whatsoever, such as going to dances and driving her car. One might describe her as being in a state of apprehension about practically everything. Jane herself is not certain what she fears, and she seems to lack insight into the etiology of her present condition.

CASE 5

Margaret, an eighteen-year-old girl, is afraid to be alone at home or to go alone more than one block away from home. She is particularly afraid of being in a room by herself. She becomes panicky when alone and reports she has the feeling that the walls are closing in on her.

CASE 6

Bill is an extremely orderly, clean, stubborn, and stingy person. He expects everything in the house to be spotless at all times. He insists that every chair, napkin, ashtray, and book be in its proper place. His wife loves him but finds it very difficult to keep the house in the rigid order he demands. He tends to have some time-consuming rituals connected with dressing and personal care, such as arranging his toilet articles in a particular order, rinsing his face exactly five times after shaving, laying out all of his clothes in a fixed sequence and making sure that he puts them on in that order.

CASE 7

Ralph is a highly impulsive person who has difficulty making plans or sticking to a job for any length of time. He has been fired from several jobs because he was caught stealing or because of frequent absences due to periodic drinking and gambling sprees. He always blames his employer for his dismissal and will not admit that his own behavior is responsible for his poor job history. Women tend to find him charming and personable, but they soon tire of his irresponsible behavior, frequent financial sponging, and general lack of consideration. His quick temper and disregard for social regulations have brought him into frequent brushes with the law, but he usually manages to charm his way out and has never been convicted of a crime. He appears to feel little guilt or anxiety regarding his behavior.

CASE 8

Following the breakup of her engagement to Fred, Martha has become very despondent. She shows little interest in her job (which previously she found stimulating and exciting) and often calls in sick. She spends a great deal of time alone in her room, sitting idly by the window or listening to the radio. When friends call to invite her out she usually refuses, pleading illness or fatigue. She complains that she feels continually tired, has to force herself to undertake such simple tasks as getting dressed or fixing a meal, and cannot concentrate enough to read a newspaper or magazine. Tears flow at the slightest provocation, and she feels worthless and inadequate. Her condition does not improve after several months have passed.

Questions For Discussion

1. Which of the symptoms shown by neurotic patients are most common (in less extreme form) among mentally healthy people?

2. In what way does the psychopathic personality differ from individuals classed as psychotic or neurotic?

3. In what way do neurotic individuals differ from those classed as psychotic?

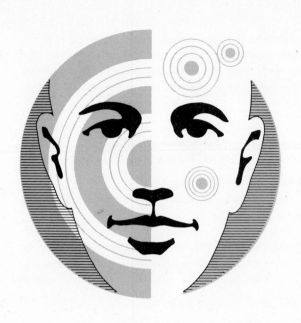

17
psychotherapy and other treatment methods

LEARNING OBJECTIVES

Be familiar with the functions of the different specialists involved in psychotherapy.

Describe and distinguish among the three major approaches to psychotherapy.

Be familiar with the techniques and advantages of group and family therapy.

Discuss the difficulties involved in evaluating the success of psychotherapeutic techniques.

Describe some of the methods of somatotherapy.

Discuss the factors that help an individual maintain a satisfactory adjustment.

PROGRAMMED UNIT

1. When a person is seriously disturbed emotionally, what can be done? *Psychotherapy* is one method of treatment. If you know that "therapy" means treatment, you can guess that *psychotherapy* is treatment by

psychological

_____ means. *Somatotherapy,* on the other hand, is a method of treatment for behavioral disorders that is not psychological, but biological, in that it treats the body (*soma*) with drugs, surgery, electroshock, or other physiological means.

Somatotherapy   **2.** Som_____ is carried out by persons with medical training and is of less intrinsic interest to a psychologist than psychotherapy   ps_____, which involves treatment by psychological means.

3. The individuals active in the treatment of behavior disorders are the *psychiatrist,* who is a physician, the *clinical psychologist,* the *psychiatric social worker,* and, in mental hospitals, the *psychiatric nurse.* Since the only person who can assume *medical* responsibility for the patient is a physician, this is the function of the

psychiatrist   _____.

4. Some psychiatrists are psychoanalysts and follow the therapeutic methods formulated by Freud, but most psychiatrists are not trained in psychoanalysis

somatotherapy   and use other methods of treatment, including somato_____.
is not   A psychoanalyst today is almost always a psychiatrist, but a psychiatrist (*is/is not*) always a psychoanalyst.

5. The *clinical psychologist* usually has a Ph.D. degree in psychology and has special training in the fields of diagnostic testing, psychotherapy, and research. Clinical psychologists are not trained in medicine, however, and cannot assume

medical   m_____ responsibility for their patients.

6. The *psychiatric social worker* usually has a Master's degree in social work and has special training in interviewing, writing case histories, and carrying treatment procedures into the home and community. Neither the psychiatric social worker nor the clinical psychologist is trained in medicine, however, and therefore they

cannot   (*can/cannot*) assume medical responsibility for patients.

7. You will remember that psychoanalysis was discussed as a theory of personality. We will now consider psychoanalysis as a method of psychotherapy. One of the foundations of this method is called *free association.* In this approach the patient is told to say, without selection or editing, everything that enters his mind. In order to get the patient to put repressed thoughts into words, the psychoanalyst will ask him to talk, to ramble, not to think too much about what

free association   he is saying, and not to suppress anything. This is the technique of _____

_____.

8. When one says a word, it will be associated, through past experience, with other words. For instance, if one says "grass," the word "green" may come to mind. If the patient allows this type of association to continue freely, without censorship, he may bring out repressed thoughts and feelings by following the tech-

free association   nique of _____ _____.

free association   9. The technique of _____ _____ assumes that as the patient continues to talk without editing his words, he will utter thoughts and feelings that are associated with his problem and that these will give the analyst and eventually the patient the information they need to work toward a cure.

10. If a person has repressed certain thoughts, feelings, and impulses, they are
unconscious   (*conscious/unconscious*). The psychoanalyst, by using the method of free association, helps the client bring to *conscious* awareness that which has been repressed.

11. A person in treatment often represses certain thoughts and feelings because they make him feel too uncomfortable. He therefore *resists* their recall during his analytic treatment. You might guess that one of the tasks of the analyst is to

resistance   help the patient overcome his _____ance so that they, together, can deal with these unpleasant, unconscious thoughts and feelings.

12. Patient C is late for her appointment and when she does show up, she states that she cannot recall something she wishes to share with the analyst. This is an

resistance   example of _____. That is, consciously the patient wishes to recall, but unconscious blocks hinder recall. And the fact that she was

resistance   late for her appointment might also be interpreted as _____.

13. In order to help Patient C to overcome *resistance* and to better understand herself, the psychoanalyst will make *interpretations* of her behavior. He may, for instance, call the patient's attention to her resistance to treatment by pointing out to her that she was late for her appointment and that she cannot recall what she wishes to share with the therapist. Psychoanalysts use

interpretation   _____ to help a client overcome resistances to treatment and to help him understand himself better.

14. The psychoanalyst helps the client understand some of the deeper meanings of his free associations as well as his dreams. He helps the client make *interpretations* of his behavior. For instance, a client may recall the manifest content of a nightmare he had the previous night, but he cannot understand the dream's latent content, or what the dream means or implies. With the help of the analyst,

interpretation   however, he may be able to make an _____ of what the dream really means.

resistance   **15.** It is not unusual for a client to have some _____ to treatment, since his symptoms are often less painful and stressful to him than the *reality* of some of his conflicts and feelings. To help him deal with what has

free   been repressed, the analyst may use _____ association and make

interpretations   _____ of the deeper meanings of the client's associations and dreams.

16. On a conscious level, the patient wishes to get well and to feel good. But on an

resistance   unconscious level, he may show _____ to treatment by coming late for appointments and by frequent blocking of what he wishes to relate to the therapist.

17. During therapy the patient will often *transfer* to the analyst emotional reactions that he has had to others who were important to him. This tendency is called

transference   tr_____ence. By analyzing these reactions, which often are not appropriate to the actual relationship of the analyst and the patient, the analyst gets clues to the patient's difficulties.

18. If a patient acts toward an analyst in the way he used to act toward his father or mother or some other significant person in his life, we would call this a

transference   manifestation of _____.

19. Sometimes a patient acts in a hostile manner toward the analyst when the latter has

transference   given him no reason to do so. This is interpreted as _____,
since the patient is responding emotionally toward the analyst as though the
analyst were someone else.

20. In the permissive atmosphere of the therapist's office it is sometimes possible for
a patient to relive a past situation that had strong emotional aspects and to
express this emotion *freely,* as he or she had been unable to do in the original
situation. This process, called *abreaction,* often brings the patient some relief
from tension. If a patient relives a situation in which her father treated her
unfairly and freely expresses the anger that she could not express then, she is

abreaction   experiencing _____.

emotion   **21.** A free expression of _____ that was felt but not expressed in

abreaction   an earlier situation is known as _____.

22. At the time of his father's funeral Peter suppressed his feelings of anguish
because they might be regarded as unmanly. Now that Peter is in therapy and
relating the experience to an uncritical listener, the former suppressed feelings
are expressed and he cries and sobs freely. We would say Peter is now experienc-

abreaction   ing what psychoanalysts call _____.

freely   **23.** Abreaction is like catharsis in that pent-up feelings are _____ly
expressed in a permissive setting.

abreaction   **24.** A form of emotional cleansing, called _____ by
psychoanalysts, sometimes takes place in therapy; by itself, it does not eliminate
the causes of conflict, though the patient may feel some relief from tension.

25. When a patient understands the roots of his conflict, he has achieved *insight.* For
instance, Sue now understands the relationship between some of her symptoms and some early life experiences. In other words, she has achieved

insight   some measure of _____ into her difficulties.

26. Stan now understands that he forms an immediate dislike of anyone in a
supervisory capacity over him because the first authority figure in his life, his
father, both bossed and belittled him unmercifully. We would say that Stan now

insight   has some _____ into his hatred for authority figures.

27. As a patient is on the road to recovery, he goes through a process known as
working through. In this process, he examines the same conflicts over and over
again as they have appeared in a variety of situations throughout his life, and

Working   learns to face them in a more mature way. _____ through is
part of the process of becoming adjusted, which is a matter of learning to face
reality.

28. Since the patient will often face his conflicts over and over again outside the thera-

working through   pist's office, it follows that the _____ _____
process will continue in many situations in everyday life.

psychotherapy

29. Psychoanalysis is a method of _____ therapy that accents the unconscious determinants of personality.

30. A form of psychotherapy that differs from psychoanalysis is *client-centered* therapy. This form of therapy assumes that the client can work out his or her own problems if the therapist provides the right psychological atmosphere. The therapist does not instruct the client to free associate, nor does he interpret the

psychoanalyst

client's statements and behavior as would a _____.
Instead the therapist attempts to *reflect* and to *clarify* the feelings of the client and to see things from the client's point of view, or *frame of reference,* as it is sometimes referred to.

31. The client-centered therapist tries to see things from the client's frame of

reference

_____. The therapist *accepts* the client and his state-

accept

ments and feelings so that the client may begin to <u>acc</u>_____ himself.

client-centered

32. In _____-_____ therapy the therapist mainly accepts, reflects, and clarifies the views of the client so that the client can understand himself better.

client-centered

33. An assumption made in _____-_____ ther-apy is that the client has the capacity to deal with his psychological situation and with himself.

34. One of the main tenets of client-centered therapy is that the therapist must try

reference

to adopt the frame of _____ of the client. That is, the

client

therapist must try to see things as the _____ sees them.

35. Thus far we have discussed two different kinds of psychotherapy.

Psychoanalysis

_____ is a form of treatment by psy-chological means in which the therapist uses free association and interpretation

client-centered

as techniques of treatment. In _____-_____ therapy, the therapist tries to adopt the frame of reference of the client and to reflect and clarify the client's feelings. The assumption in this form of treatment is that the client has resources to solve his own problems in an accepting relationship with another.

36. Still a third form of psychotherapy is *behavior therapy,* which differs from both psychoanalysis and client-centered therapy in that it is based upon the principles of learning theory. The assumption in this kind of therapy is that if maladaptive

unlearned

behavior is *learned,* it can also be <u>unl</u>_____ by having the person learn new or more appropriate responses in place of the maladaptive responses.

37. Because we are trying to change the *behavior* of a maladjusted organism by

learning

means of certain principles of _____, we call this method

behavior

_____ therapy.

38. If a severe shock is administered to a cat every time it approaches a feeding cage, it will, of course, become *anxious* and *fearful.* The cat wishes to eat because it is hungry, but it dreads the pain from the electric shock. The cat may even manifest neurotic behavior because it has been placed in an approach-

avoidance

_____ conflict that cannot be resolved. The maladaptive

anxiety

response learned by the cat in this situation is a_____.

39. The *maladaptive* anxiety reaction one has learned in one situation or under certain conditions may *generalize* to other situations. Thus, our anxious cat may refuse to eat not only in the feeding cage but also in other places in the experimental room, even though the other places are perfectly safe. Its behavior

maladaptive

is certainly mal_____, because it is hungry but re-

generalized

fuses to eat even in safe places. Its anxiety reaction has _____ to other situations.

behavior

40. We wish now to use _____ therapy on this cat so that it will learn that it is safe to eat. We shall have to eliminate, or extinguish, the

maladaptive

mal_____ behavior. How do we go about doing this, using what we know about the principles of learning?

41. Because the cat's maladaptive behavior has been learned through conditioning, per-

extinguish

haps we can use *counter-conditioning* to weaken or ex_____ the maladaptive responses by strengthening incompatible or antagonistic responses.

counter

42. Psychologists use _____-conditioning to help extinguish a maladaptive response. That is, the organism learns some new response through weakening or extinguishing the maladaptive response.

extinguish

43. The prime task is to destroy or _____ the anxiety response, or maladaptive response, by making it possible for the normal response of eating to occur.

44. Since the cat is anxious and refuses to eat anywhere in the experimental room

generalized

because its anxiety has g_____ from the feeding place to other places in the experimental room, perhaps we can get it to eat if we

far removed from

place the food (*near / far removed from*) the original feeding place.

45. Once the cat learns it can eat in one place without experiencing any pain, it can

anxiety

overcome its a_____ reactions. Then we can place the feeding cup in *gradual* steps closer to the original feeding place. If after one successful feeding at a place far from the original feeding place, we set the feeding cup very

anxious

near the original place, the cat would surely become _____

maladaptive

again and manifest m_____ behavior. Thus the

gradual

steps must be _____.

46. Once the cat is able to eat in the cage where it had originally been shocked and shows no sign of being anxious, we have probably cured it of its anxiety by

conditioning

means of counter-_____. In other words, we have extinguished the anxious, maladaptive behavior it had learned by strengthening incompatible or antagonistic responses.

47. We can treat human subjects who exhibit anxiety in a similar manner by asking them to list the sorts of situations that are anxiety producing for them. We can then rank the situations in a sort of *hierarchy* from most to least anxiety provoking. Such a list is called an *anxiety hierarchy* because we have ranked

most

these situations from the least to the _____ anxiety provoking.

48. When a therapist ranks from low to high those situations that a particular client

anxiety

finds anxiety provoking, he is establishing an _____ hierarchy.

49. From what we have learned about behavior therapy from the illustration of the maladapted cat in the feeding situation, we may surmise that, as we study the

least

anxiety hierarchy, we would start with situations that are (*most/least*) anxiety provoking for our subject.

50. We can ask our subject to *relax* with instructions to visualize the least

anxiety

_____-provoking situation. If the subject remains relaxed and appears not to be anxious, we can then *gradually* proceed to the next anxiety-provoking situation on the list.

51. We continue in this manner until the situation that originally provoked the most anxiety now elicits only relaxation. Thus, we have conditioned our subject to

relaxation

respond with _____ to situations that initially produced an anxiety response.

conditioning

52. Both examples above illustrate counter-_____,

maladaptive

whereby a _____ response is extinguished and

behavior

replaced by an adaptive one. This is one technique used in _____ therapy. (The text discusses other methods used by behavior therapists.)

53. Since most emotional problems stem from difficulties in relating to other people, it makes sense sometimes to practice therapy in *groups.* Such therapy is

group

called, appropriately enough, gr_____ *therapy.*

54. When therapy is carried out with a therapist and more than one client, we call it

group

_____ therapy. Group therapy saves time, gives the individual the feeling that his or her problems are not unique—that others are "in the same boat"—and provides opportunities to learn better ways of interacting with other people. All the methods of psychotherapy that we have discussed have been used, often in modified form, in group therapy.

55. *Encounter groups* are a popular offshoot of group therapy. The main difference

encounter

is that en_____ groups are aimed at teaching people how to relate more openly to one another rather than at solving emotional problems or treating behavior disorders.

groups | **56.** Encounter _____, also known as *T-groups* or *sensitivity groups,* emphasize learning how to express one's feelings more openly. They may help people achieve a better understanding of how to interact with others, but they

disorders | are not designed to treat emotional problems or behavior _____.

encounter group | **57.** T-group and sensitivity group are other names for a(n) _____

_____.

58. We have discussed three major approaches to psychotherapy. The method that uses free association to bring repressed impulses and thoughts to conscious

psychoanalysis | awareness is called _____. A therapist who makes no attempt to interpret what the patient says but simply reflects and

client-centered | clarifies the patient's feelings, is using _____-_____ therapy. The method of psychotherapy that is based upon learning-theory

behavior therapy | principles is called _____ _____.

59. Psychotherapy is the treatment of behavior disorders by psychological means.

somatotherapy | Treatment by physiological means is called <u>so</u>_____. Some forms of somatotherapy used in the past, such as electroshock and brain surgery, have had little success. The most promising type of somatotherapy in use today is *chemotherapy.*

60. Chemotherapy, which uses drugs to modify behavior, is the most promising type

somatotherapy | of _____ used today. *Tranquilizers,* such as reserpine and chlorpromazine, have been very effective in calming disturbed and anxious patients and making them more amenable to treatment by psycho-

psychotherapy | logical means, or _____.

61. Another group of drugs, called *antidepressants,* help to elevate the mood of

tranquilize | depressed patients. They energize rather than _____, apparently by affecting the amount of certain neurotransmitters in the brain.

chemotherapy | **62.** The therapeutic use of drugs to modify behavior is called _____.
tranquilizers | Drugs that are effective in calming anxious patients are _____;
antidepressants | those that elevate the mood of depressed individuals are _____.

TERMS AND CONCEPTS FOR IDENTIFICATION

somatotherapy _____
_____
_____
_____

psychotherapy _____
_____
_____
_____

psychiatrist _____
_____
_____
_____

psychoanalyst _____
_____
_____
_____

clinical psychologist _____
_____
_____
_____

psychiatric social worker _____
_____
_____
_____

rapport _____
_____
_____
_____

free association _____
_____
_____
_____

transference _____
_____
_____

abreaction _____
_____
_____
_____

client-centered therapy _____
_____
_____
_____

behavior therapy _____
_____
_____
_____

counter-conditioning _____
_____
_____
_____

anxiety hierarchy _____
_____
_____
_____

systematic desensitization _____
_____
_____
_____

assertive training _____
_____
_____
_____

aversive conditioning _____
_____
_____
_____

chemotherapy _____
_____
_____

SELF-QUIZ

_____ 1. Therapists are now able to offer several suggestions for people interested in bettering their mental health. Which of the following is *not* one of them?
   a. seek always to solve your own problems, turning to professionals only as a last resort
   b. discover occasions that provoke emotional overreaction, so as to be able to guard against it
   c. learn to accept your feelings as something natural and normal
   d. if emotional expression is blocked by circumstances, learn to seek permissible outlets

_____ 2. "Token economies" have been developed by behavior therapists on the basis of principles of
   a. modeling
   b. operant conditioning
   c. aversive conditioning
   d. classical conditioning

_____ 3. During the past ten years the emphasis in treatment of the mentally ill has shifted from
   a. client-centered therapy to psychoanalytic therapy
   b. somatotherapy to psychotherapy
   c. professionals to amateurs
   d. hospital treatment to community treatment

_____ 4. The use of nonprofessionals as therapists
   a. is now a well-established technique
   b. is applicable only for neurotics
   c. is exploratory, but has generated enthusiasm
   d. includes only those nonprofessionals who have themselves had problems, i.e., ex-patients or drug addicts

_____ 5. The course of improvement during psychoanalytic therapy is commonly attributed to three main experiences of the patient. Which of the following is *not* one of these?
   a. insight
   b. transference
   c. abreaction
   d. working through

_____ 6. Somatotherapies have achieved numerous successes, but in some ways are less successful than had been hoped. Which of the following is *not* one of somatotherapies' successes?
   a. antibiotics for the indirect relief of general paresis
   b. vitamin treatment for the mental disturbances associated with pellagra
   c. electric shock for schizophrenia
   d. barbiturates for epilepsy

_____ 7. In the use of behavior therapy for the relief of snake phobias the most effective approach was
   a. symbolic modeling
   b. live modeling with participation
   c. desensitization
   d. active modeling

_____ 8. An important concept in psychoanalysis is transference. This refers to the tendency of patients to
   a. transfer emotional responses to the therapist
   b. transfer their own responsibilities to the therapist
   c. show reduced resistance as therapy progresses
   d. free associate less freely as therapy progresses

_____ 9. The method of somatotherapy that holds the most promise of success in the future is
   a. psychosurgery
   b. electroshock therapy
   c. insulin-shock therapy
   d. chemotherapy

_____ 10. Carl Rogers has described what he believes to be a consistent pattern of change in encounter groups of various types. Which of the following is *not* characteristic of such groups? Members
   a. initially tend to be confused and frustrated
   b. often begin the expression of their feelings with negative comments about others
   c. express their feelings openly at the beginning

d. become impatient with defensiveness, by the final session

11. The client-centered or nondirective therapist
   a. is concerned with the patient's present attitudes and behavior
   b. gathers a detailed case history to help understand the patient's current problems
   c. carefully directs the patient's attention to overlooked problems
   d. all of the above

12. The first advocate of humane treatment of the mentally ill was
   a. Clifford Beers
   b. Hippocrates
   c. Phillippe Pinel
   d. Sigmund Freud

13. A psychotherapist who maintains an eclectic approach might include _____ in the treatment of an anxiety neurotic.
   a. tranquilizers and relaxation training
   b. a discussion of the patient's history
   c. education techniques
   d. any of the above

14. Behavior therapists believe that insight is
   a. a worthwhile goal
   b. not sufficient for behavior change
   c. not necessary for behavior change
   d. all of the above

15. Psychoanalysis
   a. represents the largest group of mental health professionals
   b. is based on a substantial body of research data
   c. has been very influential in modern thinking
   d. all of the above

16. When counter-conditioning is used as a therapeutic technique,
   a. maladaptive responses are weakened or eliminated by strengthening antagonistic responses
   b. anxiety is increased to effect an alteration in behavior
   c. the patient is placed in a restricted environment with no anxiety-provoking stimuli present

d. modification of behavior depends upon the patient's understanding of unconscious motives

17. There are several professions involved in psychotherapy and sometimes the situation seems more complicated than it really is. One complexity is that a _____ is almost always a _____ but not vice versa.
   a. psychotherapist, psychiatrist
   b. clinical psychologist, psychiatric nurse
   c. psychoanalyst, psychiatrist
   d. psychiatric social worker, psychiatrist

18. Some of the problems of assessing cure in psychotherapy are reflected in the so-called "hello-goodbye effect." In this effect
   a. therapists see the patients' problems as more severe when they enter therapy than when they leave
   b. patients exaggerate their problems at the beginning of therapy
   c. patients try to minimize their problems at the beginning of therapy
   d. patients exaggerate any of their problems that still remain at the end of therapy

19. The "basic rule" of _____ is to say everything that enters your mind, without selection or editing.
   a. interpretation
   b. transference
   c. abreaction
   d. free association

20. A consensus regarding psychotherapy is difficult to reach because of the many problems in defining cures, the interaction of therapist and patient variables, and so forth. Nevertheless some things do seem clear. Which of the following is *not* one of them?
   a. only those patients treated by the psychotherapy most appropriate to their problems show much improvement
   b. psychotherapies do help patients
   c. all psychotherapies share common features, such as a warm relationship in a special setting
   d. there is little evidence, except for phobias and specific anxieties, that one form of therapy produces better results than another

1. a	6. c	11. a	16. a
2. b	7. b	12. b	17. c
3. d	8. a	13. d	18. b
4. c	9. d	14. d	19. d
5. b	10. c	15. c	20. a

INDIVIDUAL EXERCISE

FREE ASSOCIATION

Introduction

This is a very simple exercise, but it will give you a better feeling for what goes on in therapy and a better understanding of why certain kinds of therapy take so long.

The main technique in psychoanalytic therapy is free association. The therapist instructs the client to say whatever comes into his mind. There should be no attempt to censor any material that comes to consciousness—it should all be verbalized, no matter how irrelevant, unimportant, or embarrassing it may seem.

Equipment Needed

None required, but if a tape recorder is available it would be useful.

Procedure

The technique of free association appears to be very simple. In order to get some idea of what it is like, follow these instructions: Go to a place in which you know you will not be disturbed or overheard—go to any lengths you feel necessary in order to find such a place. Some students have waited until they were at home and their family was away. When you are *sure* that you are alone and no one else can hear you, try to follow the rules for free association. Say everything *aloud* in a clear tone.

If possible it would be instructive to tape record your free associations so that you can analyze them later.

Questions For Discussion

1. Was it easy to do? If not, why do you think it was not?

2. Can you imagine what it would be like to do this in the presence of another person?

3. How long do you think it would take you to be able to do this in the presence of another person?

4. Can you trace some of the cues that made one thought lead to another?

18
social
psychology

LEARNING OBJECTIVES

Be familiar with the operation of primacy and recency effects in impression formation and in persuasion.

Discuss some of the variables that influence interpersonal attraction.

Describe how stereotypes and implicit personality theories influence our perception of other people.

Discuss the problems that biases in our attribution processes create in both inter-personal perception and self-perception.

Be familiar with the research findings on social influence.

Describe the conditions under which behavior change is most likely to lead to attitude change. Explain these findings from the viewpoints of (a) cognitive dissonance theory and (b) self-perception theory.

Discuss the theory of immunization against persuasion.

PROGRAMMED UNIT

1. *Social psychology* studies the ways in which a person's *thoughts, feelings,* and *behaviors* are *influenced by other persons.* Since most of our lives are spent in the presence of other people, we might conclude that almost all of psychology is

social   s_____.

2. But social psychologists tend to look at social influence from a somewhat different perspective than other psychologists. First, they are more apt to focus on the current or ongoing *situational influences* on behavior than on develop-

situational mental or personality factors. Social psychologists are more interested in current or ongoing _____ influences on behavior than on factors in the individual's past that may have shaped his or her personality.

3. Thus, if the leader of a teenage gang assaults a police officer, the social

influences psychologist is more interested in the situational _____ (e.g., What was the provocation? Were other gang members present?) than in experiences in the individual's past that predisposed him or her to be aggressive.

4. The social psychologist is more interested in situational factors than in develop-

behavior mental or personality influences on <u>be</u>_____.

5. A second emphasis of social psychology is on the individual's *phenomenology,* that is, on the *individual's own point of view* or *subjective definition of the situation,* as opposed to some objective measure of the circumstances. Phenomenology refers to the study of phenomena from the individual's own point

view of _____.

6. Thus, if the gang leader attacked the police officer because he believes all policemen are hostile to him, this perceived hostility *is* the cause of the individual's behavior—regardless of what the objective situation may be. Social

definition (or view) psychologists are interested in the individual's subjective _____ of the situation.

phenomenology **7.** For social psychologists the important thing is the individual's <u>phen</u>_____ rather than some objective measure of the situation.

8. Social psychology differs from other areas of psychology in two ways: its focus

situational on the ongoing _____ influences on behavior and

phenomenology its emphasis on the individual's _____.

9. One topic of interest to social psychologists is our perception of other people—

people what factors influence our impressions of other _____.

10. First impressions are important because we are biased toward *primacy effects;* that is, we tend to give too much weight to initial information and too little to

information later <u>in</u>_____ that may be contradictory.

much **11.** Primacy effects refer to the tendency to give too (*much/little*) weight to the initial information we receive about a person.

12. Agnes did very well on her first psychology test but poorly on later tests; Mark received a low score on his first test but improved markedly on subsequent tests. The instructor still thinks of Agnes as a better student than Mark. He is biased

primacy by _____ effects.

13. The tendency to stick to our initial impression of a person and to ignore later

primacy effect contradictory information is called the _____ _____.

14. Studies have shown that if sufficient *time* intervenes between the initial informa-

primacy tion and the subsequent contradictory information, then the _____ effect may be reversed. That is, the initial information may dim in memory so that we give greater weight to the *more recent* information. This is known as the *recency effect.*

15. As the name implies, the recency effect refers to the tendency to bias our

recent judgments toward the more _____ information.

16. One variable that determines whether the recency effect will be more influential

time than the primacy effect is the _____ interval between the two sets of information.

primacy **17.** If the two sets of information occur close together, then _____ effects will be important; if there is a sufficient time lapse between the two sets

recency of information, then _____ effects may occur because the

memory initial information has dimmed in _____.

18. Suppose a trial by jury hears all of the prosecution lawyer's arguments in one block and then immediately hears the arguments of the defense. Since the two sets of information come close together we would predict that the jury would be

prosecution more influenced by the arguments of the (*defense/prosecution*) lawyer in arriving at its verdict. A short time interval between two sets of information favors

primacy the _____ effect.

19. If there is a large time interval between the two arguments, then we would

recency expect the jury to be biased by _____ effects. In this case the advantage would go to the defense lawyer because his case was presented

last (*first/last*).

20. Social psychologists are also interested in interpersonal attraction. Research has uncovered a number of factors that determine whether people will be *attracted* to each other. These include *physical appearance, competence, similarity, reciprocal liking,* and *familiarity.* All of these factors help determine whether two

attracted people will be _____ to each other.

21. Although people usually do not *rate* physical attractiveness as important in their liking of others, studies indicate that appearance is more important than personality characteristics or similar interests in determining whom college students choose to date. And people tend to attribute more positive personality characteristics to photographs of attractive individuals than they do to photos of unattractive individuals. Despite what we prefer to believe, physical

appearance _____ is an important determiner of (or attractiveness) liking.

22. We also tend to be attracted to people who appear competent, are similar to us

similarity

in attitudes and values, and who like us. Thus, competence, _____, and reciprocal liking are variables influencing interpersonal attraction.

23. Familiarity is also a determiner of liking. Even if your roommate is quite different from you in attitudes and values, you may like him or her better at the end of the year than a new acquaintance who is more similar to you. In this

familiarity

instance _____ is operating to promote interpersonal attraction.

24. Other variables that influence interpersonal attraction, in addition to familiarity,

physical, competence

are _____ appearance, c_____,

similarity, reciprocal

s_____, and r_____ liking.

25. The fact that more positive personality characteristics are attributed to photographs of attractive individuals than to photos of unattractive individuals shows that physical appearance is an important determiner of interpersonal

attraction

_____. It also demonstrates the operation of *stereotypes*. Personality characteristics were attributed on the basis of appearance alone; the judges had no information other than what appeared in the photograph. Their personality evaluations must have been based on their *stereotypes* of attractive and unattractive people.

26. A stereotype is a group of *interrelated traits and attributes* assumed to be characteristic of certain kinds of individuals. Suppose I show you a picture of a long-haired, barefoot young man dressed in patched jeans and ask you to rate him on certain personality traits—e.g., friendliness, honesty, conscientiousness,

stereotype

aggressiveness, etc. Your ratings would be based on a stereo_____ of how an individual who looks like this behaves, because your only clues are his appearance.

interrelated

27. A stereotype is a group of _____ traits and attributes assumed to be characteristic of certain kinds of individuals.

28. When people are shown photographs of attractive and unattractive individuals and asked to rate the pictured individuals on a number of personality traits, they rate the attractive person as friendlier, happier, and superior in character to the

stereotypes

unattractive person. Their judgments are influenced by _____ of attractive and unattractive appearing individuals.

29. Stereotypes are misleading and often have no basis in fact. But they arise from the natural tendency to generalize about an individual (on the basis of what we know about similar individuals we have met in the past) so as to predict his or

behavior

her behavior. People use stereotypes to aid in predicting _____ until they have further information to go on.

30. Stereotypes are a special case of what psychologists call *implicit personality*

personality

theories. An implicit _____ theory is a preconceived notion about which traits and behaviors go with other traits and behaviors. For example, if a person is described to you as "warm," you probably also theory   assume that he or she is an extravert. Your implicit personality _____ assumes that the two traits are correlated.

31. An implicit personality theory is a preconceived notion that certain traits and

correlate   behaviors co_____ with other traits and behaviors.

32. If I tell you that my friend Alice is "conscientious," you probably assume that she is seldom late for appointments, turns her assignments in on time, and keeps

implicit   a neater-than-average room. Your _____ personality theory may have some basis in fact, since it depends upon past observations of what traits and behaviors seem to go together. But studies have shown that people tend to go far beyond whatever validity their implicit personality theories may have and to make unwarranted inferences about the person being observed.

33. Both stereotypes and implicit personality theories enable us to go beyond the information we are given about a person and to draw inferences about unobserved aspects even though these inferences may not be accurate. Stereotypes are

implicit personality   a special case of _____ _____

behaviors   theories; they are an implicit set of assumptions about the traits and _____ of certain classes or types of people.

implicit   **34.** In addition to _____ personality theories relating traits and behaviors, people also tend to have implicit rules for *inferring the causes of behavior.*

cause   **35.** While observing a person's behavior we usually try to infer its _____. To what do we *attribute* the individual's behavior? We may attribute it to forces

attribute   or pressures in the environment, or we may _____ it to the individual's own motives and personality traits.

36. A young man stands on a street corner giving an eloquent speech in support of a bill to legalize prostitution. To what do we attribute his behavior? To the fact that he fervently believes in legalized prostitution? That his wife is a prostitute and they need more money? That he is being paid to give the speech? That he is fulfilling an assignment for his public-speaking class? If you attribute his behavior to the first two possibilities, you are making a *dispositional attribution.* If you attribute his actions to the last two possibilities, you are making a *situa-*

attribution   *tional* _____tion.

37. *Attribution theory* attempts to make explicit the rules we use in inferring causes

behavior   of _____, and to discover the *biases* that influence our attempts to do so. When we make a dispositional attribution we infer that the cause of behavior lies in the individual's attitudes or personality traits. When we make a situational attribution we infer that factors in the external

situation   s_____ prompted the behavior.

38. Attribution theory refers to our attempts to infer the causes of an individual's

behavior   _____.

39. Research shows that there are some systematic biases in our attributions; we tend to give too much weight to personality variables as determinants of behavior and to underestimate the situational factors that caused the person to behave as he did. That is, we tend to give too much importance to (*dispositional*/*situational*) factors.

dispositional

40. In one study subjects heard an individual give a speech either favoring or opposing racial segregation. They were informed in advance that the speaker had been *told* which side of the issue to take and the specific arguments to use. Despite this knowledge, the subjects inferred that the speaker believed to some degree the point of view he was arguing. This illustrates our bias toward _____ attributions.

dispositional

41. Because another person's behavior is such a dominant aspect of any situation we observe, we tend to weight it too heavily and to underestimate _____ factors that may have led the individual to act as he or she did. The text cites evidence to show that dispositional attributions, once made, are difficult to reverse. Once we have made a dispositional judgment about a person (she's a "hard worker," "aggressive," "not very bright," etc.) it takes a lot of contradictory information to disconfirm our initial judgment. Note that the irreversibility of dispositional attributions is related to the primacy effect; initial information is taken (*more*/*less*) seriously than later information.

situational

more

42. So far we have talked about how we form impressions of other people, the factors that promote inter_____ attraction, stereotypes, and _____ personality theories, and our biases in inferring causes of behavior. Another area of interest to social psychologists is *social influence,* the influence that other people have on our attitudes and behavior.

interpersonal

implicit

43. Just the *physical presence* of another person can influence your behavior. If someone else is watching you perform (an *audience*) or working independently along with you (a *coactor*), you will behave differently than if you are alone. The physical _____ of another person can influence your behavior.

presence

44. The presence of an audience or a co_____ can either *facilitate* or *impair* performance, depending upon a number of variables.

coactor

45. College students complete more mathematical problems when working in a group than when working alone. This illustrates that coaction may (*facilitate*/*impair*) performance.

facilitate

46. But the same students make more errors when working on mathematical problems in a group than when alone. Thus, coaction can also _____ performance.

impair

47. Whether the presence of others facilitates or _____ performance depends upon the complexity of the task. *Simple* or *well-learned responses* are usually facilitated, whereas more *complex responses* are usually *impaired* by the presence of others.

impairs

48.

facilitated

Thus, if you are sorting a group of balls according to color, your performance would probably be _____ with someone watching; if you were solving a mathematical equation, your performance would

impaired

probably be _____.

49.

complexity

Whether performance is facilitated or impaired by the presence of others depends partly on the <u>com</u>_____ of the task.

50. The *presence of other people* can also have a profound influence on what you do in an emergency. The term "bystander apathy" has been used to explain why people often fail to intervene in an emergency situation. Studies have shown, however, that it is not simple indifference to the fate of the victim that prevents

emergency
is not

people from intervening in <u>em</u>_____ situations, but a host of other variables. Thus, the term bystander apathy (*is/is not*) really accurate.

people

51. The presence of other _____ decreases the probability that any given person will intervene by (a) *defining the situation as a nonemergency* and (b) *diffusing* the *responsibility* for acting.

52. Suppose you are sitting in a theater and think you smell smoke; you even imagine you see wisps of smoke coming from behind the curtain. But everyone else appears to be unconcerned. You might take action if you were alone. But the presence of other people who remain calm serves to define the situation as a

nonemergency

_____.

53. While walking down a crowded street you observe a woman fall to the pavement striking her head severely. In this case it is difficult to define the situation as a nonemergency, but the presence of other people diffuses the

responsibility

_____ for acting. If you were alone you might go to her aid. But in a crowd you don't feel responsible. Someone else will take care of her.

nonemergency,
responsibility

54. Two factors that help explain "bystander apathy" are defining the situation as a _____ and diffusion of _____.

55. One factor that will *increase* the probability of an individual's helping in an emergency is having watched someone else help in a similar situation. If you pass a car with a flat tire and notice that someone has stopped to help, you will be

more

(*more/less*) likely to stop and help the next disabled driver you pass.

56. The actions of others have considerable influence on us. Studies on conformity show that people tend to alter their judgments to conform to the opinion of the group—even though they continue to believe privately that they, not the group,

conform

are correct. In a group situation the pressure to <u>con</u>_____ is great.

pressures

57. Studies suggest that conformity to group _____ or compliance to authorities is easier to obtain than most people (including psychologists) had imagined. This finding indicates that we underestimate the

situational

importance of (*situational/dispositional*) factors on behavior.

58. A person may conform to the behavior of others or comply to the requests of authorities without changing his *attitude.* Social psychologists are interested in the circumstances that produce *attitude change.* Under what circumstances will actions taken to comply to group pressure or the requests of authorities result in

change   attitude _____?

59. In general, if a person is offered a large sum of money to change his behavior or comply with a request, he is more apt to do so than if offered a small sum. Similarly, a severe threat of punishment is more apt to result in compliance than a mild threat. Although large rewards or severe threats of punishment are

behavior   effective in producing changes in _____, they are usually less successful in getting people to believe in what they have been induced to do;

attitude   that is, to change their _____.

60. For example, in one study college students were given some dull, repetitive tasks to perform, and after completing them were bribed to go into the waiting room and tell the next subjects that the tasks had been fun and interesting. For some of the students the bribe was only one dollar; for others it was twenty dollars. Later the students were asked their actual opinion of the tasks. If small rewards are more successful than large rewards in inducing attitude change, then we

$1   would expect that the *($1/$20)* subjects would be more likely to say at a later time that they really enjoyed the tasks.

61. And this is what happened. Subjects who were paid one dollar to convince someone that the tasks were interesting, actually came to believe that they were;

twenty   subjects who were paid _____ dollars did not change their attitude. All subjects complied with the request, but only those who were given a

attitude   minimum bribe changed their _____.

62. Thus, we see that attitude change is more likely to occur when compliance is

small   obtained using a *(small/large)* incentive.

more   **63.** Two theories explain the fact that attitude change is *(more/less)* likely to occur when inducements are minimal. *Cognitive dissonance theory* assumes that people strive for *consistency* among their various beliefs and between their beliefs and their behaviors. When people engage in behavior they do not believe in, they will

consistent   be uncomfortable because their behavior is not con_____ with their beliefs.

dissonance   **64.** Cognitive _____ theory assumes that people want their behaviors and beliefs to be consistent. The feeling of inconsistency that occurs when people engage in behavior they do not believe in is called cognitive

dissonance   _____; cognitions are dissonant with each other or with behavior.

dissonance   **65.** The individual seeks to resolve this _____, and one

behavior   way is to change his beliefs so they are consistent with his _____.

66. In the one dollar-twenty dollar study the student tells another person the tasks were interesting when actually he considered them dull. Since his behavior is inconsistent with his true beliefs, we would expect this situation to produce

cognitive

_____ dissonance.

67. The student who is paid twenty dollars has a good reason for making the false statements. He can justify his behavior to himself ("I did it for the money"), so there is no longer any "dissonance pressure" for him to change his

opinions
(or attitudes)

_____ about the tasks.

68. The student who is paid only one dollar cannot justify his behavior by convincing himself he made false statements for the money. He thus experiences

cognitive dissonance

_____ _____ until he

consistent

changes his opinions so they are _____ with his behavior. He decides he must have enjoyed the tasks.

69. Cognitive dissonance theory is one explanation for the fact that attitude change

small

is more likely to occur when inducements are (*small/large*). Another theory that also can explain this fact focuses on the individual's *self-perception. Self-perception theory* assumes that sometimes we infer our attitudes from *observing our own behavior.*

perception

70. According to self-_____ theory, the individual is sometimes forced into the role of an outside observer and looks at his

behavior

own be_____ to help decide what his true feelings and attitudes are.

71. "I've been biting my nails all day; something must be bugging me." This

behavior

statement shows the person observing his own _____ to help decide how he feels.

72. "This is my second sandwich; I must be hungrier than I thought." Again,

self-perception

_____-_____ theory would say that the indi-

observing

vidual is ob_____ his own behavior to help determine how he feels.

73. Self-perception theory explains the results of the one dollar-twenty dollar experiment by assuming that the subject observes his own behavior to help decide his attitude toward the tasks. The subject who was given twenty dollars to say something he didn't really believe assumes that situational factors explain his behavior ("Most people would do the same thing for twenty dollars") and

does not

(*does/does not*) change his opinion of the tasks. The one-dollar subject assumes that situational factors (one dollar) are not sufficient to explain his behavior and he arrives at a dispositional attribution ("I must think the tasks are interesting; otherwise, I would not have said so").

74. Self-perception theory is essentially a form of attribution theory applied to self-observations rather than observations of others. The individual looks at his own behavior and attributes it to factors in the situation (a situational

attribution

_____) or to his own attitude or personality

dispositional

disposition (a _____ attribution).

75. Two theories that explain the results of the one dollar-twenty dollar study are

cognitive dissonance

_____ _____ theory, which focuses on the individual's need for consistency among his attitudes, beliefs, and

self-perception

behaviors, and _____-_____ theory, which

observer

emphasizes the individual as an _____ of his own behavior. (The text discusses other experiments where the two theories are applied to make predictions concerning attitude change.)

TERMS AND CONCEPTS FOR IDENTIFICATION

phenomenology _____

_____

_____

_____

primacy effects _____

_____

_____

_____

recency effects _____

_____

_____

_____

stereotypes _____

_____

_____

_____

implicit personality theories _____

_____

_____

_____

attribution theory _____

_____

_____

_____

dispositional attributions _____

_____

_____

_____

situational attributions _____

_____

_____

_____

self-perception theory _____

_____

_____

_____

social facilitation _____

_____

_____

_____

pluralistic ignorance _____

_____

_____

_____

diffusion of responsibility _____

_____

_____

_____

cognitive dissonance theory _____

_____

_____

_____

immunization against persuasion _____

_____

_____

_____

_____ 1. Social psychologists have found that we all rely to a large extent on stereotypes in predicting each other's behavior, a practice that is useful but often misleading. In a study of stereotypes based on physical appearance, attractive individuals were judged (in comparison to less attractive individuals) to

a. be more self-centered
b. have a better character
c. be a better parent
d. all of the above

_____ 2. "Pluralistic ignorance" is a term that has been coined to describe a phenomenon noted in research on "bystander apathy." Pluralistic ignorance refers to the fact that

a. few of us know what to do in a real emergency
b. most people are simply not attentive enough to notice the signs of an emergency
c. the presence of other people diffuses the responsibility for action
d. collective inaction in a group convinces each member that no emergency exists

_____ 3. Stanley Milgram's famous "shock" studies not only utilized a phony "shock machine" but shock us with their results. We can perhaps take some comfort, however, from the finding that

a. once the "learner" no longer answered at all, few subjects continued the shocks
b. the obedience rate dropped when subjects were made to feel more responsible for their actions
c. none of the subjects continued to administer shocks when the experimenter left the room and gave his instructions by telephone
d. all of the above

_____ 4. Primacy and recency effects can have important practical implications. For example, does it matter in what order the jury hears the arguments of the prosecution and the defense? An experiment that simulated a jury trial in order to study this question found

a. a recency effect when the time interval between arguments was long but the interval between the second argument and the moment for deciding on a verdict was short
b. a recency effect when both intervals (time between arguments and time between second argument and verdict) were long
c. an interaction with no condition showing a clear-cut primacy or recency effect
d. a primacy effect when time intervals between arguments and between the second argument and the verdict were both short

_____ 5. Self-perception theory attempts to explain the results of studies relating behavioral compliance and attitude change (such as those designed to measure cognitive dissonance) by a rather surprising proposal. Self-perception theory claims that we

a. base our interpretations of others' behavior on what we would do in similar circumstances
b. assume that situational forces are very powerful and attribute too little effect to our own motives
c. try to behave according to the way that we feel but are often unsuccessful
d. infer our attitudes by observing our own behavior as if it were that of someone else

_____ 6. Social psychologists may be distinguished from other psychologists in at least two ways: their emphasis on the individual's "phenomenology" and their focus on _____ causes of behavior.

a. situational
b. developmental
c. personality
d. systematic

_____ 7. Solomon Asch's famous studies on compliance, in which a naive subject was asked to judge the length of a line after pseudo-subjects had intentionally misjudged it, have since been replicated and extended. Which of the following statements is *not* true about this research?

a. in the basic study about 3/4 of subjects conformed on at least one trial
b. if even one confederate breaks with the

majority, conformity drops sharply

c. conformity was reduced by a noncon-forming confederate only when the confederate gave the correct answer

d. subjects in the basic study conform about 1/3 of the time (i.e., on 1/3 of the critical trials)

_____ 8. When superior persons commit embarrassing blunders we tend to like them more, provided we have
a. low self-esteem
b. average self-esteem
c. feelings of superiority
d. proof that they feel humiliated

_____ 9. Milgram's studies of compliance in a "shocking" situation have been extensively criticized on the grounds that they
a. raise moral issues that we are not prepared to face
b. were not carried out with adequate experimental methodology
c. raise serious questions of research ethics
d. did not apply enough pressure to the subjects for the results to be meaningful in the real world

_____ 10. Studies such as the forbidden-toy one, originally designed to examine cognitive dissonance effects, have been repeated and expanded to study details of the attribution process. One important finding of these studies is that dispositional attributions
a. tend to be irreversible, once they have been made
b. are not made if the situational forces are clear and unambiguous
c. can be reversed by providing new information
d. are less likely to be made than are situational attributions

_____ 11. Research shows that physical appearance is important in determining
a. whether blind dates like each other
b. whether five-year-old children are popular with their peers
c. adults' predictions of a child's personality
d. all of the above

_____ 12. Attribution theory, self-perception theory, and cognitive-dissonance theory have all been used to examine the relationship(s) of

behavioral compliance and attitude change. One general conclusion from this area of research is that
a. behavioral compliance never leads to attitude change
b. the less the inducement for compliance, the more attitude change
c. the greater the inducement for compliance, the more attitude change
d. most behavioral compliance yields some attitude change

_____ 13. Attribution theorists have studied the way in which we infer the causes of others' (and perhaps our own) behavior. In doing so they have noted several rules which they believe we all tend to use. Which of the following is *not* one of these rules?
a. we are more likely to draw dispositional inferences from an uncommon act than from a common one
b. we prefer to see how behavior varies over time before making dispositional inferences
c. we typically make "situational attributions" when the evidence says we should be making "dispositional attributions"
d. we prefer to see how behavior varies in different situations before making dispositional inferences

_____ 14. One of the best ways of helping people become more resistant to persuasion is to
a. provide supporting arguments for something the person already believes in
b. keep the person isolated from opposing views until his beliefs have become very strongly built-in
c. launch an all-out attack on the person's belief to test its strength, then yield if he seems to be weakening, so that he wins
d. launch a weak attack on the person's belief, one that he can easily refute

_____ 15. A study of helping behavior, carried out in the New York subway, attempted to minimize the processes that prevent people from intervening in emergency situations. This study found that
a. an apparently ill victim received help in over 95 percent of the trials
b. people on the subway were even more reluctant to intervene than subjects in

the laboratory

c. black "drunk" victims were aided only by black passengers

d. "diffusion of responsibility" played a major role in the results

_____ 16. Implicit personality theories
a. are predictive only for people with whom we have little personal contact
b. lead us to see people as more variable in their behavior than they really are
c. may be one cause of the primacy effect
d. have little or no basis in fact

_____ 17. When we receive mixed information about a person, we tend to base our impression on the information that is
a. favorable
b. unfavorable
c. received last
d. received first

_____ 18. When subjects who believed themselves to be in a group discussion via intercom heard one of the "group members" supposedly have a seizure
a. "pluralistic ignorance" kept many of them from responding appropriately
b. those who did not report the seizure showed more distress than those who did
c. the "diffusion-of-responsibility" effect kept subjects from defining the situation as an emergency

d. the concept of "bystander apathy" was shown to be appropriately named

_____ 19. Most of the social-psychology research on attitude change during the past fifteen years has been generated by theories concerning
a. consistency in attitudes and behavior
b. cognitive dissonance
c. self-perception
d. attribution

_____ 20. Studies of coaction and audience effects have found that cockroaches and humans share some common reactions, as do other species. Which of the following is *not* true about these findings?
a. children turn a fishing reel faster in co-action
b. human subjects lift a finger weight faster with an audience
c. human subjects make fewer multiplication errors in coaction or with an audience
d. cockroaches ran a "runway" box faster with a cockroach audience

KEY TO SELF-QUIZ

1. b	6. a	11. d	16. c
2. d	7. c	12. b	17. d
3. b	8. b	13. c	18. b
4. a	9. c	14. d	19. a
5. d	10. a	15. a	20. c

INDIVIDUAL OR CLASS EXERCISE

CONFORMITY TO RULES

Introduction

In order to function effectively and to provide for the safety and welfare of its people any society must establish certain rules and regulations governing behavior. Social psychologists are interested in the factors that produce conformity to society's rules. The purpose of this exercise is to investigate some of the variables that influence an individual motorist's conformity to the rule requiring him to stop at a stop sign.

Equipment Needed

Clipboard and pencil.

Procedure

Select a four-way stop intersection (marked by stop signs, not a traffic light) with a moderate flow of traffic. It should be an intersection where you can watch the traffic from all four directions without being too conspicuous.

For a 45-minute period observe each car that approaches the intersection and record the information specified on the data sheet given on page 266. You will need to decide first whether the car (1) comes to a full stop at the intersection, (2) slows down but does not make a complete stop, or (3) makes little or no attempt to slow down. You should spend a few minutes observing the cars before starting your recording period in order to get an idea of how to classify the various degrees of "stopping." Exclude from your records those cars that are forced to stop because they were either behind another car or blocked by cross traffic.

After deciding upon the appropriate conformity category, note the sex of the driver, approximate age (under or over 25), and whether or not the driver is traveling alone. Place a tally mark in the appropriate box on the data sheet. For example, if the driver was a female, over 25, traveling with two children, and she made no attempt to slow down, you would place a tally mark in the bottom row in the box to the far right. If the driver was a male, under 25, traveling alone, and he came to a full stop, your tally mark would go in the top box of the extreme left-hand column. Obviously, if the car does not stop you will have to make some quick judgments as to age, sex, and companion.

Treatment of Data

Either you may analyze only your own data or the instructor may collect the data sheets from the entire class and provide you with the class totals in each category for your analysis.

1. Compute the overall percentage of individuals who made a full stop (that is, those who were rated as falling in Conformity Category 1).

   _____%

2. Compute the percentage of males who made a full stop, and do the same for females.

   males _____%

   females _____%

3. Compute the percentage of individuals under 25 who made a full stop, and do the same for those over 25.

   under 25 _____%

   over 25 _____%

4. Compute the percentage of times a full stop was made when the driver was alone, and the percentage when he was accompanied by one or more riders.

   alone _____%

   accompanied _____%

Questions For Discussion

1. Do most people comply with the regulation requiring a full stop at stop signs?

2. Does the degree of compliance or conformity depend upon the age and sex of the drivers? Is compliance influenced by whether or not the driver is alone?

3. In calculating our percentages, only Conformity Category 1 was considered. Do we gain any additional information by examining the percentage of drivers that fell in categories 2 and 3?

4. What other variables besides those recorded in this study seemed to predict conformity behavior? For example, did you get the impression that factors such as type or condition of the car, or the apparent socioeconomic status of the driver, were related to conformity?

5. How accurate do you think your judgments were concerning stopping behavior and the other variables? Would it have been worthwhile to have had several judges rather than a single observer making ratings?

6. If you were to make a large-scale study of this type of conformity behavior, what changes would you make in the research procedure?

DATA SHEET

			Conformity Categories		
			1. Full stop	2. Considerable slowing but not full stop	3. Little or no slowing
Alone	Under 25	Male			
		Female			
	Over 25	Male			
		Female			
With others	Under 25	Male			
		Female			
	Over 25	Male			
		Female			

19
psychology and society

LEARNING OBJECTIVES

Be able to give illustrations of psychology's influence on public policy.

Describe psychology's three main methodological contributions to society.

Understand the notion of social indicators, listing some possible examples, and the methods discussed for forecasting the future.

Give some examples showing how society's assumptions and prejudices can affect the objectivity of the behavioral scientist's research.

PROGRAMMED UNIT

1. In addition to its role in solving practical problems, psychology, along with the other behavioral sciences, has an important influence on the formation of *public policy*. Previous chapters have provided examples of psychology's contributions to the solution of problems in such areas as learning, perception, child rearing, and the treatment of emotional disorders. In this chapter we will look at

policy   psychology's influence on public _____.

2. The United States Supreme Court, in reaching its 1954 decision declaring racial segregation in the schools to be unconstitutional, gave serious consideration to psychological research showing the detrimental effects of segregation on the self-concept of black children. This is a very clear example of psychology's

public policy   influence on _____ _____. The text also gives as an example an 1896 Supreme Court decision which shows that legislation and court decisions have always been influenced by psychological theory even though the relationship was not explicitly acknowledged.

3. Psychology's contribution to the solution of society's problems lies as much in its *methodological skills* as in its theories and experimental findings. These

methodological   metho_____ skills include *experimental methods, standardized testing,* and *opinion surveys.*

4. Three important methodological skills that psychology has contributed are

methods, testing   experimental _____, standardized _____,

surveys   and opinion _____.

5. Even though the psychologist may not know the answer to a problem, he or she

experimental   comes equipped with some well-proven exp_____
methods that will help find the answer. These include techniques for *formulating the question experimentally, testing it out,* and *evaluating the results.*

6. Among the psychologist's methodological equipment are techniques for

formulating   _____ questions experimentally, testing them

evaluating   out, and _____ the results.

7. The psychologists' know-how in designing and evaluating empirical studies provides one of their greatest contributions to the formulation and implementa-

policy   tion of public _____.

8. Many questions cannot be answered unless we know how to study them empirically. What are the most effective methods for teaching young children? How does sex-segregated advertising affect job applications? What parole policies are most effective in preventing future criminal acts? To answer these questions

experimental   we need people who are skilled in _____
(or empirical)   methods.

9. A second major contribution of psychology, in addition to knowledge of

methods   experimental _____, is *standardized testing.*

10. The development of objective methods for measuring intelligence, special abilities, aptitudes, and interests has had an enormous impact on society. More and

tests   more institutions each year adopt psychological _____ for selecting
and guiding individuals into schools and jobs.

11. The use of tests for selection of job and school applicants has helped ensure that opportunities are open to all; selection is based on *merit,* as represented by

test   scores on a _____, rather than by social class, race, sex, or political
influence.

merit   12. By ensuring that opportunities are available on the basis of _____, the
use of psychological tests has made a significant contribution to the American
ideal of equal opportunity for all regardless of race, sex, or social class. But tests

sometimes fail to achieve their goal for two reasons: (a) it is difficult to construct a test that is *"fair"* to all members of society; (b) tests may be used *inappropriately* so that they exclude individuals on the basis of factors irrelevant to the job for which they are being selected.

inappropriately

13. Requiring employers to provide evidence that their selection tests actually predict on-the-job performance is one way of making sure that tests are not used in _____.

fair

14. In using tests for job selection it is important that the test be both _____ and appropriate.

experimental

opinion

15. Two of psychology's most important methodological contributions to society are _____ methods and testing. A third contribution is the *public opinion survey.* Public _____ surveys are used to measure how people feel on a wide variety of topics.

surveys

16. Because policy makers often rely on the results of public opinion _____ as guides in making and timing their decisions, such surveys also help *shape policies.* For example, before deciding on changes in welfare programs government officials may assess the feelings of various groups of people by means of

surveys

carefully devised _____.

shape

17. Thus, public opinion surveys help to _____ policies as well as to record opinions. Survey techniques have also been used in research on the nature of *beliefs* and *attitudes.* For example, one survey study found that while many Americans oppose social welfare programs *in general,* they endorse almost all of the specific programs already in operation.

attitudes

18. Thus, surveys show some inconsistencies in our beliefs and _____.

experimental

testing, surveys

19. Psychology's three major methodological contributions are _____ methods, standardized _____, and opinion _____.

guide

indicators

20. To help in formulating and evaluating social policies and programs, we need *guidelines* based on the current status of the nation's social health. One way of providing such _____lines would be to construct *social indicators.* Social _____ would show, on the basis of available data, how well we are progressing in such areas as health, education, public safety, crime, poverty, social mobility, protection of the physical environment, and so on.

social indicator

21. The number of first admissions to neuropsychiatric hospitals each year would be a _____ _____ telling us something about the status of the nation's mental health.

22. The proportion of crimes committed each year by juveniles would be a social indicator

_____ _____ telling us how well we are coping with the problems of our youth.

23. Social indicators can be developed in many areas to show the current status of

guidelines

social health and to provide g_____ for *future policy.* Because of the psychologists' experience in survey research, test construction, and studies of attitude change, they can play a major role in the development

indicators

and interpretation of social _____.

policy

24. In recommending future _____ it is helpful to be able to make some forecasts about the future, to make predictions about the course of

future

large-scale social processes. One method of forecasting the _____ is *trend analysis.*

25. If we know the number of mental patients cared for in various private, state, and government hospitals each year for the past ten years, and we know also the rate

forecast

of population growth over these years, we can predict, or <u>fore</u>_____, with fair accuracy the number of hospital beds that will be required to care for mental patients ten years from now. We are analyzing the *trend* in population

trend

growth and the <u>tr</u>_____ in incidence of mental illness.

analysis

26. One difficulty with trend _____ is that it does not take into account new events that have not affected the trend in the past but may influence the future. For example, the trend in population growth may well be affected by widespread use of more effective methods of birth control. If this were the case, prediction of the size of the population ten years hence, based

overestimate

upon past growth, may well (*overestimate / underestimate*) the actual population size in ten years.

27. Similarly, if a new and startlingly effective treatment for schizophrenia were

prediction

discovered within the next few years, the <u>pre</u>_____

overestimation

concerning the treatment facilities required in ten years would probably be an (*overestimation / underestimation*).

analysis

28. To improve predictions based on trend _____ experts in various fields are consulted about events likely to take place in the years ahead that are not fully reflected in the current analyses.

29. When the predictions of experts in a number of fields are synthesized to take into account the interdependencies of their predictions, the method is known as

matrix

the *cross-impact matrix method.* The cross-impact _____ method

experts

synthesizes the predictions of a number of _____ to arrive at a

forecast

more accurate <u>fore</u>_____ of future events.

30. Because many social problems are wide in scope, covering a number of different professions, it is no longer efficient for psychologists, economists, engineers, biologists, and other scientists to work in isolation on such problems. An *inter-disciplinary* approach is needed, where scientists from various fields and dis-

ciplines pool their knowledge and abilities in a concerted attack on social problems. Because the problems that confront society span many scientific areas, a _____ approach would be the most effective.

interdisciplinary

Note: The final section of this chapter discusses ways in which society's assumptions and prejudices can affect the objectivity of the behavioral scientist's research. The text points out that, despite these influences, the scientific method of open and repeatable inquiry is still the best procedure yet devised for obtaining knowledge.

TERMS AND CONCEPTS FOR IDENTIFICATION

social indicators _____

_____

_____

_____

trend analysis_____

_____

_____

_____

Delphi method _____

_____

_____

_____

cross-impact matrix method _____

_____

_____

_____

_____ 1. An unconscious bias may enter into a be-
           havioral scientist's work in several ways.
           For example, it can influence the
           a. questions he chooses
           b. objectivity of his methods
           c. data he decides to publish
           d. all of the above

_____ 2. Social indicators
           a. are now routinely collected but unused
           b. include gross national product and the
              prime interest rate
           c. would consist of totally new measures
              devised for this purpose
           d. would be similar to economic indicators
              and could use some available statistics

_____ 3. The Strong Vocational Interest Blank is
           one of those tests that contribute to soci-
           etal conservatism, because it
           a. is not used widely enough to help com-
              bat such conservatism
           b. selects conservative individuals for im-
              portant vocations
           c. guides individuals to occupations made
              up of people just like them
           d. has until recently collected data only
              for men

_____ 4. The study of sex bias in advertising found
           that
           a. approximately 30 percent of women ap-
              plied for male-biased ads even before
              the ads were rewritten
           b. nearly half the women applied for for-
              merly male jobs when ads were rewrit-
              ten to appeal specifically to women
           c. the results for men showed a virtually
              identical pattern to that of women
           d. all of the above

_____ 5. The Taichung Study found that
           a. educational efforts directed at wives
              were as effective as those aimed at both
              husbands and wives
           b. efforts directed at husbands and wives
              were much more effective than those
              directed at wives alone
           c. home visits were more effective than
              group meetings
           d. most of the women were unwilling to
              change

_____ 6. When the United States was considering
           limiting immigration in the early 1900's,
           psychologists boldly used their science to
           a. protest against such policies
           b. study completely different problems
           c. support society's prejudices
           d. none of the above

_____ 7. The public opinion survey is
           a. a passive recorder of opinion
           b. limited to what the public believes at
              one moment in time
           c. generally ignored by successful politi-
              cians
           d. increasingly helping to shape opinion as
              well as measure it

_____ 8. One of psychology's major methodological
           contributions to society is standardized
           testing. Tests have been criticized, how-
           ever, on the grounds that they
           a. are not fair to all members of society
           b. may be used inappropriately to exclude
              individuals from a job
           c. are not valid predictors of on-the-job
              performance
           d. all of the above

_____ 9. Methods of future forecasting are of vary-
           ing degrees of complexity, with the most
           complex having the best chance of predict-
           ing accurately. The three methods sug-
           gested in the text, in order of increasing
           complexity, are
           a. Delphi, trend analysis, cross-impact ma-
              trix
           b. trend analysis, Delphi, cross-impact
              matrix
           c. Delphi, expert judgement, trend analysis
           d. trend analysis, cross-impact matrix,
              Delphi

_____ 10. The objectivity of science lies in
           a. the capability of scientists to avoid the
              prejudices of their society
           b. the choice of questions studied
           c. its methodology
           d. all of the above

_____ 11. One problem when aptitude tests are used
           to screen potential employees is that they
           frequently

a. predict success in the training program better than success on the job
b. are too difficult and thus screen out too many people
c. are too easy and thus do not limit the potential employees adequately
d. are especially offensive to lower-class blacks who might apply for such jobs

____ 12. A major problem in developing interdisciplinary research is the difficulty of integrating such research into existing university structures. National panels reporting on this problem have suggested
a. multidisciplinary institutes inside universities
b. multidisciplinary institutes outside universities
c. professional schools of applied behavioral science
d. all of the above

____ 13. Social problems typically are large and complex. Attempts to solve them
a. have typically also been large and complex
b. need to be both larger and more interdisciplinary than in the past
c. have typically been interdisciplinary but small in scope
d. have typically been large but too narrow in approach

____ 14. The text used two Supreme Court decisions on racial relations, one from 1896 and one from 1954, to illustrate an important point about psychology and society. These two decisions were useful for this purpose because they show
a. how much more favorable to minorities the 1954 decision was
b. that little changed between 1896 and 1954
c. that both decisions mirrored the psychology of the times
d. that only recently have psychological theories been influential in court decisions

____ 15. The thinking of behavioral scientists affects the society and vice versa. The text points out that in this relationship
a. the primary influence is that of society on behavioral scientists
b. the primary influence is that of behav-

ioral scientists on society
c. these influences are about evenly matched
d. it is not possible to compare such influences

____ 16. By "the hidden conservatism of testing" the text means that testing
a. is regulated by comparatively unseen members of the "Establishment"
b. as a field, attracts psychologists who are conservative in their beliefs
c. too often includes political bias in non-political tests
d. tends to freeze the status quo by its very success

____ 17. Psychology's major contribution to the solution of society's problems is
a. psychological theory
b. specific information obtained from research
c. methodology
d. both a and b

____ 18. The technique of future forecasting in which estimates of future trends provided by panels of experts are combined into a single estimate is the _____ method.
a. test analysis
b. cross-impact matrix
c. trend analysis
d. expert judgment

____ 19. The "KAP" surveys are a good start toward coordinated, large-scale, systematic inquiry of a social problem. These surveys
a. sought information on population control
b. examined sex bias in advertising
c. sought knowledge, then action, on problems
d. examined political attitudes in the United States

____ 20. As a result of the two studies of sex bias in classified ads described in the text
a. AT & T has rewritten all of its advertising and has launched a campaign featuring sex-reversed ads
b. the Pennsylvania case was won by NOW
c. most newspapers have "desegregated" their want-ad columns
d. all of the above

INDIVIDUAL EXERCISE

REVERSING SEXISM

Introduction

One of the major social concerns of our time is the achieving of true personal equality for all individuals—of different races, ages, and sexes. One of the difficulties in dealing with such problems is to be able to recognize them. Daryl Bem of Stanford University has written about the difficulty many of us have in identifying sexism—in ourselves, in others, and in the institutions which shape and support us.[1] Bem calls the result a "nonconscious ideology" and has suggested the technique for learning to recognize it, which forms the basis of this exercise.

Equipment Needed

None

Procedure

1. First, read the following description of a modern egalitarian marriage:

Both my wife and I earned Ph.D. degrees in our respective disciplines. I turned down a superior academic post in Oregon and accepted a slightly less desirable position in New York where my wife could obtain a part-time teaching job and do research at one of the several other colleges in the area. Although I would have preferred to live in a suburb, we purchased a home near my wife's college so that she could have an office at home where she would be when the children returned from school. Because my wife earns a good salary, she can easily afford to pay a maid to do her major household chores. My wife and I share all other tasks around the house

[1] Bem, D. (1970) *Beliefs, attitudes and human affairs.* Belmont, Calif: Brooks-Cole.

equally. For example, she cooks the meals, but I do the laundry for her and help her with many of her other household tasks.

2. Do you agree that this is a truly nonsexist marriage? Or are you uncertain? It may seem different from the older stereotype of a sexist marriage, but is it truly equal?

3. The technique proposed by Bem for analyzing such questions is very simple. If you can substitute "he" for "she" and vice versa in any such description, it is truly nonsexist. Can that be done with the above description? Read the results below and see what you think.

Both my husband and I earned Ph.D. degrees in our respective disciplines, I turned down a superior academic post in Oregon and accepted a slightly less desirable position in New York where my husband could obtain a part-time teaching job and do research at one of the several other colleges in the area. Although I would have preferred to live in a suburb, we purchased a home near my husband's college so that he could have an office at home where he would be when the children returned from school. Because my husband earns a good salary, he can easily afford to pay a maid to do his major household chores. My husband and I share all other tasks around the house equally. For example, he cooks the meals, but I do the laundry for him and help him with many of his other household tasks.

4. As you have no doubt noted, the marriage described is far from equal. The husband is simply generously sharing some of the tasks that are jointly produced—such as laundry—but which are by stereotype the wife's duties. This technique is a good general one for you to keep in mind. It allows you to spot and recognize sexist stereotypes that might otherwise slip by.

5. As a variation on this technique try substituting a male person for a female, and vice versa, in thinking about situations. For example, the liberated women

among you might consider the situation in which a male friend picks up a lunch tab for you. Would you accept the same from a female friend? If not, you're supporting sexism.

6. This procedure is so convincing that it makes a useful demonstration for others whose consciousness may not be as raised as yours. The next time you wish to convince someone that a procedure is sexist try turning it around in this way.

Questions For Discussion

1. If one wishes to be egalitarian, why is it not easy simply to be so? Why do we have to use such tricks as this?

2. What would have to happen for such tricks to become unnecessary? Is it likely to? How soon, do you think? (Hint: are pink and blue blankets equal?)

appendix:

statistical methods and measurement

LEARNING OBJECTIVES

Be familiar with measures of central tendency (mean, mode, and median) and measures of variation (range and standard deviation).

Be able to explain the logical basis on which one makes a statistical inference. Be particularly familiar with the procedure for testing the significance of a difference between two means (e.g., between the means of an experimental group and a control group).

Be familiar with coefficients of correlation (the product-moment correlation and the rank correlation). Be able to compute correlation coefficients for sample sets of data.

Understand the logic of a correlational study, and its limitations regarding cause-and-effect relationships.

PROGRAMMED UNIT

1. If we administer a test to 1000 students and enter their scores in a notebook, we will be recording information about the test results in the form of *raw scores.*

   raw   The scores are called _____ because these are the data as they were collected; they have not been changed in any way.

2. The number a person receives on any measure (height, weight, a test, and so on)

   raw   is called a _____ score because it has not been manipulated in any way—it remains just as it was collected.

3. Raw data become comprehensible if they are presented in the form of a *frequency distribution.* If we follow a common procedure, we may list each possible score and record next to it the number of people who made that score.

distribution   In this way the raw data is rearranged as a frequency _____.

4. Whenever we take raw data and arrange it so that we can tell how many people

frequency   made each possible score, we have a _____
distribution
_____ .

5. Since we cannot keep 1000 raw scores in mind at any one time, it would be very convenient if we could *describe* these scores more simply. There are a number of ways to describe (or summarize) frequency distributions; all of them, so long as they merely *describe* the distribution, are classified as *descriptive statistics.* Whenever we use a number (for example, an average) to describe a distribution,

descriptive   we are using a _____ statistic.

6. Professor X, who has given a test to a large class, wishes to compute the average score in order to describe how well her students as a whole have performed. The

descriptive statistic   professor is using a _____ _____.

descriptive   **7.** Anyone who describes a distribution of scores by the use of summarizing or
statistics
simplifying scores is using _____ _____.

8. One descriptive statistic, used very often, is called the *mean;* it is nothing more than the familiar arithmetic average. In order to determine the *mean* of a distribution of scores, one merely sums (that is, adds up) all the scores and *divides* by the *number* of scores. If you sum the raw scores and divide by the

mean   number of scores, you have computed the _____.

9. John has taken eight tests during a semester, each of which counts equally toward his final grade. To get an idea of how well he has done, he sums the numerical grades received on the tests and divides the sum by eight. He has

mean   computed a _____ grade.

10. In order to compute a mean, one sums all the raw scores and divides by the

number   _____ of scores.

11. Another descriptive statistic is called the *median.* The *median* is defined as the middle score of the distribution. This statistic is obtained by arranging all the scores from low to high and counting in to the middle from either end. The

median   middle score is the _____ score. If the number of cases is even, one simply averages the cases on either side of the middle. For instance, with 10

median   cases, the _____ is the average of the fifth and sixth scores when they are arranged from low to high.

12. Put another way, if we find the score that divides the distribution in half, we

median   have found the _____.

13. The *mode* is the score that appears most *frequently* in the distribution. We find the mode by merely examining the distribution; it requires no computation. Whenever we are talking about the score that occurs most frequently, we are

mode

talking about the _____.

frequently
(or synonym)

14. The mode, then, is the score that appears most _____ in the distribution.

descriptive

15. The mean, the median, and the mode are all _____ statistics. They simply describe the distribution of scores.

16. Let us illustrate the way these three statistics may differ by using an example. Let us consider the salaries of five men. Assume that Jim earns $5000 a year, Tom earns $10,000, Harry also earns $10,000, Bob earns $20,000, and Mack earns $155,000. First let us compute the *mean* salary. To make this computa-

divide

tion, sum all the salaries and _____ by the number of salaries. (*Use a separate sheet for this computation and keep it in view.*)

5

17. When we sum the salaries of the five men, and divide by ___, we arrive at a mean

$40,000

salary of $_____.

18. Next find the *median* salary. The median is the salary in the middle of the distribution. Arranging the five salaries in order from high to low and counting

$10,000

in to the middle yields a median of $_____.

19. Finally we examine the distribution to find the *modal* salary. It is obvious that

$10,000

the *mode* of the distribution is $_____, since this is the salary that appears most often in the distribution.

20. It now becomes clear that these three statistics may be very different from one another. In this particular example, the mode and median both take on the

same, larger

_____ value, but the mean is much _____. If you were given the mode of a distribution and thought that you were getting the mean, you would be receiving a distorted picture of the true state of affairs.

21. Once we have a mean, it is often helpful to know whether the scores are all very close to the mean or whether they are spread from very low to very high. In other words, we would like to have a *measure of variation* to describe whether the scores vary a lot or just a little. One measure of variation is the *range,* which is the spread from the lowest to the highest score. If the instructor says that the scores on a test went from a low of 32 to a high of 93, he is giving the

range

_____ of scores.

variation

22. The range is one measure of _____.

23. Joyce got a 63 on a test. Her roommate asked her how well the others in the class did, and she replied that the scores ran from 40 to 74. Joyce was describing

range

the variation of scores in terms of their _____.

mean	**24.** Most scores are not the same as the mean; that is, they deviate from the mean. The *standard deviation* is a frequently used measure of the amount by which scores deviate or depart from their _____. The standard deviation is thus
variation	another measure of _____.

25. The lower case Greek letter σ is frequently used as an abbreviation for the
deviation   standard _____. The formula for computing the standard deviation is as follows:

$$\sigma = \sqrt{\frac{\text{Sum of } d^2}{N}}$$

The deviation, *d,* for each score is first computed by subtracting the score from the mean. Next, the *d* for each score is squared, and then the squared deviations for all the scores are summed.

26. Statisticians use *N* as a shorthand for the number of scores. When we divide the
deviations   sum of the squared _____ by *N,* we are dividing by
scores   the number of _____.

27. In computing the *standard deviation,* then, the first step is to determine the
square   deviation of each raw score from the mean. The second step is to _____ each of these deviations.

28. In the third step, sum these squared deviations and then divide by *N.* To review:
deviation   The first step is to determine the _____ of each raw
square   score from the mean. The second step is to _____ each of these
N   deviations. Third, sum the squared deviations and divide by ___.

29. When we then take the *square root* of the result of step three, we arrive at the
standard deviation   _____ _____.

30. To recapitulate: First, determine the deviations of the raw scores from the
mean, deviations   _____; second, square each of these _____;
sum   third, _____ these squared deviations and divide by *N.* Finally, take the
root, standard   square _____ of the result to obtain the _____
deviation   _____.

31. Let us consider the following example to show how a standard deviation is calculated. For the sake of simplicity, we will use only a few scores. Suppose a test is given to five people and the scores are as follows: 11, 13, 14, 15, 17. In
14   this case the mean would be _____. (*Use a separate sheet of paper.*)

32. For the score of 11, the deviation from the mean (obtained by subtracting the
9   score from the mean) is 3. Squaring this we would arrive at the number ___.

1   **33.** The deviation of the score of 13 would be ___. Squaring this we would arrive at
1   the number ___.

0, 0   **34.** The deviation of the score of 14 would be ___. Squaring this yields ___.

35. The deviation of the score of 15 would be −1 (14 − 15 = −1). Squaring −1 yields

1   ___.

−3, 9   **36.** The deviation of the score of 17 would be _____. Squaring this yields ___.

37. We now have the squared deviation of each of the scores. In other words, we have completed steps one and two in the sequence mentioned above and are ready to move on to step three in the computation of the standard deviation. In

sum   step three we _____ the squared deviations and divide by N. In this case N

5   equals ___.

4   **38.** When the operations in step three are carried out, we arrive at ___ (*number*) as a result.

39. We now perform the final operation; we take the square root of the result of

2   step three. The square root of 4 is ___.

2   **40.** Therefore the standard deviation of this distribution of scores is ___.

standard   **41.** We have examined two *measures of variation:* the range and the _____ deviation.

variation   **42.** The range and the standard deviation are both measures of _____. Since these two statistics merely *describe* the distribution, they are classified as

descriptive   _____ statistics.

43. We often wish to say something about large groups of people, for example, the population of China, or the population of the United States, or all college students, or all students at a particular college. The group we wish to talk about is called the *population,* whether it contains 50,000,000 or 100 people. In research, the total group we wish to make our statements about is called the

population   _____.

44. Professor Jones wishes to find out whether English males are taller than German males. Since he wants to say something about both English males and German

populations   males, these are his _____s.

45. It is obvious that Professor Jones will not have enough time or money to test all English and German males. Therefore he will have to be satisfied to test fewer than all of them. In a way he has the same problem that a customs inspector has. The customs inspector wants to make sure that no one brings in contraband, but he hasn't time to inspect everyone's luggage. Therefore he selects some of the people and inspects their baggage thoroughly. He has drawn a *sample* of the total

sample   population. A _____, then, is a smaller number of cases that is

population   drawn from the _____.

46. Whenever one selects and tests a smaller number of cases from the total population he is interested in, he has drawn a _____ from the population.

sample

47. A sample should be selected in such a way that it is *representative* of the total population. Otherwise, we cannot make reasonable *inferences* about the total

population

_____ based solely on information obtained from the sample.

48. A sample that is not representative of the population will not allow us to make reasonable _____ about the population.

inferences

49. One way of obtaining a representative sample is to select it at *random.* To do this, we can put the names of the members of the population in a hat and draw out the number we need, or use any other means of selection that will guarantee that *every person in the population has an equal chance of being chosen.* When we draw a sample in such a way that each individual in the population has an

random

equal chance of being chosen, we have drawn a r_____ sample.

50. A key feature of a random sample is that each individual in the population has

equal chance

an _____ _____ of being chosen.

51. If we collect data on a sample of 100 people in a town of 1000 people and then make statements about the *entire* population of the town on the basis of this data, we cannot be *sure* our statements are correct. Only if we collect data on

population

the entire _____ of the town can we be sure that any statements based upon the data will be correct for the whole population.

52. When we make statements about a population on the basis of a sample, we *infer* that what is true about the sample will also be approximately true for the entire population. A statement about a population based upon a sample of that

inference

population is called a(n) _____ence. We can never be com-

sure (or synonym)

pletely _____ that such an inference is correct.

53. Another way of putting this is to say that when we make an inference about a population from a sample, we have only a certain probability that our statement is correct for the population as a whole. The probability of our statement being true would be 100 percent only if we had data on the

entire (or synonym)

_____ population.

54. The smaller the size of the sample, the smaller the probability of making a correct inference about the population. Since we are making inferences about

population

the _____, based on *statistics* that are computed

sample

from only a _____ of the population, we call this process *statistical inference.*

55. When the Gallup poll interviews a small number of people and makes a prediction about who will be elected President of the United States, a statistical inference _____ _____ is being made.

56. Suppose a researcher is interested in the population of a particular college with 10,000 students. She goes to the college directory and takes each hundredth

random name, thus drawing a _____ sample of the population of students at that college.

57. She tests this sample of students and, on the basis of their scores alone, she

population makes statements about the entire _____ of the

statistical inference college. When she does this, she is making a _____

_____ .

58. Suppose we gave an intelligence test to all the people in the United States and then plotted on a graph the scores and the number of people who got each score. We plot the number of people on the vertical axis and their scores on the

horizontal hor_____ axis. In schematic form the graph would look like the illustration below.

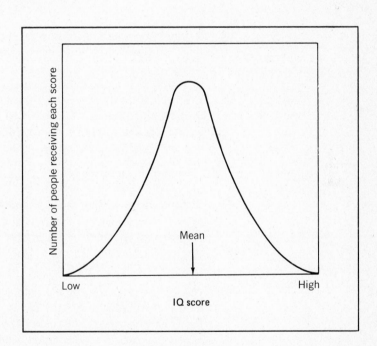

59. This graph represents a *frequency distribution* of scores. Looking at the graph, we find that there are relatively few people who got very low scores and that the

increases number of people who got any particular score (*increases*/*decreases*) as we move upward toward the mean. As we move past the mean to the right, there are fewer and fewer people getting the higher scores and very few getting the highest scores.

60. Note that the curve of the frequency distribution is *symmetric* in form; that is,

above the part of the curve below the mean is a mirror image of the part _____ the mean. Symmetry implies that for every score a fixed distance above the

below

mean there is a corresponding score the same distance _____ the mean, so that the number of people receiving each score will be the same.

frequency

61. The curve of the _____ distribution shown above is not only symmetric in form but also is shaped very much like a bell. A frequency-

bell

distribution curve that is symmetric and also _____-*shaped* is called a *normal curve.*

distribution

62. When we plot a frequency _____ and get a

normal

curve that is bell-shaped, we call this curve a _____ curve.

63. For a normal curve the mean, median, and mode all have the same value. There are the same number of cases below and above the middle of the distribution; for every score below the mean there is another score the same distance above the mean; and the number of cases receiving a score a given distance below the mean is matched by an equal number of cases receiving a score the same distance

symmetric

above the mean. In other words, the two halves of the curve are _____.

fifty

64. If fifty people have a score of 80 and the mean is 100, then _____ (*number*) people can be expected to have a score of 120 if the curve is a normal curve.

65. If we actually administered the Stanford-Binet intelligence test to all the people in the United States, we would find that the frequency distribution of scores would take the form of a normal curve. The *mean* of the scores would be 100 and the *standard deviation* would be 16. The standard deviation, as you will

variation

remember, is a measure of var_____.

66. Statisticians often talk about a score as being one or more standard deviations away from the mean. If the mean of the scores on an intelligence test is 100 and the standard deviation is 16, a score of 84 would be said to be one standard

below

deviation _____ the mean.

67. One of the properties of the normal curve is that *68 percent* of all the cases in the distribution will have scores that lie between one standard deviation below and one above the mean. The normal curve is so defined that this will *always* be true. If a distribution of intelligence test scores fits a normal curve,

68

_____ percent of the cases will have scores between one standard deviation

above

below the mean and one standard deviation _____ the mean. This characteristic of the normal curve is shown in the illustration below, in which new labels have been added to the normal curve with which you are already familiar.

68. As you already know, the Greek letter σ is the abbreviation for standard

below

deviation. Thus -1σ means one standard deviation _____ the mean.

69. Referring again to the intelligence test with a mean of 100 and a standard

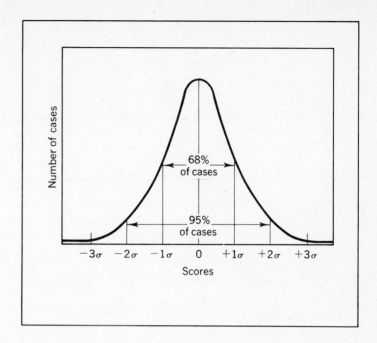

deviation of 16, the score that is one standard deviation below the mean is

84   _____ (*number*).

116

70. The score that is one standard deviation above the mean would be _____.

71. Therefore, if we group all the people with scores between 84 and 116 on the

68   intelligence test, we will have _____ percent of the population.

72. If we look again at the new illustration of the normal curve, we see that 95 percent of the population have scores that lie between *two* standard deviations below the mean and two standard deviations above the mean. To go back to the intelligence test with a mean of 100 and a standard deviation of 16, 95 percent

132   of the population will have scores between 68 and _____.

73. If 68 percent of the population have scores that lie between one standard deviation below the mean and one standard deviation above the mean on the

34   normal curve, then it follows that _____ percent of the population have scores between one standard deviation below the mean and the mean itself.

74. In other words, in our example, 34 percent of the population have scores

100   between 84 and _____.

75. If 95 percent of the population have scores between two standard deviations below the mean and two standard deviations above the mean, then 47.5 percent of the population have scores between two standard deviations above the mean and the mean itself. In our example, then, 47.5 percent of the population have

132   scores between 100 and _____.

76. Again looking at our illustration of the normal curve, we can see that almost all of the people (over 99 percent) have scores that lie between three standard

above   deviations below the mean and three standard deviations _____ the
mean. Thus for practical purposes virtually all of the scores fall between minus

three   and plus _____ standard deviations from the mean.

77. To use our example once more, we would expect that practically all the people
who took the intelligence test (mean = 100, standard deviation = 16) would have

52, 148   scores between _____ and _____.

78. As a quick example of how one can use the concept of the standard deviation on
the normal curve, let us suppose that Susan had a score of 148 on the
intelligence test. Knowing the mean and the standard deviation of that test,
Susan can be sure that she has earned one of the very highest scores, since her

three   score is _____ standard deviations above the mean. In other words,
she knows how her score compares with those from the population at large.

Note: The Appendix in the text can be only an introduction to the subject of
statistics. In turn, this programmed unit can be only an introduction to that
material. You have learned about some of the basic terms and techniques of
statistical analysis, but several concepts that are treated in the text have not even
been mentioned in this program. You should, however, find it easier to master
the text treatment if you have understood the concepts presented here.

TERMS AND CONCEPTS FOR IDENTIFiCATION

descriptive statistics _____

_____

_____

_____

frequency distribution _____

_____

_____

_____

mean _____

_____

_____

_____

median _____

_____

_____

_____

mode _____

_____

_____

_____

range _____

_____

_____

_____

standard deviation _____

_____

_____

_____

population _____

_____

_____

_____

sample _____

_____

_____

_____

normal distribution _____

_____

_____

_____

statistical inference _____

_____

_____

_____

standard error of the mean _____

_____

_____

_____

product-moment correlation (r) _____

_____

_____

_____

rank correlation (ρ) _____

_____

_____

_____

_____ 1. A coefficient of correlation is significant if
a. its sign is positive
b. it exceeds .80
c. its standard error is less than 1
d. its critical ratio is greater than 2

_____ 2. Suppose scores on test A have a mean of
20 and a standard error of the mean of 1,
while scores on test B have a mean of 25
and also have a standard error of the mean
of 1. Can we depend on the difference
between the two means, i.e., is it significant?
a. yes, since the critical ratio is high
b. no; the difference is not significant
c. maybe, since the critical ratio is close to
the significance level
d. we cannot tell from these data

_____ 3. The curve which results from a large number of chance events occurring independently is a _____ curve
a. standard
b. normal
c. random
d. chance

_____ 4. What two measures of central tendency are
identical for this distribution: 1, 1, 3, 4, 6?
a. mean and mode
b. mode and median
c. mean and median
d. all of the above

_____ 5. Suppose you take a midterm and a final in
this course. Will you be able to tell on
which one you do better when there are
different numbers of questions? If the midterm has a mean of 50 with a standard
deviation of 10, the final has a mean of
120 with a standard deviation of 20, and
your scores are 55 and 135, you will have
a. done better on the final
b. done worse on the final
c. stayed the same on the final
d. failed the course

_____ 6. It should always be remembered that correlation
a. does not measure linear relationships
b. cannot show statistical significance

c. does not yield causal relationships
d. all of the above

_____ 7. A measure of variation
a. is the range
b. tells us how representative the mean is
c. is the standard deviation
d. all of the above

_____ 8. A rank correlation
a. is designated by r
b. is a simpler method for determining correlations than is the product-moment
correlation
c. should probably be done on a computer, because of the complexity of the
formula
d. does not go below zero, because ranks
are involved

_____ 9. If we wished to know whether the average
of a distribution is typical of the scores
within it, we would look at the _____
for a simple indicator but would compute
the _____ if we wished a
more sensitive measure.
a. range, standard deviation
b. range, standard score
c. mean, standard deviation
d. mode, critical ratio

_____ 10. The most widely used graph form for plot-
ting data grouped into class intervals is the
a. frequency distribution
b. symmetrical distribution
c. frequency histogram
d. normal distribution

_____ 11. A standard score is
a. based on the standard deviation
b. offers a way of scaling the data
c. tells us how one score compares to the
others in a distribution
d. all of the above

_____ 12. The conventional rule of thumb for an
acceptable level of statistical significance is
_____ percent, i.e., we are willing
to risk a chance result occurring _____
in 100 decisions.
a. 1, 1

b. 2, 2
c. 5, 5
d. 10, 10

_____ 13. If a normal distribution has a mean of 100 and a standard deviation of 5, we know that
a. 68 percent of the scores fall between 95 and 105
b. 95 percent of the scores fall between 85 and 115
c. approximately half of the scores fall between 80 and 120
d. the range of scores is 75 to 125

_____ 14. A correlation of $r = -.80$
a. is significant
b. means that increases in x are accompanied by decreases in y
c. means that increases in x are accompanied by increases in y
d. makes the relationship between x and y unclear

_____ 15. The median is
a. obtained by adding the scores and dividing by the number of cases
b. that part of the scale where most cases occur
c. the score with the highest frequency
d. the middle score in a distribution

_____ 16. We can have confidence in a statistical inference if the
a. sample is significant
b. effect is large relative to the sampling error
c. population is normal
d. all of the above

_____ 17. If a general round of wage increases were to be combined with a reduction of extremely high incomes, the
a. mean income would tend to go up

b. distribution of income would become less skewed
c. median would tend to go down
d. distribution of income would become more skewed

_____ 18. Since the standard error of the mean is a special case of the standard deviation, it tells us about the distribution of the *population* made up of *sample means.* For example, we know that if a sample has a mean of 50 and a standard error of the mean of 5, the population mean almost certainly falls in the range of
a. 45-55
b. 40-60
c. 35-65
d. 30-70

_____ 19. The _____ is very useful, in that it gives us a mathematical way of stating the degree of relationship between two variables.
a. rank correlation (*rho*)
b. coefficient of correlation
c. product-moment correlation (*r*)
d. all of the above

_____ 20. In order to make a judgment about a population without testing all members of it, we
a. draw a random sample for testing
b. examine the normal distribution
c. develop a standard score
d. examine the standard error of the scores

KEY TO SELF-QUIZ

20. a	15. d	10. c	5. a
19. d	14. b	9. a	4. c
18. c	13. a	8. b	3. b
17. b	12. c	7. d	2. a
16. b	11. d	6. c	1. d

INDIVIDUAL EXERCISES

Introduction

Although a mastery of statistical techniques requires time and training, the basic notions of statistics can be understood by those with a minimum of mathematical background. The following exercises use simple data in order to make computations easy. These exercises are designed to illustrate how the formulas work rather than to provide skill in their use; you should attempt the exercises only after you have read the Appendix in the textbook. (The answers to these exercises are given in the Appendix of this book, page 297.)

Equipment Needed

None

Procedure

Read carefully the instructions given for each exercise and then make computations.

FREQUENCY DISTRIBUTION

Eleven applicants for an office job made the following scores on a typing test:

25 53 42 64 38 43 56 36 38 48 47

Complete the table below by counting the scores in each class interval; then plot the diagram.

FREQUENCY DISTRIBUTION

Scores on typing test	Number of applicants making these scores
20–29	_____
30–39	_____
40–49	_____
50–59	_____
60–69	_____

FREQUENCY DIAGRAM

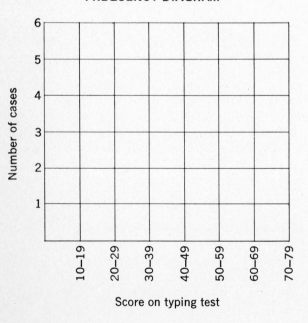

Score on typing test

Questions

1. What is the class interval?

2. Is the distribution symmetric?

MEASURES OF CENTRAL TENDENCY

Questions

3. Determine the *median* score for the above data by arranging the scores in order and finding the *middle* case (that is, the 6th from either end of 11).

    Median = _____

4. Calculate the *mean* for the above data by adding the *raw scores* and dividing by the number of scores.

    Mean = _____

5. Under what circumstances do the mean and median differ?

6. If the person getting the high score of 64 had in fact gotten a score of 75, how would it have affected the mean and the median?

MEASURES OF VARIATION

Consider the following weekly earnings reported by five part-time taxicab drivers:

Driver	Weekly earnings
A	$50
B	$60
C	$70
D	$80
E	$90

Questions

7. What is the *range* of weekly earnings? _____ the *mean?* _____

8. Compute the *standard deviation* by completing the following table.

Driver	Weekly earnings	Deviation from mean (d)	Deviation squared (d²)
A			
B			
C			
D			
E			

Sum of d^2 = _____

$\dfrac{\text{Sum of } d^2}{N}$ = _____

Standard deviation = $\sqrt{\dfrac{\text{Sum of } d^2}{N}}$ = _____

STANDARD ERROR OF THE MEAN

The more cases that enter into the computation of a mean, the more confidence we have that our obtained mean represents the total group from which our sample has been drawn.

Suppose that we draw successive samples of increasing size in order to measure some psychological characteristic, such as speed of reaction, among college students. How does our confidence increase with the size of the sample?

Suppose that the means of our reaction-time measurement fluctuate around 150 milliseconds (0.150 seconds), with standard deviations around 15 milliseconds. Where does the true mean reaction time fall?

These problems will be dealt with as you answer Questions 9 and 10.

Questions

9. Let us compute the *standard error of the mean,* assuming different numbers of cases (persons) in our sample. Complete the following table, using the formula:

Standard error of the mean (σ_M) =

$\dfrac{\text{Standard deviation } (\sigma)}{\sqrt{N}}$

Number of cases (N)	$\sqrt{N}$	Standard deviation (σ)	Standard error of mean (σ_M)
25	5	15	
100	10	15	
400	20	15	

Note that the standard error of the mean decreases as N increases. How can we convert this into some kind of statement about the true mean?

10. *Confidence limits.* We can state that with repeated measurements we can expect our means to fall within the range from -2.0σ to $+2.0\sigma$ in 95 percent of the cases. Using the table below determine the confidence limits for the mean reaction times of the three different sample sizes.

Sample size	Mean reaction time (milliseconds)	95 percent confidence limits	
		Lower limit (mean less 2.0 × standard error)	Upper limit (mean plus 2.0 × standard error)
25	150		
100	150		
400	150		

Thus far nothing has been said about the true mean of the population. Setting the confidence limits as we have, we may infer that the true mean lies within our confidence limits 95 percent of the time.

SIGNIFICANCE OF A DIFFERENCE

Suppose that we are comparing the mathematics scores of boys and girls in the fourth grade, with the following results:

	Number of cases (N)	Mean	Standard error of mean (σ_M)
Girls	50	72.0	0.4
Boys	50	70.5	0.3

Questions

Do the girls score significantly higher than the boys? To find out, we compute a *critical ratio,* but first we have to find the *standard error of difference,* according to the following formula.

11. The formula for the standard error of difference is

$$\sigma_D = \sqrt{{\sigma_{M_1}}^2 + {\sigma_{M_2}}^2}$$

where σ_{M_1} and σ_{M_2} are the standard errors of the means for girls and boys. Work out this formula using the data above.

$$\sigma_D = \sqrt{(\quad\quad)^2 + (\quad\quad)^2} =$$
$$\sqrt{(\quad\quad)} = \underline{\quad\quad\quad}$$

12. Compute the critical ratio, using this formula:

$$\text{Critical ratio} = \frac{\text{Difference between means}}{\sigma_D} =$$

$$\frac{(\quad\quad) - (\quad\quad)}{(\quad\quad)} = \underline{\quad}$$

13. If the absolute size of the critical ratio is over 2.0, we usually call the difference *significant*. In our example, is there a significant difference between the mathematic scores of boys and girls?

COEFFICIENT OF CORRELATION

Salesmen were given a test of sales ability before being hired. Then their scores were compared with subsequent performance on the job (as shown in first table below).

Questions

The degree of relationship between scores and sales is expressed by the *coefficient of correlation.* This index may be computed from two different formulas.

14. The most frequently used method yields the *product-moment correlation, r.* What is the product-moment correlation between the salesmen's test scores and earnings? Complete the computations indicated in the table on page 293 and copy

your result here: $r = \underline{\quad\quad\quad}$.

15. When there are few cases, an approximate method, known as *rank correlation,* yielding *rho* instead of *r,* is useful. The data are converted to ranks and then the following formula is used:

$$rho = 1 - \frac{6(\text{Sum } D^2)}{N(N^2 - 1)}$$

where D is difference in ranks for the measures and N the number of cases. Compute the rank correlation, using the table below.

16. On the basis of this correlation, what can be said about the cause-and-effect relations between test scores and sales performance?

	Anderson	Brown	Cook	Dodge	East
Test score:	50	60	70	80	90
Sales (in thousands of dollars):	$60	$80	$90	$70	$100

COMPUTATION OF RANK CORRELATION

Subject	(1) Sales test score rank	(2) Earnings score rank	Difference in rank $D = (1) - (2)$	Squared difference (D^2)
Anderson				
Brown				
Cook				
Dodge				
East				

$$rho = 1 - \frac{6(\quad\quad)}{(\quad)(\quad\quad)} = 1 - \frac{(\quad\quad)}{(\quad\quad)} = \underline{\quad\quad\quad}$$

COMPUTATION OF PRODUCT-MOMENT CORRELATION (r)

Correlation between a sales test and later sales in thousands of dollars

Subject	Scores on the sales test and computation of σ_x			Sales success and computation of σ_y			Cross-products used in computing r
	Test score (x)	Deviation from mean (dx)* (mean = 70)	$(dx)^2$	Sales score (y)	Deviation from mean (dy)* (mean = \$80)	$(dy)^2$	Product of deviations (dx)(dy)
Anderson							
Brown							
Cook							
Dodge							
East							
		Sum $(dx)^2 =$ $\dfrac{\text{Sum }(dx)^2}{N} =$ $\sigma_x = \sqrt{\dfrac{\text{Sum }(dx)^2}{N}} =$			Sum $(dy)^2 =$ $\dfrac{\text{Sum }(dy)^2}{N} =$ $\sigma_y = \sqrt{\dfrac{\text{Sum }(dy)^2}{N}} =$		Sum (dx)(dy) =

* Subtract mean from score: respect the sign of the difference.

$$\text{Coefficient of correlation, } r = \frac{\text{Sum }(dx)(dy)}{N\,\sigma_x\,\sigma_y} = \frac{(\quad)}{(\quad)\times(\quad)\times(\quad)} = \frac{(\quad)}{(\quad)} = \frac{(\quad)}{(\quad)} = \underline{\qquad}$$

appendix

Note. This Appendix includes answers to exercises and problems presented in the *Study Guide.* The student should not read this material until reference is made to it in the text of the *Guide.*

CHAPTER 11 (PAGE 162) MEASURING MOTIVATION

Score your completed sentences as follows:

P . . . . if your response indicates a positive, humorous, or hopeful attitude

C . . . . if your response indicates conflict, antagonism, pessimism, emotional disturbance

N . . . . if your response is neutral, that is, not clearly positive or conflictful

Examples of how your responses should be scored:

Boys _____.

P. . . . . are friendly, are easy to get along with, are nice, are good sports, are considerate, are fun at a party, are good friends, are O.K.

C . . . . are a pain in the neck, get on my nerves, can't be trusted, bother me, give me a headache, think they are superior, are rude, are stupid.

N . . . . are human beings, are taller than girls, are stronger than girls, are the opposite sex, are the same sex.

Count the total number of P, C, and N scores. Your instructor may ask you to write these on a slip of paper so that he can determine the distribution of results for the entire class. (You may then complete the table below and determine the median score.) You need not identify yourself. Compute your score by adding fifty to the number of C responses and subtracting the number of P responses. Any omissions (incompleted sentences) are not scored.

Score	Number of students	Score	Number of students
96–100		46–50	
91–95		41–45	
86–90		36–40	
81–85		31–35	
76–80		26–30	
71–75		21–25	
66–70		16–20	
61–65		11–15	
56–60		6–10	
51–55		1–5	

Median score

CHAPTER 14 (PAGE 204) INDIVIDUAL DIFFERENCES

The unscrambled sentences are as follows:

1. The good that men do lives after them.
2. Don't shoot until you see the whites of their eyes.
3. The most valuable thing in the world is the free human mind.
4. Tell your yarn and let your style go to the devil.
5. It is only at rare moments that we live.
6. Do not blame me too much for not knowing all the answers.
7. The greatest of faults is to be conscious of none.
8. It is better to understand a little than to misunderstand a lot.
9. The worst use that can be made of success is boasting of it.
10. Better a witty fool than a foolish wit.
11. First love is only a little foolishness and a lot of curiosity.
12. The power of laughter is astonishing.
13. Money cannot cure unhappiness.
14. Your reputation grows with every failure.
15. Talk to a man about himself and he will listen for hours.
16. The truth is the one thing nobody will believe.
17. My way of joking is to tell the truth.
18. It is not pleasure that makes life worth living.
19. I had rather be right than President.
20. Very simple ideas lie within the reach only of complex minds.

CHAPTER 16 (PAGE 237) CLASSIFICATION OF BEHAVIOR DISORDERS

The cases are designed to illustrate the following disorders:

Case 1. Psychosis—manic-depressive reaction, manic phase (or hypomania)
Case 2. Psychosis—schizophrenia
Case 3. Neurosis—conversion reaction
Case 4. Neurosis—anxiety reaction
Case 5. Neurosis—phobic reaction
Case 6. Neurosis—compulsive reaction
Case 7. Psychopathic personality
Case 8. Neurotic depression

APPENDIX: STATISTICAL METHODS AND MEASUREMENT (PAGE 290)

Answers to the *Individual Exercises.*

1. 10
2. No
3. Median = 43
4. Mean = 44.55
5. When the frequency distribution is not perfectly symmetric about the mean
6. Increased the mean, no effect on the median
7. Range from $50 to $90, or $40; Mean = $70
8. Standard deviation = 14.14
9. Standard errors: for 25 cases, 3.0; for 100 cases, 1.5; for 400 cases, 0.75
10. Confidence limits: for 25 cases, 144–156; for 100 cases, 147–153; for 400 cases, 148.5–151.5
11. Standard error of difference = 0.5
12. Critical ratio = 3.0
13. Yes
14. $r = .70$
15. $rho = .70$
16. No definite conclusions about cause-and-effect relations can be drawn from correlational evidence. See discussion of this topic in text.